Weathering Risk in Rural Mexico

Weathering Risk in Rural Mexico

Climatic, Institutional, and Economic Change

Hallie Eakin

The University of Arizona Press   Tucson

The University of Arizona Press
© 2006 The Arizona Board of Regents

Library of Congress Cataloging-in-Publication Data
Eakin, Hallie Catherine, 1970–
   Weathering risk in rural Mexico : climatic, institutional, and
economic change / Hallie Catherine Eakin.
      p. cm.
   Includes bibliographical references and index.
   ISBN-13: 978-0-8165-2500-3 (hardcover : alk. paper)
   ISBN-10: 0-8165-2500-5 (hardcover : alk. paper)
      1. Agriculture—Economic aspects—Mexico—Puebla (State)
2. Agriculture—Economic aspects—Mexico—Tlaxcala (State)
3. Farmers—Mexico—Puebla (State) 4. Farmers—Mexico—
Tlaxcala (State) 5. Climatic changes—Mexico—Puebla (State)
6. Climatic changes—Mexico—Tlaxcala (State) 7. Crops and
climate—Mexico—Puebla (State) 8. Crops and climate—Mexico
—Tlaxcala (State) 9. Globalization—Economic aspects. I. Title.
HD1795.A23E35 2007
338.1'4–dc22   2006019925

Publication of this book is made possible in part by the
proceeds of a permanent endowment created with the
assistance of a Challenge Grant from the National Endowment
for the Humanities, a federal agency.

Manufactured in the United States of America on acid-free,
archival-quality paper containing a minimum of 50% post-
consumer waste and processed chlorine free.

11 10 09 08 07 06   6 5 4 3 2 1

A Judith

Contents

Illustrations and Tables

Acknowledgments

I owe the success of this project first and foremost to the hospitality of the residents of Plan de Ayala, Ranchería de Torres, and Nazareno and their willingness to share with me the details of their livelihoods. I am particularly indebted to Don Manuel Santos and his family (Aida, José Manuel, Judith, and Josefa), who made my project their own and accepted me as a member of their household. Doña Vicky of San Miguel Xaltepec kindly let me stay in her home, and Doña Julia also opened many doors for me. Don Fernando Durán, Don Emeterio, and Don Toribio were also particularly supportive of my project and tolerant of my many questions. I am also grateful to the family of Don Miguel Leal Hernández for their warm welcome and continued interest in my research.

My research was generously funded through a National Science Foundation graduate fellowship, a National Security Education Program Boren fellowship, a FISPE North American Consortium grant, and a Foreign Language and Area Studies fellowship. Elements of this research first appeared as articles in the *Journal of Environment and Development* and *World Development*, and I would like to thank these journals for permission to present the material in its expanded form in this book.

If I had not had the good fortune to study with Diana Liverman at the University of Arizona, I probably would have never come to know Mexico as I now do, and this book would not have been written. Dr. Carlos Gay, Dr. Cecilia Conde, and Dr. Victor Magaña of the Center for Atmospheric Sciences of the National Autonomous University of Mexico have continually offered institutional and scientific support for my research in Mexico, and in many ways this book is the fruit of this collaboration. I am particularly appreciative of the support of Dr. Luis Bojórquez and his students at the Laboratory for Spatial Analysis of the Institute of Ecology at UNAM, and José Jiménez López of the University of Tlaxcala, for help in implementing the household surveys. I would like to thank Dr. Nestor Estrella, director of the Colegio de Postgraduados, Campus Puebla, the extension staff in the Tecamachalco office of SAGARPA, Ing. Carlos Pérez in Tecamachalco, Ing. Enrique Oviedo Hervert of Tlaxcala's Ministry of Agriculture and Livestock Development, SEFOA, Ing. Gustavo Jiménez of PEAT in Puebla, and the rural development experts of Fundación Desarrollo Rural for sharing their expertise and knowledge of the region. I am grateful to Allyson Carter and the University of Arizona Press for enabling me to bring this project to fruition. This book would undoubtedly never have reached a broader audience without the close reading, careful editing, and unwavering support of my parents, Sybil and John Eakin. Last, but definitely not least, I want to thank Luis for his enthusiasm, love, and encouragement and for sharing with me his Mexico.

Además, gracias a Hugo Morales Torres por darme permiso usar su foto en la portada del libro.

Weathering Risk in Rural Mexico

1 Globalization, Climatic Uncertainty, and the Smallholder

Local Complexity, Global Uncertainty, and Farming in Mexico

I was visiting Plan de Ayala on a Saturday in mid-May 2000. May is one of the hottest months in the Mexican state of Tlaxcala, and I appreciated having been invited in to the cool dimness of the large concrete hall where the community was holding its monthly meeting. The farmers—men in well-worn sombreros and women in braids and aprons, mainly in their sixties—were listening attentively while the *técnico*, a young man from the Ministry of Agrarian Reform in the state capital, explained the steps required for the agrarian community (an *ejido*) to permit a few of its member households to sell some prime farmland to Kimberly-Clark, whose factory was slowly expanding into the ejido's property. I knew that despite the ejido's relatively large landholdings, access to good farmland was still a concern in the village. Just two weeks before, I had watched as the *comisariado ejidal*, the ejido's leaders, organized the community to clear the last remaining arable land at the top of a nearby hill, in order to increase the availability of land in areas considered to be at less risk to frost, as well as to ensure that every *ejidatario* (the community's members with land-use rights) had exactly the same amount of land.

The possibility of the land sales was not being well received. Several farmers were scowling and grumbling with displeasure. A tall thin man requested permission to speak, and in short words suggested that selling the land was an unfortunate proposal, not in the spirit of the ejido. The ejido was one of the last to be constituted in Tlaxcala, and the hard-won fight for land was recent in the memories of many of its members. In the brief speeches that followed, it was clear that selling land to the factory was viewed by some as a betrayal of the original revolutionary motivations for the ejido's formation.

Perhaps it was not the ideal moment for me to ask for the ejidatarios' cooperation with my project, yet I took courage in the fact that weather and climate are typically perceived as relatively neutral topics. When I stood up to talk, I explained that I was interested in learning about the agriculture they practiced and in particular about their experiences with the variable climate of Tlaxcala. I asked if anyone was interested in speaking with me on my next visit to the community. Immediately two middle-aged ejidatarios volunteered, asking whether they could talk not only about the late frost that had already destroyed their recently planted maize, but also "el TLC" (the Spanish acronym for the North American Free Trade Agreement) and how it was eliminating their opportunities to sell their harvests. They did not want to wait for me to return to their village the following week. They were ready to talk now.

While some farmers were considering the potentially lucrative offer from a multinational corporation for their land, unexpected climate events were encouraging the ejido's leadership to bring more land into production. Meanwhile, all the market signals were telling the ejidatarios that farming anything at all was increasingly a losing proposition. When I embarked on my project to understand vulnerability in rural Mexico, I knew that the farmers' responses to climate risk would be tied up with their struggles to survive Mexico's agricultural reforms of the 1990s. Economic integration with the agricultural powers of the United States and Canada has made the inadequacies in Mexican agriculture all the more obvious since Mexico began to aggressively liberalize its agricultural markets in the mid-1980s, and climatic hazards have accentuated the negative implications of globalization for Mexico's farmers. I was surprised, however, that the interactions of economic globalization, market reforms, and climatic shocks were tied so directly to the choices being debated in this tiny community, over a thousand miles from the U.S.–Mexico border.

Now that the words "globalization" and "climate" are beginning to appear together in debates about vulnerability (e.g., Handmer, Dovers, and Downing 1999; O'Brien and Leichenko 2000, 2003), it is increasingly obvious that economic and climatic change are not only linked as cause and effect but also interact in unpredictable and complex ways in the context of regional political and trade relationships, national economic and social programs, and in the decision making of institutions, enterprises, and individuals. While occurring on different temporal and spatial scales, the simultaneity of the processes of globalization and climatic change results in populations that are, in the words of Karen O'Brien and Robin Leichenko, "doubly exposed" and thus particularly vulnerable (O'Brien and Leichenko 2000).

Small-scale farmers in developing countries are one such social group. In a world where there is increasing pressure for countries to drop agricultural subsidies and open their markets to free trade, smallholders are increasingly left without infrastructural and institutional support. These farmers often lack the organization and political clout of agricultural groups in more industrialized countries that would facilitate their participation in more competitive international and domestic markets. Transportation costs and reductions in state support for agricultural research and technology compound the difficulties these farmers face. Insurance industries and disaster management institutions are often absent or inadequate, despite the fact that the nature of climatic variability in the tropics and subtropics can result in frequent and intense extreme events.

In academic circles, vulnerability to climate and vulnerability to economic change have, until quite recently, been considered as independent and unrelated processes. In research on climate vulnerability and adaptation, the social context of climate impacts has often been held constant or, for the sake of simplicity, is assumed to change gradually and linearly. The opposite can also be said of research on social change: if mentioned at all, climate is often considered to be part of the physical background against which social and institutional upheavals occur. Rarely are global political-economic and global environmental change considered together as dynamic and interacting drivers of local vulnerability.

Over the last decade, analysts have developed elaborate models to simulate the sensitivity and response of agricultural production to climatic variability and climate change. Increasingly the heterogeneity of farm systems and thus the variable decision-making contexts of different farm groups, are being incorporated into new climate impact assessments (e.g., Antle et al. 2004; Polsky 2004). Yet as the complexity of these models increases, so do the uncertainties embedded within them (Reilly 1999). Among other sources of uncertainty are the relatively limited knowledge available on the behavior and responses of different types of farmers to climate signals and how farmers make decisions as they interact with other actors, with markets, and with the variety of institutions that govern their production (Bryant et al. 2000; Reilly 1999; Risbey, Kandlikar, and Dowlatabadi 1999). This is particularly the case in many developing countries where common economic assumptions about the motivations and purpose of agricultural decisions may not be applicable. Even in the context of industrialized agriculture, assumptions about farmers' responses to future climatic signals have been questioned (Brklachich et al. 1997; Chiotti et al. 1997; Hanemann 2000; Risbey, Kandlikar, and Dowlatabadi 1999).

In our increasingly complex world, direct interaction with farmers about their decision-making process may be one way in which new insights can be gained into the process of adaptation. In the field of global change, where research has tended to emphasize processes extending far into the future and covering broad geographic areas, interacting directly with decision makers often means turning to the present time and integrating the local scale into research frameworks (see, e.g., Chiotti et al. 1997; Kelly and Adger 2000). While the knowledge gained from understanding present-day management of risk may not necessarily be directly transferable to future conditions (Burton 1997), it can provide important insights into the factors driving potentially adaptive decisions and the social complexity inherent in human responses to environmental risk. The challenge is to situate the dynamics of individual choice in particular places into a far broader landscape of temporal and spatial change.

This book is a response to this challenge. My hope is that it will contribute to strengthening the bridge between two lines of research—the human dimensions of climate variability and change, and the social implications of institutional change—that have been too seldom considered together in studies of vulnerability. Uniting these two lines of research is complicated not only by the intricate and often indecipherable webs of cause and effect relationships observable at different scales but by the simple fact that neither global warming, whether manifest as shifts in climate means or as alterations in the distribution of extreme events, nor economic globalization are necessarily *experienced* as such by particular individuals in specific places (Bryant et al. 2000). In twenty years of farming, a smallholder may perceive a shift in climate patterns: an increased frequency of drought, for example, or more intense cold spells or heat waves. Is this climate change? At what point and under what circumstances is a defined shift in production or livelihood strategy, an adaptation, warranted? And if, while struggling with a series of losses from climate hazards, a farmer faces abrupt shifts in agricultural policy, increasingly volatile prices, and rising costs, at what point does he or she consider such changes indicators of broader trends or the reorganization of global market structure?

For many if not most smallholders, global change may be experienced essentially as subtle and not-so-subtle shifts in variability and volatility—both inherent characteristics of agriculture and yet also determinants of the pace and evolution of agricultural systems (Bryant et al. 2000; Smit, McNabb, and Smithers 1996; Smithers and Smit 1997; Weber 1997). Farmers' responses to the climate patterns they perceive (whether or not, with scientific hindsight, such variability can be directly attributed to global change) illustrate not only how differential resource access and entitlements structure risk perception and choice, but also how the types of livelihood strategies evolving from such choices may alter the flexibility of farm households in dealing with future risk. It is the cumulative impact of individual interannual decisions about production and livelihood that collectively create new social contexts of vulnerability and that structure capacities for adaptation.

For this reason, while this book is designed to contribute to the growing literature on vulnerability and adaptation to global environmental change, the focus is on farmers' experiences with the here and now: climate variability, extreme events, and the simultaneous disruption of rapid change in sector policy. My hope is that by viewing the world through the words and experiences of the farmers in the three communities in the Puebla-Tlaxcala Valley who participated in this study, we can gain insight into what matters most in farmers' decision making, and what the implications of their actions may be for both the future vulnerability of their families and for the regions in which they live. While it is now almost commonplace to say that most decisions at the farm level are the result of multiple factors both internal and external to the household, relatively little is known about how these factors interact and the implications of this interaction for local vulnerability.

The book uses two concrete developments during the 1990s in Mexico as proxies for how global climate and economic change are experienced at the local level: the impacts of the El Niño–Southern Oscillation (ENSO) events in 1997, 1998, and 1999 (described in chaps. 2 and 5) and the institutionalization of neoliberalism and free-trade principles under the Salinas de Gotari and Zedillo administrations (described in chap. 3).

The floods, forest fires, and droughts that devastated Latin America during the 1997–98 El Niño made global headlines. In Mexico, the 1990s were marked by a prolonged multiyear drought, repeated floods, and anomalous frosts in different parts of the country, making the decade particularly difficult for the country's farmers. There is now some evidence that El Niño warm events have increased in frequency since the late 1970s, and that this increase may be associated with changes in the intensity of drought and wet events worldwide over the 1990s (Trenberth and Hoar 1996, 1997). Although the relationship between ENSO and global temperatures is complex, these observed changes are thought by some to be at least partly influenced by warming global temperatures (Trenberth and Hoar 1997; Tsonis, Hunt, and Elsner 2002).

The climate extremes of the 1990s were not the only events that rocked Mexico's agriculture sector. Mexico's proximity to the United States, the so-called engine of economic and cultural globalization, also has made the country especially sensitive to the dynamics of the international economy. Although Mexico has always courted international investment, particularly from the United States, the degree to which neoliberalism has been internalized domestically has surpassed all expectations. Not only has the country overhauled its agricultural institutions and policy in line with free-market principles, but the year 2000 also marked the first time in Mexico's postrevolutionary period that the country held democratic multiparty elections—elections that ended seventy years of the Partido Revolucionario Institucional's domination of rural politics. While the social and climatic circumstances of the 1990s cannot be viewed as directly analogous to what might be experienced under climatic change, the

simultaneous intensity of both climatic events and institutional reforms in Mexico during this period provide an exceptional opportunity to understand how rural populations respond to risks and adjust
to real-time uncertainty.

A Livelihoods Approach to Understanding Vulnerability

The argument of this book is centered on unraveling the perplexing interactions of *both* climatic risk and institutional change in
the vulnerability of rural households. Inspired by the pragmatic and
unassuming approach of eminent cultural ecologists Robert Netting
and Gene Wilken, I chose a relatively simple tactic in my research:
I asked the men and women working as farmers, housewives, farm
laborers, carpenters, agronomists, extension agents, community ac-
tivists, civil servants, and private-sector merchants about what affected their lives and livelihoods, how they made their decisions, and
what those decisions meant for their households. As farmers make
their decisions, the multiple uncertainties and sometimes conflicting
priorities they face intersect. In the context of economic globalization and neoliberal reform, the relationship of peasant households to
markets, whether input markets, markets for agricultural harvests,
or for labor and other goods and services, becomes a central issue in
farmers' strategies. By tracing the links from farmers' livelihoods outward to prices, policies, public programs, and private development,
I was able to develop a structure through which I could empirically
document the important and relevant cross-scalar and intersectoral
linkages in the farm households' vulnerability.

I used a variety of techniques to understand farmers' strategies:
a household survey, in-depth interviews, numerous informal conversations, and group discussions, as well as simply observing and
participating in the daily activities of those households who most
welcomed my company (see appendix B). I did not assume linkages
between local lives and global environmental change, international
markets, and national policy but rather let the people I interviewed
identify and delineate those linkages for me. As my initial encounter
with the ejidatarios in Plan de Ayala revealed, this was far easier than
I imagined.

Ian Scoones defines livelihoods as "the capabilities, assets (including both material and social resources), and activities required for a means of living" (Scoones 1998: 5). Drawing from his experience in the Andes, the geographer Antony Bebbington uses a broader definition, arguing that people's assets and capabilities are not only the means to accumulation but also what give meaning to people's lives and thus serve as a source of empowerment to change and control their circumstances (Bebbington 1999: 2022). It is this idea of meaning that I feel is particularly relevant in understanding the decisions peasant households make and the persistence of small-scale agriculture in Mexico. While it is easy to despair at the incredible odds facing households in rural Mexico as they struggle to keep their footing in an increasingly unsupportive and rapidly changing economy, it is important to recognize the agency that resides in each of these households to make the most of the resources they have available.

A livelihoods approach recognizes that the assets on which livings are based are not simply financial resources and physical property, but also social networks, bonds of trust and investment in institutions and organization (social capital); health, skills, knowledge formation, and education (human capital); and access to and investment in the maintenance and sustainability of natural resources (natural capital) (Ellis 2000; Scoones 1998). What resources the different members of a household have, and what they can and may do with their endowments, affects the range and type of strategies they can pursue and the effectiveness of those strategies in managing risk. In fact, increasingly livelihoods are being evaluated in terms of their sustainability over time, and that sustainability arises from the capacity of households to cope with and build resistance to diverse stresses and shocks (Batterbury and Forsyth 1999; Ellis 2000).

A particular household's asset endowment and capacities are mediated by informal and formal policies, laws, norms, and rights, as well as by physical organizations constituted at different scales of governance. These are the "institutions" I refer to. Institutions and political-economic change not only produce vulnerability by structuring the range of livelihood options available to any household, but also can act as additional sources of stress.

Neoclassical development efforts often have focused on the economic inefficiencies and lack of profitability of smallholder agriculture, often declaring its failure in terms of monetary gains and losses.

A livelihoods approach, in contrast, in recognizing that many rural households *are* surviving, "inefficient" or not, asks how and why. Recent livelihoods research has drawn attention to the fact that rural areas are coevolving in relation to change in urban sectors, demonstrating that traditional divisions of urban/rural, agriculture/industry, or local/global may no longer have much utility in the globalized contexts of smallholder production (Bryceson 1996; de Janvry and Sadoulet 2001; Francis 2000). In other words, as I hope to show through the experiences of so many farmers, a farm household's survival of a drought depends not only on the rain that falls on its cornfields but also on the employment opportunities in the cement factory in the next state, the price of milk, the cost of medicine, or the peso's exchange rate with the U.S. dollar.

Although livelihoods approaches are only beginning to be used to understand households' adaptive capacities in the face of climatic variability and climatic change (see, e.g., Adger 1999; Mortimore and Adams 1999), the emphasis of the livelihoods framework on diversity, flexibility, and strategic decision-making lends itself directly to research on household adaptive capacity. In particular, livelihoods research facilitates an analysis of the interaction of multiple stressors at various scales on a household's assets and choices.

While the importance of viewing vulnerability as the product of interacting diverse stressors may seem obvious, analyses of vulnerability to climate at the local scale have not always been considered in this light. In the early years of natural hazards research in geography, vulnerability to climatic events was defined largely by the physical impact and intensity, frequency, and spatial extent of climatic hazards. A population was vulnerable to climate impacts primarily by happenstance of location, faulty infrastructure or poorly planned settlements, and by the disjoint between individual perceptions and behavior and the objective risk posed by hazards to lives and property. Managing this vulnerability was largely an issue of overcoming nature's chaos through appropriate technology and modifying human behavior with better information and policy (Burton, White, and Kates 1978; White 1973).

The devastating famines of the 1980s in the African Sahel provided the grounds for a widespread critique of the tenets held by early natural hazards' researchers on how vulnerability was produced. The famines tragically illustrated the fact that while living in risky and fragile environments can make an agricultural system particularly sensitive to climate events such as drought, ultimately the social, political, and economic circumstances in which rural households live play determinant roles in vulnerability (Copans 1983; Hewitt 1983; Mortimore 1989; Watts 1983). Central to this critique was Amartya Sen's concept of entitlements—the set of rights, norms, and institutions that govern what a person is able to do with the resources he or she has available at any given moment (Sen 1981, 1990). In the 1990s, the theoretical contributions of academics and practitioners studying famine coalesced in the development of definitions of vulnerability that drew heavily on political-economic and structural explanations of poverty, marginalization, and risk exposure, yet did not abandon the critical importance of the environmental hazard and its impacts on exposed populations (Blaikie et al. 1994; Downing, Watts, and Bohle 1996; Ribot 1996).

Today climate vulnerability is often defined in three dimensions: the exposure of a population to hazards, stresses, and shocks; the sensitivity of the population to such hazards; and the capacity of the population to make the necessary adjustments in order to regain previous standards of living, or to maintain the integrity of their livelihood strategy in the aftermath of the period of stress or shock (Blaikie et al. 1994; Dow 1992; Downing, Watts, and Bohle 1996). In this way, the concepts of adaptive capacity and vulnerability are presented as essentially two sides of the same coin: vulnerable populations are inhibited in their capacity to adapt and, because of this constraint, are considered more vulnerable.

Although almost a decade has passed since these theories of vulnerability were articulated, putting such definitions into practice has proven difficult. In climate change research the use of quantifiable climate impacts (e.g., change in crop yield, monetary losses) as a proxy for vulnerability is still often a preferred method of measurement, particularly at the broad regional and global scale of social analysis that best fits the resolution of climate models. Impacts can be modeled and mapped, and on this basis vulnerable populations can, theoretically, be identified. In addition to impacts, aggregated measures of poverty, inequality, human capital, and infrastructure are also being used to target vulnerable populations and rank and compare vulnerable places (Adger et al. 2004; Moss, Brenkert, and Malone 2001).

Yet the relative ease of using such indicators in vulnerability analysis belies the complexity of the concept, particularly at the scales at which the experience of climate risk often takes place. As numerous farmers have explained to me, their vulnerability to drought, frost, or floods is not *produced* by the climate event, nor is it a direct function of characteristics such as wealth or education. Instead, when I ask why a farmer did not suffer as extensive losses as a neighbor, I am provided with more circumstantial arguments: "I was able to prepare my fields on time; my neighbor is lazy"; or "My daughter works in a factory, the income helped to buy tortillas"; or "So-and-so has little time to dedicate to farming; he works in Mexico City"; or "My land is good; some of us weren't here for the original distribution of land of the ejido and weren't so lucky." Their vulnerability reflects the coincidence of climate shocks and opportunity, opportunity constrained by history, politics, economics, and the resources available to them before, during, and after the moment of crisis. Their comments show relationships between livelihoods, risk, and resources that are difficult to capture in aggregated statistics. The vulnerability of these farmers is here and now, and is not necessarily independent of their vulnerability in a modeled future state. Who will be facing future risks in Mexico's countryside, where, and with what resources has a lot to do with how today's farmers address their present challenges.

Hence the relevance of livelihoods research to understanding local vulnerability. To implement this type of analysis, the household or the individual decision maker becomes an appropriate unit of analysis. As Jesse Ribot argues, vulnerability analysis thus "builds outward from the household" and "includes the multiple temporal, spatial, and social scales that impinge on the production and reproduction of everyday life" (Ribot 1996: 9). The snapshot of vulnerability I will provide in the subsequent chapters attempts to make these cross-scalar linkages, illustrating how Mexico's agrarian history, tumultuous political economy, and its dynamic geography and climate have affected the ways in which farm households in three Mexican communities have organized their livelihoods, and how their actions differently enable them to manage the various challenges they face. While climate impacts can be simulated fifty years into the future, adaptation to climate change occurs through the combined decisions of numerous individuals in the time frame of seasons or years, decisions that cumulatively can result in structural adaptations (or *mal*-adaptations) for an entire sector of the economy (Smithers and Smit 1997).

Adaptation and Adaptive Capacity

Although the concept of adaptation, and more specifically *adaptive capacity*, is integral to the definitions of vulnerability described above, this capacity merits some independent discussion, particularly as it is now the focus of considerable attention by government agencies and politicians who are eager to say they have been preparing for the eventuality of climatic catastrophes. The IPCC defines adaptation as "adjustment in ecological, social, or economic systems in responses to actual or expected climatic stimuli and their effects and impacts" (IPCC Working Group II 2001: 879). In practice, adaptation is frequently interpreted in the climate literature in terms of technologies, programs, and policies and evaluated in terms of the costs and benefits of these measures for reducing climate impacts (Burton et al. 2002; Hanemann 2000; Wheaton and Maciver 1999). In short, the concept of adaptation has been largely addressed through the prescriptive science used for public policy and planning (Kandlikar and Risbey 2000).

This perspective differs from the long contemplation of adaptation in human geography and cultural anthropology, in which cultural ecologists set out to understand how the human race has modified the physical environment to suit its needs and ambitions, and how climate, soils, and vegetation have set constraints on human social development (Alland 1975; Bennett 1976; Robbins 2004). In the 1970s, inspired by evolutionary theory and systems ecology, some cultural ecologists argued that much of human behavior and social institutions could be understood as the outcomes of strategic and adaptive processes of populations competing for scarce resources in efforts to assure their survival (Alland 1975; Bennett 1976).

Within the broad subfield of cultural ecology, geographers and anthropologists studying "peasant farm systems" turned the focus of analysis away from systems theory to the process of individual decision making and the complex knowledge and experience that individuals and communities develop in response to environmental, social, political, and economic challenges to their livelihoods (Barlett 1980; Cancian 1980; Netting 1993). Latin America has frequently provided the geographic context for such research (see, e.g., Cancian 1980; Denevan 1980; Doolittle 2000; Whitmore and Turner II 1992; Wilken 1987). A wide diversity of climatic-risk mitigation strategies employed by rural populations, involving soil moisture conservation techniques, tillage practices, seed selection for stress tolerance, intercropping, and other forms of microclimate adjustments have been meticulously documented in the forms and features of Latin American landscapes and environmental history, and a few of the practices that sustained high population densities and elaborate cultural development can still be observed in many traditional agricultural systems in Mexico (see, e.g., Altieri and Trujillo 1987; Bellon 1991; Brush, Bellon Corrales, and Schmidt 1988; Doolittle 1989; Trujillo 1990; Wilken 1987). From Boserup's explanations of the importance of land scarcity and population density in the evolution of farm systems, and Chayanov's argument of a separate "peasant economics" to explain smallholder behavior, cultural ecologists used agrarian studies to move from systems analysis to a more overtly political agenda, arguing that contrary to much of development theory, smallholder farmers were in fact efficient, experienced, flexible, and essentially *adaptive* (Brush 1977; Netting 1993; Turner and Brush 1987).

While I would not argue that farmers' livelihood strategies necessarily represent adaptations, or that their management of resources, risks, and uncertainty always lead to positive outcomes, I do believe that looking at how farm households organize their lives can reveal a lot about adaptive capacity—the sets of assets, skills, and opportunities that allow a household to mitigate their sensitivity and exposure to shocks and stresses. I believe that looking at livelihoods also can illustrate how external factors—not only the biophysical environment, but also stresses from the economy and political spheres of production—introduce new instabilities into rural households while challenging their efforts to adjust to change.

Over the last three decades, the subdiscipline of political ecology has set out to expand traditional cultural ecology by concretely linking explanations of local environmental change to the political economy of production, politicized perceptions of the environment, and power struggles over resource use at interacting scales of geography and management (Blaikie 1999; Bryant 1998; Greenburg and Park 1994). This literature not only addresses how global environmental change affects local places, but also explores local responses to economic globalization, neoliberalism, and other aspects of broadscale political-economic change, and the implications of those responses for the environment (see Bassett and Zimmerer 2003). Often using the tools and techniques of livelihood analysis, political ecology research challenges the very notion of what it means to be "rural" in the twentieth and twenty-first century, recognizing that the strategic choices of households have increasingly less to do with local environmental constraints and community cultural practices than with the relationship of households to social organizations and institutions that traverse history and political boundaries (Batterbury, Forsyth, and Thomson 1997; Bebbington and Batterbury 2001; Nigh 1997; Zimmerer 1991).

Some of this research has shown that the implications of economic globalization at the local level are not necessarily negative. The opening of markets and increased flow of information and resources associated with globalization may provide some new opportunities for rural households, or even reinforce traditional practices and identities (Bebbington 1993). Others have argued that agricultural globalization directly undermines the economic and ecological basis for the type of small-scale agriculture that is so common in the Americas, and thus may be eroding the viability and adaptive capacities of smallholders (Buttel 1997; Gledhill 1995; Wilkinson 1997).

The implications of the rapid institutional changes associated with the agricultural globalization process for farmers' livelihoods, and thus their adaptive capacities, is the subject of this book. Although I discuss households' differential sensitivity and exposure to both climate hazards and policy reforms at length, household adaptive capacity is the core theme of the book. In the chapters that follow, I illustrate how farmers' livelihood strategies, conditioned by each household's particular suite of resources and entitlements, either enhance or restrict their flexibility of choice in responding to the twin challenges of climatic risk and political-economic change. Defining the concrete linkages between policy reforms, household production and livelihood choices, and vulnerability to climatic risk is no easy task. Although this book focuses on just two sources of stress to farmers' livelihoods, climate variability and changing agriculture policy and markets, it should be recognized that farmers face a wide variety of other sources of uncertainty and risk, a detailed analysis of which was beyond the scope of this project. Soil degradation, deforestation and land-use change, pest proliferation, aquifer depletion, and technology change (e.g., the introduction of genetically modified agricultural products) are among the many issues pertinent to farmers' livelihoods and production strategies. These other "stressors" are brought up at various points in the text where the farmers made it clear that these additional stressors were directly interacting with their risk-management decisions and livelihood outcomes.

In chapter 2, I present the evolving geography of the Puebla-Tlaxcala Valley and describe the types of climatic stress and variability farmers were facing in the late 1990s. Again, here the emphasis is not on the full diversity of environmental constraints on production but rather on climate hazards and some of the more dynamic biophysical and economic elements of the regional context of production.

Chapter 3 reviews the variety of policy reforms implemented in the 1990s and the high social costs associated with them. As is illustrated in detail in chapter 5, under these new institutional conditions, the options for responding to climatic risk that may be available to producers in more industrialized systems—irrigation, alternative (yet lucrative) crops, capital investments to enhance temperature or moisture control, or market orientation—are unrealistic for the majority of Mexico's producers. The different livelihood strategies of the farmers of Plan de Ayala, Ranchería de Torres (henceforth called Torres), and Nazareno (described in chaps. 4 and 6 through 9) reveal that the most viable means of stabilizing incomes and welfare may be outside the agricultural sector entirely, entailing long-distance migration, peri-urban wage employment, shifts in the meaning and purpose of rural land use, as well as basic education. These actions complicate our understanding of agricultural vulnerability. The documentation of farmers' evolving strategies demands not only cross-sectoral and cross-scalar research, but also sophisticated policy coordination in order to address the new risks posed by their changing livelihoods.

For these reasons, it is difficult to generalize about what factors enhance adaptive capacity at the household level. While broadscale economic models may illustrate that, in the long run, changes in market prices and new technology will allow agricultural systems to adapt so that aggregate global food security is never truly threatened (Helms, Mendelsohn, and Neumann 1996; Rosenzweig and Parry 1993), the reality is that these results mask important social and cultural costs within regions, nations, and communities (Chen 1994; Reilly and Schilmmelpfenning 1999). The importance of immediate economic, technological, and institutional incentives and constraints in farmers' decisions also implies that there is always the potential that agricultural adjustments to climate will be either overreactive (Reilly and Schilmmelpfenning 1999: 756) or, what is more likely, *underreactive*, as farm households fail to respond to climatic signals because imperfect markets and policy provide incentives for contrary behavior. Ultimately, without a better understanding of the process of decision making in the face of uncertainty, we still are unsure whether or not particular agricultural systems can and will adapt, and whether or not policy intervention is needed to encourage adaptation (Downing et al. 1999; Reilly and Schimmelpfenning 2000; Smit, McNabb, and Smithers 1996).

Some scholars in search of a theoretical approach to understanding adaptation are now borrowing the ecological concept of "thresholds," particular degrees of change beyond which adjustment is unavoidable, or, in the worst case, which cause the shift of an entire system to a new state (Reilly and Schimmelpfenning 1999). The complexity of social systems and human perception defies efforts to identify a specific threshold in temperature change or precipitation that would trigger catastrophe. It may be only in hindsight that the causes and consequences of truly transformative periods in history are apparent. For example, David Hodell and his colleagues (1995) and Bruce Dahlin (1983) have linked the abrupt collapse of the Mayan civilization in the Yucatán peninsula with evidence of a dramatic change in precipitation and water availability in the region. Enrique Florescano (1980), Friedrich Katz (1988), and Escobar Ohmstede (1997) present arguments that the 1810 War of Independence and 1910 revolution in Mexico's more recent history were driven, in part, by food shortages and price spikes caused by multiyear droughts occurring in the context of public policy that systematically under-mined the food security of Mexico's working class.

Although our understanding of the implications of current pro-cesses of change is myopic and distorted by our position in the pres-ent, it is quite possible that we are now witnessing one such trans-formative period in the history of Mexican agriculture. As this book was being written, farmers all over Mexico were taking to the streets and plazas of the capital in mass marches, blocking border crossings with their tractors, and staging hunger strikes to demand a renego-tiation of the North American Free Trade Agreement and a system-atic review of the government's responsibilities for rural economic well-being. Their protests followed four years of highly variable and unfavorable climatic conditions that have depressed yields and exac-erbated indebtedness.

It is difficult to predict the outcome of the interaction of these processes of change on the future vulnerability of smallholder house-holds and the future adaptability of Mexican agriculture. Yet while the political-economic systems that circumscribe decision making are in constant flux, there is also an element of path dependency in this change: institutional and political choices made yesterday or today have, and will have, an influence on the choice sets available to any particular actor in the future. Thus contemporary policy that marginalizes small-scale producers and aggressively "de-develops" (Yapa 1996) alternatives for the rural economy would seem, in light of the vast social and environmental uncertainties of Mexico's fu-ture, shortsighted. As E. O. Wilson writes of the problems of the pro-liferation of Green Revolution crop varieties: "In a world created by natural selection, homogeneity means vulnerability" (Wilson 1992: 301). Broadening this argument to address agricultural systems, Bebbington argues, "'Diversification' in this context should therefore imply not only diversification of crops (which can impart both eco-nomic as well as agroecological resilience) but also a diversification of other farm management skills and socio-institutional resources to help the farmer cope with or recover from economic shocks to the farm" (Bebbington 1990: 206). As I argue in the concluding chap-ter, the challenge for those of us interested in facilitating the process of adaptation is not to find the degree and extent of diversification necessary to enable adjustment to any particular set of anticipated

exogenous changes, but rather to create a process of policy development and evolution that self-consciously sets out to expand choice
and opportunity in the future while working with the constraints
and capacities of the present.

In the course of the surveys, interviews, and casual conversations
I had with the farmers of Plan de Ayala, Torres, and Nazareno, I always took pains to explain that I was not working for the government
(this point was particularly important in 2000, an election year) and
could not resolve the many problems they related to me about their
daily efforts to make farming work for them. I did promise, however,
that I would do what I could to enable the farmers of Tlaxcala and
Puebla to speak to a broader audience about what has helped and
hindered their efforts to secure their livelihoods, and by giving a bit
of academic weight to their words, perhaps increase the chances that
someone with the power to change things would listen.

2 Agriculture and Climate in the Puebla-Tlaxcala Valley

Agrarian Roots in the Puebla-Tlaxcala Valley

The farmers whose strategies I relate in this book were residents of the villages of Torres, Plan de Ayala, and Nazareno, three communities in the Puebla-Tlaxcala Valley, just east of Mexico City (fig. 2.1). While their stories reflect to a large extent the history of the region, and their particular relationship to the resources and opportunities of their location, I could have done the same research in almost any region of the Mexican highlands. Households all over rural Mexico are struggling with the same political and economic changes and, in a broad sense, share a common agrarian history and culture. They are also, to different degrees, facing similar environmental and climatic challenges to production, and thus all would have something particular to say about surviving under dynamic and uncertain conditions.

The Puebla-Tlaxcala Valley, however, is particularly fascinating from the standpoint of agricultural history and adaptation. Archaeologists have found evidence of squash and maize cultivation dating back to 6000 and 2000 BC near the town of Tehuacán, Puebla, not far from where I was working in the town of Nazareno (Nolasco and Bonfil Batalla 1972: 18). Remains of raised-bed agriculture (*chinampas*) and irrigation canals have also been found in that area as well as farther west near Cholula, Puebla, and at the archaeological site of Cacaxtla in southwestern Tlaxcala (Martínez Saldaña 1997: 123–26; Nolasco and Bonfil Batalla 1972: 12–13). Many people believe that maize may have been first domesticated in the valley. What most astonishes historians is the density of population that is thought to have been supported by pre-Hispanic agriculture. By one estimate there may have been a population as large as 159,000

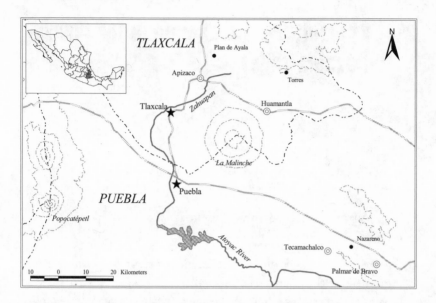

Figure 2.1 The Puebla-Tlaxcala Valley. (Map prepared by Armando Peralta Higuera, Instituto de Geografía, UNAM.)

in the Tehuacán Valley at time of the arrival of the Spanish (Licate 1981). Given the poor soils and arid environment, food production on such a large scale would not have been possible without the elaborate earthen dams, maguey-lined terraces, and rainwater harvesting techniques developed by the early settlers in the valley (Rojas 1991). As Hernán Cortés marched up from the Veracruz coast through the Puebla-Tlaxcala Valley, he is reputed to have expressed great admiration for the elaborate irrigation systems and productive fields he encountered. The Tlaxcalan farmers were so admired by the Spanish colonists that they were brought into northern Mexico to teach northern settlers about farming (Martínez Saldaña 1997).

With the spread of disease and the establishment of the first colonial settlements, the Spanish were rapidly able to control most of the land in the valley. Under the Spanish feudal-like system, the indigenous farmers continued to plant maize, squash, and beans for their own subsistence, but the majority of land in the valley was dedicated to wheat, sugar, and livestock for the colonists' consumption. According to some historians, lack of labor for land maintenance practices together with the changing production priorities of the Spanish colonists contributed to an increase in the sensitivity of the region to climate events. Droughts and frosts repeatedly affected the region in the sixteenth, seventeenth, and eighteenth centuries, causing widespread hunger and food scarcity (Castro Morales 1972: 22–23; Romero 1991).

By the middle of the nineteenth century, although 80 percent of Mexico's population was in rural areas, the majority survived as landless laborers for the haciendas, or in many cases were allowed to rent or sharecrop small landholdings to produce subsistence crops, a practice encouraged by the colonists because it effectively subsidized the cost of maintaining the labor force. Legal reforms in the early nineteenth century, accelerated under Porfirio Díaz's dictatorship (1876–1911), facilitated foreign investment in Mexican land. Land of indebted smallholders was seized, and investors were encouraged to bring any land considered "abandoned" into commercial production. Determined to modernize Mexico, Díaz dramatically expanded Mexico's railway and roads networks, enabling the haciendas for the first time to operate as commercial exporting enterprises, financed with international capital (and often owned by it) and facilitated by Mexico's rapidly expanding banking industry (von Wobeser 1991).

The Puebla-Tlaxcala Valley was crossed by two railways, making the region particularly auspicious for commercial production. The valley became a primary source of wheat, barley, and livestock, as well as of pulque, the alcoholic beverage of the Aztecs appropriated by the Spanish. By 1900, almost all of the cultivable land in Tlaxcala was under the control of 259 haciendas and ranches, and a third of the economically active population served as peons for the haciendas' production (Ramirez Rancaño 1990).

The expropriation of land formerly under peasant subsistence cultivation also placed new demands on food production, which was not the primary focus of Porfirato agriculture. By the end of the nineteenth century, Mexico was, for the first time, importing maize to meet its domestic demand. Not surprisingly, a severe drought in the 1890s precipitated a subsistence crisis in the country. In 1910, the country erupted in revolution, and, after seven violent years, the revolution's rural basis claimed victory. The constitution was amended, and land was to be returned to Mexico's family farmers. Although this process was slow to be implemented, and fraught with violence, by the second half of the twentieth century land in the Puebla-Tlaxcala Valley was once again largely in the hands of smallholder farmers.

Today the Tlaxcala-Puebla Valley is populated by small-scale mestizo (of mixed Spanish and indigenous ancestry) farmers of the sort that make up the majority of Mexico's agricultural population. Neither the most socially marginalized nor the most privileged, ranging from semicommercial to subsistence, ejidatarios to *pequeños propietarios* ("private" landholders with individual title), the farmers in the region today can be considered representative of both the diversity and commonalities of Mexico's smallholders.

Environmental Constraints to Production

Despite the fact that central Mexico is considered the birthplace of Mesoamerican agriculture, the climate, topography, soils, and water resources of the central highlands create highly variable production conditions that constrain the type of agriculture that can be viably practiced. The soils in both Puebla and Tlaxcala are relatively young, with poorly developed profiles and little depth (Secretaría de Programacíon y Presupuesto 1981). Not far beneath the surface is an impenetrable and erodable substance called *tepetate* (derived from the Nahuatl words for rock and mat) (Altieri and Trujillo 1987). Data from the Ministry of Environment and Natural Resources (SEMARNAT) also indicates that 85 percent and 37 percent, respectively, of Tlaxcala's and Puebla's soils exhibited moderate (e.g., soils with reduced productivity) to severe (e.g., economically unproductive soils) levels of erosion in 2001. An additional 27 percent of Puebla's soils showed signs of extreme erosion (SEMARNAT 2002).

Farmers in Tlaxcala and central Puebla have adapted to these constraints by continuing to rely largely on draft animal power as their primary tool for plowing and tillage activities. The rows of maguey (*Agave salminae*) that traditionally outlined the cultivated terraces of the arid slopes of eastern Tlaxcala and Puebla are still visible and, in places, well maintained, as part of what Wilken has called the *"zana/bordo"* system for maintaining soil moisture and slowing erosion (Altieri and Trujillo 1987; Wilken 1987: 104–5).

While the maguey terraces inhibit soil erosion, farmers have also long practiced plowing under their crop stubble to improve the organic content of their soils, and burning their fields in preparation for planting (Wilken 1987). Both these latter practices have been associated with both erosion and forest fires in Mexico by SEMARNAT, although the extent to which farming practices are primarily to blame is debatable. Throughout the 1990s both states reported over one hundred forest fire sites annually. An unprecedented number of fires (439 in Tlaxcala and 544 in Puebla) were reported in 1998—a year of intense drought associated with climate anomalies around the globe. Over eight thousand hectares in Tlaxcala and nineteen thousand hectares in Puebla were consumed by fire that year, making it the most devastating fire season in living memory (SEMARNAT 2002).

As in most of Mexico's semiarid and subhumid highlands, water resources for agricultural use in the Puebla-Tlaxcala Valley are limited both in quantity and in distribution. The meager flow of Tlaxcala's Zahuapan River runs through the state's most densely populated *municipios* (the administrative unit roughly equivalent to a county in the United States), and the water it carries is exploited for domestic, agricultural, and industrial use only in the immediate vicinity of the river. The cost and scarcity of groundwater resources has limited irrigation development in other regions of the state such that in 2000, just over 11 percent of the state's agricultural area was irrigated (INEGI 2000b).

In Puebla, the Atoyac River brings runoff from the volcano Iztaccíhuatl and Tlaxcala's waterways into western and central Puebla, providing the most important source of water for both the city of Puebla and the agricultural valley that extends south of the city. Southeast of the city of Puebla, the Atoyac supplies the Manuel Avila Camacho (Valsequillo) reservoir, which in turn channels water into the irrigation district of Tecamachalco.

Exploitation of the Atoyac waters is limited by its poor quality: the river is so contaminated from sewage and industrial wastes from Puebla that its use for irrigation is permitted only for grains and forage crops, which are thought to be at less risk of being exposed to the contaminants in the water. Any vegetables produced in the valley must be irrigated with groundwater extracted from deep wells in the Tecamachalco Valley. The use of this water is also increasingly constrained by its growing scarcity. According to the most recent data, water extraction in the valley exceeds recharge by 32 Mm^3/year (Comisión Nacional del Agua 2002).

Climatic Variability, El Niño, and Production

The most important biophysical challenge to the valley's production, however, is not its soils, slopes, or water resources, but rather its climate. Mexico's climate system has always exhibited significant variability, and the impact of extreme events has long been a feature of the country's agricultural and social history (Florescano 1980; Mosiño Aleman and García 1974).

The location of the Puebla-Tlaxcala Valley on the margin of Atlantic, Gulf, and Pacific weather systems means that the region's climate is highly sensitive to change in both synoptic-scale and more local climatic processes. The rainy season, or the *temporal*, begins in April and May when the subtropical high-pressure belt, which maintains dry conditions over central and southern Mexico in winter, shifts north. The steep pressure gradient between the subtropical high and the summer placement of the Intertropical Convergence Zone (ITCZ) draws the moist easterly trade winds across the highlands, creating the atmospheric instability that leads to the onset of the rainy season in central Mexico (Mosiño Aleman and García 1974). Eighty percent of annual rainfall occurs between May and September, with the heaviest rains falling in June and September. The Puebla-Tlaxcala Valley receives between 400 and 700 mm of rainfall annually, which in good years provides farmers with just enough precipitation for subsistence maize production. Subtle shifts in the reach of the ITCZ and the position and strength of the summer easterlies can suddenly deny the highland's farmers the rains on which they depend.

One of the most important features of the rainy season is midsummer drought, called the *canícula* by farmers. It is technically not a drought, but a decrease in the number of rainy days during the months of July and August, causing the regions that it affects to have a "bimodal" precipitation pattern with two peaks, one in June and the other in September (Magaña, Amador, and Medina 1999). Farmers in Tlaxcala typically do not view the canícula as a drought event, but rather report that the period can be "with water" or "without water" (Eakin 1998). According to farmers in central and eastern Tlaxcala, neither characterization is particularly beneficial for agriculture: a canícula "with water" also may bring hailstorms that can do significant damage to crops. A canícula "without water" is, according to the farmers interviewed, often characterized by cool, dusty conditions in which frost is a risk, or it can cause significant water stress to maize at the point when the crop is most thirsty (Eakin 1998).

The region in which the canícula is observed extends from the northeastern states down to the southeastern and south-central coast (Magaña, Amador, and Medina 1999). Of the three communities, the canícula was most pronounced in the area of Torres and Nazareno, in the eastern part of the Puebla-Tlaxcala Valley. Farmers in Plan de Ayala, for example, do not typically experience a "dry" canícula: often there is very little decrease in monthly rainfall totals during July and August. Thus, the occurrence of a "dry" canícula for these farmers is an anomaly for which farmers may be unprepared.

Even in areas where the canícula is a standard feature, it can occur with unexpected duration and timing. For example, data from a climate station in Tecamachalco, the nearest commercial town to Nazareno, shows that in 1960 the canícula was entirely absent. In 1950 it was subsumed in a drought that lasted almost three months. The range of total rainfall for the months of July and August underlines this variability: in 1982, Tecamachalco received only 21 mm of rainfall in those months, while in 1979 a total of 334 mm was reported (half of the total rainfall received that year).

While the canícula effectively interrupts the already short rainy season, frost risk is perhaps more constraining to production. Temperatures in the valley average 12°C–18°C, with winter minimums near 0°C. Maximum temperatures rarely exceed 22°C in the lower elevations. The risk of late frosts and cool soil temperatures prevents farmers from planting earlier than April, and the event of an early frost often damages the almost mature grain in September. Those crops or crop varieties that have particularly long growing seasons (i.e., five months or more, as is the case with many certified commercial maize varieties) can be planted only in areas where frost risk is low or where irrigation permits planting earlier.

Over the last few decades, the understanding of the primary drivers of Mexico's climate variability has improved. Through the analysis of tree rings, precolonial and colonial documents, observational records, and the use of statistical models, scientists have illustrated that many of the more severe droughts and floods in Mexico have been associated with the El Niño–Southern Oscillation and other synoptic-scale climate patterns (Acuna-Soto et al. 2005; Dilley 1997; Magaña 1999; Mendoza et al. 2005). Some climatologists now believe that as much as 65 percent of variability in Mexican climate conditions is caused by large-scale circulation processes such as the El Niño–Southern Oscillation (ENSO) or the Pacific–North American Oscillation (Hewitson and Crane 1992).

During El Niño events, the jet stream is generally displaced southward over North America, enhancing the flow of cold fronts across north and central Mexico (Magaña and Quintanar 1997). As a result, winter precipitation tends to increase, particularly in the northern regions of the country, while temperatures tend to be lower than normal (Magaña 1999). The opposite pattern tends to occur during the winters of cold sea surface temperature (La Niña) events.

The relationship of ENSO to summer rainfall is more critical for agricultural households in the central highlands, which are dependent on summer rainfall for their production. Summer rainfall is only partially related to large-scale factors like ENSO. Sea surface temperatures in the immediate vicinity of Mexico's coasts and lower-level circulation patterns also have a strong influence on summer precipitation. That said, it appears that during the summer months of El Niño events the ITCZ does not travel as far northward as in non–El Niño years, and thus the amount of convective activity off Mexico's southern coasts is reduced and rainfall in the central highlands decreases. Some scientists believe this lack of convection reduces the cloud cover over south and central Mexico and increases solar radiation on the highlands and rates of evapotranspiration (Magaña, Amador, and Medina 1999). Increased evapotranspiration in turn increases the probability of "black" or radiative frosts in the summer months (also called "killing frosts," occurring when temperatures drop below freezing in very dry conditions) (Morales and Magaña 1999).

My own analysis of temperature and rainfall data from five stations in central and eastern Tlaxcala (Apizaco and Huamantla) and in central Puebla (Acatzingo, Palmar de Bravo, and Tecamachalco) supports these findings, particularly in the eastern part of the Puebla-Tlaxcala Valley where the effect of ENSO appears more pronounced (Eakin 2002). The observational record is relatively short for these stations (twenty-five to fifty years), and thus the data are not conclusive. However, the observational records suggest an association of El Niño events with warmer, wetter winters and cooler, drier summers and a more accentuated (dry) canícula. During El Niño years, the frequency of early and late summer frosts also tends to be higher in these stations, a finding that became particularly relevant as I documented farmers' strategies for dealing with the droughts and frosts of the 1990s.

Understanding the link between ENSO and local climate is also important for anticipating how climate patterns are likely to change in the region under global warming. In central Tlaxcala, observational data show that maximum temperatures have risen between 1.5°C and 2°C since 1961, primarily in the winter months (Conde, Ferrer, and Gay 1998). Rainfall also appears to have increased during this period, although there is some evidence of a more pronounced midsummer drought in the early 1990s (Conde, Ferrer, and Gay 1998). Although the quality of the data does not permit a rigorous analysis of trends, the time-series data from the Tecamachalco meteorological station in Puebla also show similar patterns of changing rainfall distribution in the early 1990s, as well as an unusual number of summer frost events associated with drier conditions (figs. 2.2, 2.3).

The observed changes in monthly rainfall patterns in the 1980s and early 1990s coincide with a defined shift in the dynamics of the El Niño–Southern Oscillation since 1976 that some scientists believe may be associated with rising global surface temperatures (Trenberth and Hoar 1997; Tsonis, Hunt, and Elsner 2002). The prolonged El Niño conditions in the 1990s were particularly anomalous and unprecedented in the climate record (Trenberth and Hoar 1996). According to some global climate-change scenarios, El Niño-like climate patterns may become far more common and contribute to an increase in interannual climate variability (IPCC Working Group I 2001; Tsonis, Hunt, and Elsner 2002).

To date, the climate-change models used for scenario construc-

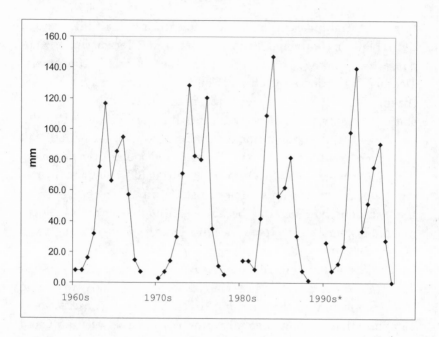

Figure 2.2 Average monthly rainfall in Tecamachalco by decade, 1960–90. *Source:* Comisión Nacional de Agua.
*Rainfall data are missing for this station between 1995 and 1998. The 1990s data presented represent average monthly rainfall 1990–94.

tion in Mexico have not been able to adequately simulate ENSO conditions or the possible implications of increased climatic variability accompanying warming temperatures. However, all models anticipate that the warming trends observed in the country will continue (Liverman and O'Brien 1991; Magaña et al. 1997). One scenario produced by the Canadian Climate Center model includes a significant increase in drought severity in both Puebla and Tlaxcala under conditions of a doubling of atmospheric carbon dioxide (Hernández Cerda, Torres Tapia, and Valdez Madero 2000).

Impact assessments conducted on the basis of these scenarios for Mexico's agricultural sector also paint a relatively pessimistic picture, with potential declines in rainfed maize yields of between 20 percent and 60 percent, withholding any adaptive action (Liverman et al. 1992). The impact of climate change on maize production is of particular concern for smallholder producers who depend on maize

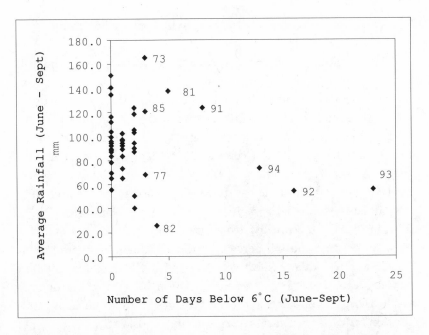

Figure 2.3 Frequency of summer frost days and average summer rainfall, 1941–94, Tecamachalco, Puebla. A frost day is defined in relation to maize, which does not tolerate temperatures below 6°C. *Source:* Comisión Nacional de Agua.

as a source of subsistence as well as a source of income, and for whom adaptation technologies may not be as accessible (Liverman 1991).

Thus, while no single extreme event or even a series of extreme events can be said to be evidence of climate change, the observed climate trends in the Puebla-Tlaxcala Valley combined with the ENSO-linked variability of the 1990s are troubling. Given the possible links between ENSO and warming temperatures, it may not be such a stretch to consider the type of variability experienced in the 1990s—for example, an increase in the occurrence of "canículas without water" and anomalous summer frosts—as a plausible scenario of future climate variability, with particularly negative implications for farmers in the Puebla-Tlaxcala Valley.

Agriculture in the Valley's Contemporary Economy

Despite the characteristic climatic variability of the valley, its poor soils, and scarce water resources, agriculture has continued to be an important economic activity, if not in terms of its
economic value, then in terms of the number of households supported in some way by agricultural activities. According to the most
recent national population census, 28 percent and 18 percent of
the economically active population in Puebla and Tlaxcala, respectively, were employed in the primary economic sector in 1999,
and agricultural activities continue to dominate land use (INEGI
2000a, 2000b). In contrast, the agricultural sector accounted for
only 6.9 percent and 6.7 percent of the gross domestic product of
Puebla and Tlaxcala, respectively, in 1999 (INEGI 2000a, 2000b).

At the national level, the contradiction between the economic
productivity and population involved in agriculture was a strong motivation for the agricultural reforms of the 1990s. Official documents
in Puebla and Tlaxcala narrate the same story line: the apparent failure in the productivity of the sector is attributed to unprofitably small
production units, unfavorable climatic and environmental conditions,
farmers' lack capital and organization, and an implied cultural stub-
bornness of farmers, reluctant to abandon their subsistence tradi-
tions for more commercial and more profitable crops (SEFOA 2000).
The consequent solution to such a problem is more intensive and
more commercial production on larger landholdings, run by far fewer farmers.

The size of the average landholding in both states would support
the conclusion that landholdings may indeed be a development constraint (in Puebla average landholdings are just 3.3 ha, and in Tlaxcala they are just under 2 ha). There are other issues, however, that
perhaps are given short shrift in official evaluations—the critical importance of maize, for instance, in rural livelihood security. Maize
is Mexico's principal crop, and the maize tortilla is still the essential
staple of the Mexican diet. Although urbanization has increased the
demand for commercially manufactured tortillas and maize flour,
outside of urban areas tortillas are still largely made with locally
grown maize.

Despite efforts during the colonial era to transform the state into barley and wheat plantations, Tlaxcala and Puebla are today, as they were in pre-Hispanic times, states of *maiceros*, or maize farmers. According to the state government, the very name Tlaxcala comes from the Nahuatl word *tlaxcalli*, or "place of tortillas." In 1998/99, maize occupied 51.7 percent of the total area planted and accounted for 26.2 percent of the total agricultural value (INEGI 2000b). Nearly 90 percent of Tlaxcala's maize area is rainfed (INEGI 2000b), and, in 1990, 65.5 percent of Tlaxcala's maize farmers produced solely for their own subsistence, a figure that is not likely to have changed considerably over the last fifteen years. In Puebla, 63.6 percent of agricultural land was devoted to maize in 1998/1999 (INEGI 2000a). Maize is planted in all 217 municipios of the state and remains the livelihood security of most of the rural population.

In general, rainfed maize yields are low. In Tlaxcala, the average yield was between 1.2 ton/ha and 2.4 ton/ha in the 1990s (SEFOA 2000). However, the maize production system in central Mexico has also been recognized as being genetically diverse, even in regions well connected to urban areas and commercial markets (Altieri and Trujillo 1987; Perales R., Brush, and Qualset 2003). Many of the local varieties planted by farmers *(criollos)* have been selected not necessarily for yield but rather for their particular color or taste, their resistance to pests, wind lodging, or water stress (Altieri and Trujillo 1987, Perales R., Brush, and Qualset 2003).

Tlaxcala's other principal crops, barley *(Hordeum vulgare)* and wheat *(Triticum aestivum)*, are considered commercial crops, normally sold as grain or as forage. Some vegetables are planted in irrigated fields in southwestern Tlaxcala, and potatoes have become an important crop in the Huamantla Valley in the eastern part of the state, not far from the community of Torres. A greater diversity of commercial crops is planted in Puebla, including a wide variety of vegetables in the Tecamachalco irrigation district in the center of the state. In the northern sierra, coffee and peanuts are grown for regional and international markets.

Despite Tlaxcala's fame as a producer of quality bulls for bullfighting (a fame that dates back to the colonial era), livestock production and animal products do not contribute substantially to Tlaxcala's economy (SEFOA 2000). The majority of farmers raise livestock purely on a small-scale subsistence basis. The production of sheep, goat, and pigs declined significantly after the economic crisis of 1994; beef and milk cattle, however, have maintained a small but steady growth rate through the 1990s. Livestock activities play a greater role in Puebla, representing approximately a third of the state's agricultural gross domestic product (INEGI 1999a). A Bachoco egg factory in Tecamachalco (established in 1993) has contributed to making Puebla one of the country's primary producers of eggs and poultry. Recently, Puebla has also begun to market goat meat and pork on an industrial scale (Morales Flores 2000).

The ongoing struggle and decline in productivity in the region's agriculture sector is balanced by the growth of urban, peri-urban, and rural industry. In the 1980s and 1990s, Tlaxcala's economic policy was designed to encourage diversification away from its traditional economic base of agriculture and textiles (Ornelas Delgado 1994: 106–7). Through investment incentives and active promotion of its economic assets, Tlaxcala is now home to small- and large-scale companies specializing in petrochemicals, pharmaceuticals, electronics, food products, paper, furniture, and clothing (Industrial Development Ministry 2000).

According to one recent study, Puebla has not been as aggressive as Tlaxcala in promoting its industrial sector, and the economic growth that has occurred in the state in the last decade has tended to concentrate opportunities and services in the capital to the neglect of Puebla's large rural population (Sánchez Daza 1998). In 1996, 53 percent of Puebla's industries and 75 percent of the industrial jobs were located in just two of the state's seven regions (García Güemez 1998: 17). A new national development plan, Plan Puebla-Panama, is expected to promote the decentralization of industrial growth in Puebla, bringing foreign and domestic industries to industrial corridors in the central valley. In 1999, approximately 21 percent of Puebla's working population was employed in manufacturing or industry (INEGI 2001a).

In the future, the importance of manufacturing and industry will undoubtedly increase and gradually absorb more of the rural labor force. Yet surprisingly, given the effort to accelerate industrialization in the valley as well as the increasingly acute crisis in the profitability of rural activities, neither state has witnessed a dramatic decrease in the proportion of the population living in rural areas over the last decade. In the 1990 census, approximately 39 percent of Tlaxcala's and 46 percent of Puebla's population lived in communities of less than 5,000 inhabitants (INEGI 1992a, 1992b). According to the latest census (INEGI 2001a), Tlaxcala's and Puebla's populations were, respectively, 37 percent and 42 percent rural.

In the near future it is reasonable to expect that the welfare of the states' rural populations will continue to be a social, economic, and political concern. The history of the region illustrates the smallholders' impressive capacity to adapt to the changing political circumstances of production in the valley and to modify the environment to suit the demands of their subsistence. The challenges they now face, however, are not necessarily related to the familiar constraints to production, but rather to the need to accommodate and adjust to the unexpected, or to new circumstances that make familiar responses no longer effective. The following chapter presents one of the major sources of nonclimatic uncertainty that farmers in the valley are now facing: the reversal of nearly a century of agrarian policy.

3   Neoliberalism and Agricultural Restructuring

Adaptive Capacity in the Age of Globalization

On January 31, 2003, thousands of farmers from all over the country took to the streets of Mexico City in angry protest. Marching under the slogan "¡El campo no aguanta más!" (The countryside can't take it anymore!), the farmers threw the blame of fifteen years of progressive impoverishment and marginalization on the doorstep of the federal government. While forty years earlier land would have been their unifying cause, in 2003 it was something far more intangible, something far more complex: the North American Free Trade Agreement (NAFTA). Ten years into NAFTA, the farmers wanted out. They demanded that the agricultural chapter be renegotiated, they demanded a guaranteed living wage from farming, and they demanded that their contribution to national food security be recognized. They declared the countryside in a state of emergency.

The massive mobilization took the administration of Vicente Fox Quesada (2000–2006) by surprise, although the crisis had been brewing for over a decade. In 2003, NAFTA had come to represent all that was wrong with Mexico's agricultural policy: the embodiment of globalization, U.S. imperialism, agribusiness greed, and urban arrogance. And the farmers had had enough. In a country in which Emiliano Zapata is a national symbol, President Vicente Fox was quickly reminded that ignoring smallholder agriculture can have revolutionary consequences.

It was not only NAFTA that had driven farmers to the streets. Since I began doing fieldwork in Mexico in 1997, losses to climatic hazards have totaled over one million hectares annually. While this figure is still small in comparison to the twenty million hectares planted every year in Mexico, maize, a crop largely planted by smallholders, typically accounts for one-third to one-half of those losses (SIAP 2003). The relationship between these losses and the agricultural policies that the farmers were protesting is complex. The joint impacts of climate and policy on one level could be considered simply an unhappy coincidence of hardship. Yet it is also increasingly clear that as a result of the policy changes of the 1990s, the range of choices that farmers face about technology, crops, and livelihoods is also changing, and these limitations are affecting their flexibility in responding to climatic shocks.

Philip McMichael defines globalization as the "worldwide integration of economic process and of space" and the "growing homogeneity . . . of a singular market culture" (McMichael 1994: 227). The meaning of globalization for agricultural systems is complicated by the fact that environmental constraints to farming—climate, soils, solar radiation—make agriculture in some ways incompatible with the flexible and mobile globalized economy (Goodman and Watts 1997). Yet the process of globalization has had profound impacts on agriculture, particularly in countries for which agriculture is not one industry among many, but rather an important source of livelihood for large segments of the population.

Agriculture has traditionally been one of the more manipulated and managed productive sectors in both developing and developed countries. Historically, systems of food production and consumption policies were determined largely by national political and socioeconomic objectives in concert with international trade commitments. In today's integrated economies, national agricultural policies are increasingly driven by transnational conditions, such as multilateral regulations on food-product quality, regulations on trade and protectionism, quality and quantity demands of transnational agro-industries, and cosmopolitan consumer tastes and preferences (Friedmann 1994; Marsden 1997). In Latin America, agricultural populations that were protected and supported for decades for diverse reasons— among them, national food security and political stability—have now been defined as "nonviable" and dismissed as economically unproductive (Bebbington 1999).

Perhaps more than any other nation, Mexico provides an ideal opportunity for the exploration of implications of agricultural globalization and climatic variability for smallholder vulnerability. While

Mexico's economic dependency on the United States has always been strong, Mexico's entry into the General Agreement on Tariffs and Trade (GATT) in 1986 and its subsequent signing of the North American Free Trade Agreement (NAFTA) in 1994 marked a new era in Mexican trade and domestic economic development policy. Over the course of the last two decades, the implementation of free trade and antiprotectionist policies, accompanied by state retrenchment, the core elements of what is dubbed "neoliberalism," has caused an upheaval in Mexico's agricultural sector. The sections that follow describe how the globalization process, articulated through the implementation of neoliberal economic policies, is changing the context of vulnerability and the potential for adaptation for Mexico's smallholders.

Globalization and "Viable" Agriculture in Mexico

To understand the meaning of the recent neoliberal reforms in Mexican agriculture, it is necessary to review briefly the vision of "viable" agriculture that was gradually institutionalized in Mexico's agricultural sector over the last century. When the technocrats were deciding the direction of agricultural reforms in the late 1980s, their general conclusion was that the sector was inefficient and technologically behind: a drastic overhaul was needed. Yet despite the arguments of "inevitability and rationality" of free traders, how and by what measures agricultural productivity is evaluated are inherently ideological (Marsden 1997).

Throughout Mexico's history, biases in the distribution of resources, in access to markets, in the objectives of research and technology investment, and in the orientation of subsidies for energy use and finance have defined the country's agricultural geography (Yates 1981). During what some call "the first wave of globalization," coinciding with the Porfirato in Mexico (1870–1911), the models of efficiency in agriculture were the sprawling hacienda and the capitalists that linked Mexico's cash crop industry to foreign markets (see chap. 2). The economic viability of this system was made possible in large part by the indebted labor of the country's peasant population.

When land began to be returned to Mexico's *campesino* farmers, the ejidatarios, in the land distribution program after the 1910 revolution, it was thought that this would be an opportunity to demonstrate that smallholder farming was not only viable but a national necessity. Article 27 of the 1917 constitution had institutionalized the agrarian movement by legally allocating land use and production rights to agrarian communities called ejidos whose members (ejidatarios) had usufruct rights to farm (Cornelius and Myhre 1998; Reyes Castañeda 1981). Although the land distribution process resulted in the creation of more than 27,000 ejidos on over 50 percent of Mexico's arable land, the quality of the distributed resources varied considerably. By some assessments, the most productive regions remained in private hands (Heath 1992). Although it was thought that the ejidatarios might become a source of economic vitality in rural areas, over time the relationship that the state developed with the smallholder and ejidal sector was one in which the rural population primarily served to ensure the legitimacy of Mexico's dominant political party, the Partido Revolucionario Institucional (PRI), through small infusions of resources and the often patronizing influence of a variety of public institutions (Foley 1995; Fox 1995).

In the mid-1940s, Mexico's President Manuel Ávila Camacho created the Office of Special Studies to develop a program of "scientific agriculture" in close collaboration with the Rockefeller Foundation (Jennings 1988). This research pact was the birth of what later was called the Green Revolution, a three-decade period of rapid transformation in agricultural technology and policy. During this period the federal government supported intensive development of irrigation infrastructure, mechanization, and adoption of commercial inputs in the northern states, where the flat topography, availability of surface water, and scale of landholdings were considered particularly appropriate for the model of "modern" agriculture the Office of Special Studies was advocating. The yields of wheat and sorghum, crops destined for the flour and livestock feed industries, surged. The Green Revolution was applauded globally as a successful example of the transformative potential of science.

Yet not all of the implications of the Green Revolution were positive, particularly for the smallholders and indigenous farmers in Mexico's central and southern states that were essentially excluded from the agricultural research agenda. Maize was not a focus of Green Revolution research, and the capital-intensive technologies that were promoted during this period were inappropriate for the environments in which most of Mexico's smallholders were farming. Yapa argues that one of the more disturbing results of the Green Revolution was the manner in which the commitment to one ideology of production (capital-intensive, high-input technology) "de-developed" alternatives that could have more appropriately addressed the demands of the majority of farmers and the productive needs of the economy over the long term (Yapa 1996).

Perhaps even more damaging was that designating Green Revolution technology as "modern" and "progressive" rendered the practices of peasants who were not participating in the modernization project by definition "backward" and "inefficient" (Cotter 1994; Loker 1996; Yapa 1996). When the objective of improving adaptive capacity to future risks and uncertainties requires providing society with greater flexibility and an increasing diversity of choice, such narrow ideas of what is viable, efficient, and modern are troubling.

Neoliberalism in Mexican Agriculture

Although the Green Revolution vision of modern agriculture was adopted in Mexican research and policy in the 1940s and 1950s, the power of this "devaluation" of small-scale agriculture did not take full force until it was legitimized in the rhetoric and practice of neoliberal economic policy thirty years later. By 1970, Green Revolution technology and public investment had created a strong commercial agricultural sector in the northern states, in which many ejidos of that region were participating. The neglect of the smallholder sector in the south and central states, however, was generating economic and social costs that were beginning to be felt at the national level. From being a food exporter in the late 1950s, Mexico became increasingly dependent on food imports to meet its domestic needs (Austin and Esteva 1987; Escalante and Redón 1987). As the more industrialized agricultural regions such as the Bajío Valley in Guanajuato and the irrigated valleys in the north turned to forage crops and specialty produce for export, Mexico faced an increasing deficit in its basic consumption crops of maize, beans, and wheat (Barkin 1990).

By the mid-1970s in many regions of the country, landless campesinos who had been waiting to participate in Mexico's agrarian reform for decades mobilized to demand what they felt was entitled to them (Gates 1989). Facing a loss of political control over the countryside, President Luis Echeverría's administration (1970–76) began to explore ways of increasing the uptake of Green Revolution technology in Mexico's central and southern states. It was in this period that small-scale maize farmers in the Puebla Valley became the focus of research and extension efforts in the Plan Puebla experiment (Díaz-Cisneros 1994; Felstehausen and Díaz-Cisneros 1985; Redclift 1983).

Through encouraging collective land management in the ejidos, President Echeverría's administration hoped to overcome what were perceived as problems of scale inefficiencies and land fragmentation (Gates 1989). Echeverría also revitalized the stagnant land distribution process, distributing over sixteen million hectares during his administration (de Janvry et al. 1995; Gates 1989). Under the Mexican Food System program (the Sistema Alimentaria Mexicana, or SAM) of President José Lopez Portillo (1976–82), the ejidatarios benefited from increased availability in credit, inputs, and technical assistance, financed by Mexico's booming oil industry. For the first time in decades, maize production increased, and Mexico was once again aiming for self-sufficiency.

In 1982, the economy slipped into crisis. Under the tutelage of the IMF and World Bank, President Miguel de la Madrid (1982–88) embarked on a series of structural changes to the economy and the agricultural sector involving dramatic cuts in public spending and strict fiscal policy. Over the course of the 1980s there was a 62 percent decline in gross public fixed investment in agriculture (Ochoa 1994: 11). The federal government began an aggressive effort to decentralize its operations, reduce its interference in markets, and privatize many of its institutions, shifting many of its responsibilities and services to the private sector, decentralized quasi-public agencies, or nongovernmental organizations. When Mexico signed NAFTA in 1994, the country's ideological commitment to neoliberalism—"the key mechanism through which globalization will achieve the economic benefits it promises" (OECD 1997: 10)—was complete. As the following discussion will illustrate, while many public institutions were dismantled, the government has also devised new ways of intervening in the agricultural sector through an (often bewildering) array of public sector welfare programs.

Price Liberalization and Privatization

One of the central policies of Mexico's new policy agenda of the 1980s and 1990s was that of price liberalization. Mexico's farmers had benefited for decades from a guaranteed price for maize, barley, wheat, beans, rice, and other basic grains that ensured the economic viability of their production (OECD 1997). These supports were particularly important in states such as Puebla, Tlaxcala, Hidalgo, Guerrero, and Oaxaca where maize and beans were the dominant crops of poor smallholder farmers. Throughout the de la Madrid administration, both food consumers and producers were rocked by hyperinflation and periodic devaluations, and the purchasing power of peasant households was dramatically eroded (Appendini 1992/2001; Calva 1994; Gates 1989).

As guaranteed producer prices were withdrawn for many products over the course of the 1980s, the role of CONASUPO (Compañía Nacional de Subsistencias Populares; National Company of Popular Subsistence), the state-run grain marketing agency, was gradually reduced. By 1988, the real guaranteed producer price for corn and beans had dropped 70 percent and 61 percent of their respective 1981 values (Ochoa 1994: 12), and producer support prices for all other grain crops had been dropped (Appendini 1994). In 1998 CONASUPO was shut down in the midst of a corruption scandal, leaving farmers with the sole option of selling to the private sector either directly or through intermediaries.

In 1990, President Carlos Salinas de Gotari (1988–94) launched the Agricultural Modernization Program, designed to single out the most competitive farmers for support, and to promote the crops for which Mexico was thought to have a comparative advantage in international markets. Corn prices continued to fall in real terms, and grain imports were made comparatively even less expensive by an appreciating exchange rate (de Janvry, Gordillo, and Sadoulet 1997). Simultaneously, the costs of farm inputs, particularly imported products, were rising, challenging the finances of even the most commercial producers (Hewitt de Alcántara 1994).

In 1994, Salinas finished his six-year term by signing NAFTA with the United States and Canada, an act that effectively ended any hope that Mexico would be able to fulfill its identity as a country of maiceros in globalized markets. Since 1994, maize imports have steadily climbed. Although under NAFTA Mexico is allowed to charge a tariff on corn imports above a threshold set annually, this tariff has rarely been collected (Appendini 1992/2001; Dussel Peters 2000; Fritscher Mundt 1999: 142). Mexican maize prices have fallen by at least 35 percent in real terms since the implementation of NAFTA, reflecting parallel declines in the international price of maize as well as a policy that sets domestic prices for white corn on par with imported U.S. yellow corn (Dyer-Leal and Yúnez-Naude 2003: 9).

Instead of uniformly promoting greater efficiency and a more "modern" agricultural sector, the new policies have pushed many semicommercial smallholders to the margins of the agricultural economy. Several analysts have observed that the loss of an easily accessible market for small volumes of grain has induced the growth of a "peasant economy" in which production for subsistence, often under traditional means (e.g., draft animal power and intercropping techniques), has increased. For example, de Janvry, Gordillo, and Sadoulet found that the use of all purchased inputs—chemical and natural fertilizers, improved seeds, pesticides and herbicides—declined significantly in the first half of the 1990s among ejidatarios, as access to production technology from official (public/government) sources dropped by 85 percent in the same period (de Janvry, Gordillo, and Sadoulet 1997: 78). In other cases, particularly in situations where ejidatarios and other small-scale producers were already involved in the production of commodities such as sugar, tobacco, fruit, or coffee, farmers have begun to forge new production relationships with intermediaries and private producer associations in order to find affordable inputs and accessible markets (see, e.g., the collection of Snyder 1999).

Credit

Credit availability was one of the first things to contract as Mexico's markets opened to greater foreign competition. For decades the public agricultural bank, BANRURAL, was the primary source of finance and technology for the ejidal sector (Myhre 1998; Pessah 1987). In addition to providing loans, BANRURAL also dictated the choice of crop, seed, and inputs that farmers would use and provided technical assistance on farm management. In 1990, staggering under poor management, corruption, and unpaid loans, BANRURAL and its insurance agency, ANAGSA, were restructured to focus operations on low-risk and economically viable clients, a group that was estimated to incorporate at most 600,000 farmers in all of Mexico (Myhre 1998). BANRURAL remained in limited operation until 2003. ANAGSA was reopened as AGROASEMEX, but by the end of the 1990s was providing only reinsurance services to the agricultural sector.

A variety of alternative financial mechanisms began to be offered to smallholders in the early 1990s. PRONASOL, or Crédito a la Palabra, is the best known of these funds. By the mid-1990s it was covering only 600,000 some farmers, less than 20 percent of BANRURAL's former clients, with loans so small that most experts believed that the program was doing little to finance production (Myhre 1998). A variety of other funds, such as FIRA (Fideicomisos Instituidos en Relación con la Agricultura; Trust Funds for Agriculture), FIRCO (Fideicomiso de Riesgo Compartido; Trust Fund for Shared Risk), or FONAES (Fondo Nacional de Empresas Sociales; National Fund for Solidarity Businesses) were also created to finance motivated rural groups in entrepreneurial activities (de Janvry et al. 1995; Myhre 1998; OECD 1997). PRONASOL and FONAES are considered part of Mexico's "poverty alleviation" programs, not agricultural finance, and are administered by Mexico's Ministry for Social Development. Today these funds, together with a new institution, Financiera Rural, work with private commercial banks to provide small subsidized loans and risk management support to farmers, although the beneficiaries of these programs represent only a small fraction of rural households. Since 1985, the total maize area covered through the government's official bank (either BANRURAL or now Financiera Rural) dropped by 87 percent (Fox Quesada 2004).

Ironically, the dismantling of the rural credit system came just at the moment that many ejidatarios and smallholders were beginning the transition to more expensive purchased fertilizers and hybrid seeds, after the introduction to these inputs through the modernization programs of the 1970s. Without easy access to insurance, smallholder farmers are even less likely to invest in the costly fertilizers, seeds, and other inputs that they need to compete in commercial markets of the NAFTA era.

Research and Extension

The withdrawal of public price supports and subsidies and the closure of admittedly inefficient public marketing agencies might have been less devastating to the flexibility and adaptability of smallholders if the public sector had simultaneously engaged in investment in research and extension. This type of investment might have facilitated the transition of households to alternative strategies appropriate to the farmers' capacities and the biophysical constraints of smallholder production. However, in the late 1980s and early 1990s, the public extension service offered by the national agriculture ministry was reformed, decentralized, and reduced in size (OECD 1997). As a result of this restructuring, the overall number of publicly funded extension agents was cut in half (de Janvry et al. 1995).

A national ejidal household survey in 1994 showed an 85 percent decline in the use of technical assistance in the ejido sector between 1990 and 1994 (de Janvry, Gordillo, and Sadoulet 1997). The majority of national extension support expenditure is now concentrated in the specific organizations that are affiliated with the provision of credit to entrepreneurial farmers and other rural residents. Technical support and advice for farmers on issues of primary production are now largely left to the private sector, or are offered via particular projects run by financial agencies such as FIRA that are designed to promote the development of particular commercial crops (such as organic coffee).

Land Reform

The institutional changes that took place in the 1980s and 1990s were implemented with the firm belief that Mexico's smallholders, the ejidos in particular, were a prime source of "dead weight" and inefficiency in Mexican agriculture (Cebreros 1990). In 1991, President Salinas de Gotari initiated the reform of article 27 of the Mexican constitution, giving Mexico's ejidatarios legal title to their fields, allowing them to legally rent and sell their parcels, use their land as collateral, and engage in joint ventures with private agents (Cornelius and Myhre 1998). The hope was that by removing the legal obstacle to land markets, there would be increased flows of investment in agriculture and ultimately a concentration of land in the hands of the most promising and entrepreneurial producers (Calva 1994; Cornelius and Myhre 1998; García Zamora 1994).

Many ejidatarios had already been engaged in informal land markets, without legal title. Gaining title through PROCEDE (Programa de Certificación de Derechos Ejidales y Titulación de Solares Urbanos; Program for the Certification of Ejido Land Rights and the Titling of Urban House Plots) is also only the first step in the process of land privatization. Under the new law, ejidatarios cannot sell their land without majority consent of the ejido assembly. Regardless of whether or not an ejidatario decides to fully privatize his or her ejidal property, it is quite common for an ejidatario to have both ejidal property and *pequeña propiedad* (land under private land tenure, often adjacent to the ejido), the latter acquired through existing formal or informal land markets.

As of 2005, 83 percent of Mexico's 29,932 agricultural ejidos had completed the titling process (through PROCEDE). All of Tlaxcala's ejidos and 77 percent of Puebla's ejidos have now completed the program. However, the land-titling process is generally not viewed by academics as having successfully stimulated private investment in the agricultural sector. Nor has it caused a mass transfer of land from the hands of marginalized ejidatarios to large-scale commercial agricultural producers (Cornelius and Myhre 1998). As I learned from observing the ejidatarios of Plan de Ayala debate the sale of their land to Kimberly-Clark, it is more probable that in many areas the outcome of PROCEDE will be a transfer of land out of agricultural activities altogether (see also Gledhill 1995).

PROCAMPO, Alianza Para el Campo, and PROGRESA

In the absence of agricultural credit, insurance, and technical assistance, rural households now rely principally on three federal programs. The first, PROCAMPO (Programa de Apoyo directo al Campo; Direct Rural Support Program), was launched in 1994 with the stated objective of easing the transition of small-scale producers into a more competitive, modern agricultural sector, while not distorting the function of agricultural markets through price supports (Gómez Cruz et al. 1993). PROCAMPO consists of a direct payment to the farmer of a standard per-hectare amount for the total land area that was planted in any of nine basic crops at the time of the program's initiation in 1994. In order to encourage diversification into higher-value alternative crops, PROCAMPO payments continue even if the farmer switches crops. PROCAMPO will be discontinued in 2008, fifteen years after the signing of NAFTA.

In 2003, PROCAMPO was reaching over two million farmers, or 35 percent of the agricultural population (Fox Quesada 2003). While some critics point out that the annual increase in the subsidy masks a decline over time in real terms (see editorial by Marquez Ayala, *La Jornada*, 2 Sept. 2000), PROCAMPO has become the only source of support for the vast majority of Mexico's small-scale producers. With the loss of agricultural financing and the escalation in input costs with the liberalization of diesel, fertilizer, and seed prices, PROCAMPO payments have begun to serve as the principal source of short-term credit available to smallholders (Nadal 1999: 117).

The government in recent years has established a system by which farmers can trade in a PROCAMPO voucher to a group of private fertilizer and chemical companies, receiving a credit for their input purchases in the amount of their PROCAMPO payment. Farmers' participation in this input purchasing program is voluntary, but is encouraged as a means to influence farmers' technology choices and improve rates of chemical and fertilizer adoption (Nadal 1999: 118). While this new policy facilitates access to specific inputs, it does not give farmers much flexibility in their choice of inputs or the option to use the voucher for alternative investments.

The other agricultural program that formed the basis of Mexico's agricultural policy in the 1990s was actually a series of smaller programs under the umbrella program Alianza para el Campo (Alliance for the Countryside). This program was launched in 1995 and includes support for improvements in irrigation, pasture establishment, dairy farming technology transfer, livestock genetic improvement, phyto-sanitary education, and mechanization. Additionally, funds are available for small-scale rural development projects, some oriented toward improving the participation of women in productive activities in rural households. Alianza is designed to foster entrepreneurial initiatives among farmers by requiring them to organize and request the services they need. Most of Alianza's programs require farmers to commit to paying up front a significant proportion of the investment costs of any project they embark on (typically 50 percent, with an upper ceiling on farmers' expenditures) (Gobierno del Estado de Puebla 1999). As a result, many of the programs under Alianza are oriented toward farmers with private land titles who already have some resources to invest.

One of the Alianza para el Campo projects that received a large proportion of the program's funds in 1999 and 2000 was the program Kilo por Kilo. In the 2000 Alianza budget for Tlaxcala, for example, Kilo por Kilo represented 13 percent of total expenditures (Gobierno de Tlaxcala 2000). Kilo por Kilo was intended to facilitate the adoption of hybrid maize, sorghum, barley, or oat seed by heavily subsidizing the cost of the seed. Like PROCAMPO's link to fertilizer and other input purchases, Kilo por Kilo was designed to facilitate the adoption of commercial inputs and thus modernize the small-scale agricultural sector. Despite its relatively large share of the agricultural budget, in Tlaxcala only 4,119 farmers participated in Kilo por Kilo annually between 1996 and 1998, representing at most 6 percent of that state's farmers (SEFOA 2000).

While not agricultural, PROGRESA (Programa de Educación, Salud y Alimentación; Education, Health, and Nutrition Program; now, under President Vicente Fox, called Oportunidades) is the third program that directly affects the livelihoods of rural families and their capacity to survive declining purchasing power and terms of trade. Since its inception in 1997, the program has provided food rations, medical support, and educational scholarships for impoverished households with school-age children. In the face of stagnant producer prices, rising consumer costs, and few alternative income sources, this welfare program has become an important support for many rural families. As of December 2000, 12,018 families in Tlaxcala and 200,000 households in Puebla were receiving support through PROGRESA. Over four million families participated in Oportunidades nationally in 2002 (Fox Quesada 2003).

Institutional Change and Rural Livelihoods

Given the profound nature of the institutional changes in the agricultural sector over the 1990s, the violence and anger that surged in the streets of Mexico as the country neared the ten-year anniversary of NAFTA should not have surprised anyone. Various comprehensive studies of agricultural development, rural welfare, and poverty since 1990 have come to the same conclusion: on the whole, the reforms of the 1980s and 1990s have had a negative effect on Mexico's ejidatarios.

One of the most comprehensive assessments at the national level was de Janvry, Gordillo, and Sadoulet's analysis of the 1994 ejido survey undertaken by the Ministry of Agrarian Reform (Secretaría de la Reforma Agraria, SRA) and the Economic Commission for Latin America and the Caribbean (Comisión Económica para America Latina y el Caribe, CEPAL). Their analysis revealed a general shift of land into maize production in the mid-1990s, contrary to what one might expect under the opening of Mexico's agricultural markets. In fact, between 1990 and 1994, cultivation of corn on irrigated ejidal land grew by 68 percent. This trend was most apparent in the North Pacific states, where the ejido survey also showed a concentration of landholdings in fewer hands. Yet they also found evidence that intercropping of rainfed maize and beans had increased, particularly among smaller landholdings in the southern states and those ejidos without irrigation, suggesting a retreat from entrepreneurial activities (de Janvry, Gordillo, and Sadoulet 1997).

In his analysis of maize in the post-NAFTA economy, Alejandro Nadal also perceived an expansion of maize cultivation in both ecologically marginal zones and irrigated areas (Nadal 1999). In the face of rising consumer prices relative to rural wages, subsistence production seems to make more and more sense to many smallholder families. There is also some indication that rural smallholders value their home-grown maize for its quality, taste, and multiple uses far more than the maize grain they can find in local markets (Dyer-Leal and Yúnez-Naude 2003). Facing highly competitive and uncertain markets after NAFTA, many larger farmers may have initially found greater security in planting maize, particularly with PROCAMPO support. More recently, however, national data on maize production suggests that if larger farmers were seeking stability by planting maize a few years ago, this is no longer likely to be the case. PROCAMPO does not bind farmers to planting maize (they may plant alternative crops as long as they were initially registered as farmers of basic grains in 1994). Commercializing maize in Mexico is increasingly difficult and unprofitable, and as maize imports from the United States have increased, commercial maize production in Mexico has becomes less secure. According to official statistics, since 1997 the area planted in maize has declined by 29 percent (SIAP 2003).

For those farmers who are turning to subsistence maize production as a source of livelihood stability and food security, it is unlikely that this strategy will facilitate their integration into the increasingly competitive agricultural economy. These farmers no longer have a guaranteed buyer of their harvests, and the continued support prices for maize have not kept up with rising consumer costs and inflation. In the words of de Janvry and colleagues, farmers have been forced to confront an "alarming institutional vacuum precisely at the moment when they needed to diversify and modernize their crops to remain competitive in the context of the broader economic reforms" (de Janvry, Gordillo, and Sadoulet 1997: 83). Smallholders no longer farm under the patronizing heavy hand of BANRURAL, yet their alternative financial resources are inadequate to meet the demands of the competitive economy.

As in many parts of Latin America, producer unions, state-level organizations, nongovernmental groups, and the private sector are increasingly participating in rural activities (Foley 1995; Krippner 1997; Myhre 1994; Snyder 1999). These groups have been especially involved in those commodity subsectors where public agencies once played strong roles in organizing production, inputs, and commercialization. Other case studies have shown that farmers who have always been on the margins of commercial markets have continued to operate using traditional marketing schemes for selling small volumes of their maize harvests, in spite of changing economic and institutional conditions (see Dyer-Leal and Yúnez-Naude 2003).

There is increasing evidence that one of the most viable livelihood strategies for smallholder producers involves migration, both to the United States and within Mexico. A recent study commissioned by the National Population Council in Mexico (Consejo Nacional de Población, CONAPO) reported that in the second half of the 1990s, as many as 360,000 Mexicans were leaving annually to look for work in the United States, and that as many as 18 percent of Mexican households have close relatives in the United States (Tuirán 2002: 78–79). The same report indicates that total quantity of remittances entering Mexico increased by an estimated 429 percent between 1989 and

2002, such that remittances are now one of Mexico's primary sources of foreign exchange. Many scholars of rural affairs in Mexico believe that without the safety valve of rural emigration in the 1990s, the extremely difficult straits of Mexico's rural sector would have come to the fore far earlier in the 1990s, and perhaps would have forced an entirely different presidential campaign strategy in the 2000 presidential elections.

The implications of this trend for the vulnerability of smallholders to climatic risk are difficult to assess. Remittances from migrants could give households additional flexibility in production decisions by providing financial backing for agricultural investments and thus facilitate agile responses to climate signals. The income could also serve as an important buffer against crop losses. Research suggests, however, that households receiving remittances tend to dedicate the largest proportion of this income to meeting basic household needs rather than production activities (Tuirán 2002: 85). There is also some concern that the instability in remittance income could make households more vulnerable to transnational economic crises. And of course, any migration that does not result in increased flows of capital to the farm could also increase vulnerability by denying households the labor required to adjust their production strategies appropriately to climatic risk.

More and more of Mexico's rural households are also turning to nonfarm economic activities as part of an apparent trend toward income diversification. By one calculation, the contribution of nonfarm income to total income ranges anywhere from 38 percent of income on larger farms to 77 percent on smaller farms (de Janvry and Sadoulet 2001). Participation in nonfarm activities has always been a feature of rural household livelihoods (Netting 1993); some observers, however, argue that the neoliberal projects of economic decentralization and privatization, as well as increased natural resource scarcity, have resulted in an altered landscape of economic opportunity in rural areas (Bryceson 1996). While on initial consideration, income diversification would seem to represent an ideal strategy for spreading livelihood risk and reducing exposure to climatic shocks, not all income-diversification activities result in increased livelihood stability, nor is it yet clear what the aggregate implications will be for rural welfare (Ellis 2000: 63; Hussein and Nelson 1998). Household demographics and assets, location, education, and skill levels, as well as whether or not the income diversification is driven by necessity for survival (push factors) or by the availability of new opportunities (pull factors), all contribute to determining whether or not the strategy adopted diminishes or increases vulnerability.

A Future for "Nonviable" Agriculture?

In summary, Mexico's farmers today face a production environment quite different from the one that they were accustomed to at the beginning of the 1980s, an environment in which the flexibility of their productive activities within the agricultural sector has been severely limited. The importance of subsistence maize in rural household strategies is being reinforced by the decline in public financing for agricultural research and extension tailored to the production goals of rural households and their growing economic insecurity. As Appendini persuasively argues, without credit, support for fertilizer use, and technical assistance, the state has effectively written off smallholders as potential contributors to the future of Mexico's agricultural sector (Appendini 1998). Ironically, the success of Mexico's neoliberal agenda depends critically on the productivity of the country's vast rural population (Appendini 1998; Cornelius and Myhre 1998). By failing to address seriously the unique development requirements of rural agriculture, the federal government may find that it lacks the social and political capital to make globalization work for Mexico.

Although Mexico's agriculture minister under President Fox has reportedly pronounced that "A small farmer, no matter how productive, is not going to be able to make enough money to survive" (Thompson, *New York Times*, 22 July 2001), the truth is that Mexico's peasant farmers have survived and evolved as an economic and social class over centuries of economic change and political transformation. There is no reason to think that they will not continue to survive in some form, despite the minister's pessimistic predictions. Yet the trends in income diversification and migration, the privatization of landholdings, and the growing presence of industries in rural areas suggest that the current process of rural transformation is profound and will have lasting implications for household livelihoods and identities, as well as vulnerabilities to future economic and environmental change.

Already social indicators give rise to some cause for concern. According to some recent studies, over the 1990s the absolute poverty of rural households has increased (CEPAL 2000; Kelly 2001). Agricultural wages have been falling in real terms (Dussel Peters 2000: 63), leaving farmers with few alternatives to subsistence production. While the increasing rural poverty rates demand programs such as PROGRESA (or Oportunidades), it now appears that such support may come at the expense of simultaneous investment in the productive capacity and self-sufficiency of farmers and their families. There is also a danger that households that are forced to rely more heavily on welfare support will become increasingly vulnerable to abrupt shifts in such policies at the national level.

In short, the political economy of agricultural vulnerability is undergoing rapid change in Mexico. For some households, the changes of the 1990s represent new opportunities, as Mexico's new commercial openness and political democratization bring changes in rural and urban industry, migration patterns, and access to information. For hundreds of thousands of others, despair and anger over their livelihood insecurity has mobilized them in massive protest. Since 2000, farmers across Mexico have repeatedly closed border crossings, blocked highways, taken over ministry offices, and marched in the capital. As yet they have made little progress in halting the implementation of NAFTA, or the inevitability of agricultural globalization.

In the spring of 2000, as I began to unravel the complexities of rural life in the Puebla-Tlaxcala Valley, I could see the frustration mounting. The farmers of Torres, Plan de Ayala, and Nazareno, the three communities I had chosen for my research, knew the policies of the 1990s intimately. Whether maize farmers, migrants and factory workers, livestock owners, or vegetable producers, they shared a common goal: how to guarantee their subsistence in spite of declining producer prices, rising costs, insufficient services, and, increasingly, climatic risks.

4   Three Communities in Central Mexico

One of the most daunting tasks at the start of this project was to decide exactly where, geographically speaking, to start. While I knew I could find households adapting to climatic and socioeconomic uncertainties in almost any agricultural community in central Mexico, I wanted my selection to be both purposeful—in that I was looking for communities that were on a continuum of increasing involvement in agricultural markets, yet were similarly exposed to climatic risk—and sufficiently random, in that I did not want the research to be overly swayed by circumstances that were unrepresentative of what one might find in other communities in the region that I was studying.

In this chapter, I introduce the three communities, drawing from the initial group interviews and some of the descriptive results of the household surveys, in order to characterize the general types of production systems practiced by farmers in each site. Although each community reflects the particular geographic, historical, and social characteristics that have given each place a unique identity, together the three communities capture a range of land tenure arrangements, agricultural practices, livelihood activities, and exposure to local and regional economic processes that, I would argue, typify Mexico's smallholder agriculture at this moment in history.

While the farmers I worked with faced similar challenges and risks, I quickly discovered that the farmers' livelihood choices reflected different degrees of flexibility in dealing with climate impacts. Subsequent chapters will explore in detail the resources and opportunities that give rise to some livelihood strategies while inhibiting the development of others as the households in each community managed in their own ways the dynamic uncertainties in both the physical and socioeconomic environment.

Torres: Maize, Maguey, and Migration

Torres, the least commercially oriented of the three communities, was also, not surprisingly, the most remote and isolated. The small cluster of houses that make up the village center is located at an elevation of 2,660 m above sea level in the steep maguey-terraced foothills of the Tlaxco-Huamantla range that forms Tlaxcala's northeastern border with the state of Puebla. La Malinche, the graceful gray volcano named for Cortés's Tlaxcaltecan princess, rises up on the opposite side of the valley floor, and on many days it's possible to see the volcano Popocatépetl letting off gentle clouds of vapor in the distant west.

The nearest meteorological station to Torres is in the valley below the community in Huamantla, where recorded annual rainfall averages just over 600 mm (1961–95). The ridge on which the community perches is relatively arid, and the farmers commented on the frequency of drought conditions, although they claimed that the ridge's exposure tended to protect their fields from frost. Approximately half of the land farmed was considered by the farmers to be flat, located on the top of the ridge where the village itself was located. The remaining farmland was sloped as the foothills declined toward the valley in steep terraces lined with maguey.

The bustling commercial town of Huamantla is only eleven kilometers away on the valley below the community, yet, because of limited transport and the condition of the road, the distance appears greater. By car, it takes almost a half hour to cover the distance between Huamantla and the community, and then only when the unpaved road is dry and relatively easy to traverse. Very few of the inhabitants of Torres have cars, trucks, or even horse and carts, and thus most have to walk the distance or depend on the public bus that rumbles up the ridge twice daily.

According to the 2000 National Population Census, the population of Torres is approximately 255, living in forty-five households. With the help of a graduate student from the Autonomous University of Tlaxcala, I surveyed twenty-two of these households in late 2000

Figure 4.1 A view toward the west from the mesa of Torres.

(see appendix B). In 1995, the National Population Council (CONA-PO) classified the community as "highly marginal" on the basis of a relatively high rate of illiteracy (26 percent of the adult population), almost complete absence of plumbing, and the fact that the majority of households reported having dirt floors in their homes (CONAPO 1998). When I was there in 2000, the community had a primary school and a small administration building, but no church or clinic. For groceries, the community was limited to one small dispensary of government-subsidized foods. The poverty of the community was obvious: not only from the lack of services and infrastructure, but also in the adobe bricks and corrugated tin roofs that characterized the majority of the houses.

Nearly a quarter of the farmers I interviewed had had no formal education, and over half had not finished primary school. These figures improved for the adult population in general, although still half of the adults had had no or incomplete primary school education. For those who wished to continue their education beyond primary school, the problem was access. Children who wished to attend secondary school had to travel to the town of Benito Juárez at the foot of the ridge, a long seven kilometer walk into the valley. Only six adults in the households surveyed reported having completed a secondary school education.

History of Torres

In pre-Hispanic times, the Otomí and Tlaxcaltecans cultivated maguey in the hills above the Huamantla Valley for the production of pulque, a fermented drink prized by the Otomí. The fiber of the maguey's thick spiny leaves was also used in textile and paper manufacturing, and the spines for weapons and tools (Gobierno de Tlaxcala 1998: 35). During the colonial and post-independence period, the valley and the hills to the north of the city of Huamantla were divided among large haciendas, which continued to produce pulque for domestic and export markets, as well as wheat, maize, sugar cane, and livestock. In the mid-1800s, pulque was extremely profitable, stimulating a boom in production that produced new settlements in the region (Gobierno de Tlaxcala 1998: 32).

According to residents in Torres, the ranchería was originally part of the hacienda Buena Ventura, which was run at the turn of the century by the *hacendado* Ramón Mantilla. Other sources suggest that Torres was most probably part of the large Guadalupe hacienda, which was subdivided in the early 1900s between various relatives of the Ramón Mantilla family (Ramirez Rancaño 1990). This family rented some of the hacienda's land to small farmers in the region, who in turn provided labor for the hacienda. In the early 1920s, anticipating land invasions and federal land reform, the Mantilla family decided to sell some of the land to these renters. The farmers who purchased the property were the founding families of Torres (and their landholdings were transferred to them as pequeña propiedad, with formal land titles). Two of these farmers became *pulqueros* (processors and merchants of pulque) in addition to producing both maize and grain for cattle feed. The village's remaining households complemented their subsistence production by serving as suppliers of raw material to the two pulque processors in the village, scraping the maguey plants that lined their maize fields for *aguamiel*, the sap that is the key raw ingredient in pulque production.

Pulque remained a central component of the livelihood strategies of Torres farmers until the early 1990s, when, in an ironic turn of the globalization tide, the growing popularity of commercial beer contributed to the collapse of the pulque market. In 2000, although some households were continuing to extract aguamiel for pulque processing, most farmers reported that the number of maguey plants had declined over the last decade and the demand was no longer sufficient to make the activity more than a minor assistance in household expenses. The two pulque-processing households were continuing to produce pulque, but on a much smaller scale.

Land and Agricultural Production

The majority of residents surveyed in Torres have pequeña propiedad landholdings (59 percent). These farmers had purchased land from the haciendas or other smallholders. Just over a quarter of the households (27 percent) are ejidatarios. The ejidal property in the village actually forms part of the Mesa Redonda ejido, which has its urban center on the other side of a ridge from Torres, in the municipio of Altzayanca. At the time of the survey, a few households were either renting or sharecropping land, and thus although they were in charge of all production decisions, they were not landowners.

Land was not equally distributed in Torres. With the exception of the two households that descended from the original founders of the community and produced pulque, the average landholding size in the community was four hectares. The two households with relatively large landholdings were together responsible for 46.6 percent of the planted area recorded in the survey, farming on twelve hectares and fifty hectares, respectively.

Since the mid-1990s, the households in the community have been primarily subsistence maize and bean producers, relying on the sale of aguamiel to the two pulque processors in the village for additional income. A few households were planting oats and barley, but as I will show in chapter 6, these tended to be the households with larger landholdings (table 4.1).

In general, the members of the households undertook all of the farm work themselves. For the tillage, weeding, and furrowing of the maize fields, the vast majority of households relied only on the mule and plow (a *yunta*). Maize is quite labor intensive, requiring, after planting, three *labores* at different stages in the production process. These activities entailed weeding the rows of corn and plowing dirt

Table 4.1 Planted Area by Crop, Torres (% of Total Area)

Crop	Year			
	1998a	1998b	1999a	1999b
Maize	49	55	83	73
Oats	14	24	10	16
Bean (black and fava)	11	18	7	11
Barley	24	0	0	0
Unplanted	2	3	0	0

a. Planted area of all households. b. Excludes area planted by largest landholder (50 ha).

up around the base of the maize plants with the use of draft animal power. Only a third of the surveyed households owned their own yunta, and thus the majority rented the mule and plow. The two largest landholders owned tractors, which they also rented out to a few households. In all, less than half of the households owned the power they needed for their production activities.

Livelihood Activities

To elucidate the distribution of livelihood resources and activities in the community, I used a statistical technique to classify the surveyed households according to the similarities and differences in their assets and incomes (see appendix B) (table 4.2). The resulting classification showed me that the income, land, and livestock of the community were concentrated in only three of the village's households. For lack of better names, I called one of these the "Pulquero" household (because most of its off-farm income came from pulque sales), and the other two I called "Livestock Specialists" (one of these was also a pulque producer who had diversified into livestock; the other was focused on goat raising). The remaining nineteen households in the survey, which I called "Subsistence Maize" households, reported levels of income and material wealth that at best were only half that of the three larger landholders, and tended to rely heavily on their own maize production for their subsistence.

Most households reported raising small livestock (chickens, turkeys, or rabbits) for their own consumption, and those that had

Table 4.2 Household Classes, Torres (Standard Deviations in Parentheses)

	Pulquero	Livestock Specialists		Maize Subsistence	
% of total sample	5.0	9.0	*	86.0	*
Households in class	1	2	*	19	*
Land per household member (ha)	16.6	1.8	(0.7)	0.7	(0.7)
Average ha	50.0	9.5	(3.5)	3.4	(2.2)
% ha lost to hazards	100.0	65.0	(21.0)	84.0	(22.0)
% of total ha in oats	0.0	46.0	(6.0)	5.0	(14.0)
% of total ha in maize	100.0	54.0	(5.0)	84.0	(23.0)
Average ha in maize	50.0	5.3	(2.5)	2.7	(1.8)
Avg. number of crops planted	1.0	2.0	(0.0)	<2.0	(0.6)
Avg. number of large animals	0.0	4.0	(4.0)	2.0	(1.0)
Avg. number of medium animals	0.0	51.0	(12.7)	2.0	(2.0)
Total average income (10^3 pesos)	145.5	54.3	(24.4)	19.4	(11.1)
Per capita income (10^3 pesos)	48.5	14.0	(14.0)	3.6	(2.5)
Avg. material goods index[a]	8.0	8.5	(0.7)	3.0	(1.5)
% Off-farm income[b]	34.0	55.0	(19.0)	52.0	(29.0)
% Nonfarm income[c]	7.0	4.0	(5.0)	22.0	(30.0)
% Crop sale income	1.0	0.0	(0.0)	0.0	(0.0)
% Animal sale income	33.0	26.0	(36.0)	4.0	(8.0)
% Government transfers	24.0	15.0	(11.0)	22.0	(16.0)

Source: Household survey data, 2000. 1 US dollar = 9.4 pesos. Data refer to 1999 unless otherwise indicated.

*No standard deviation for these variables.

a. The material goods index was constructed from a binomial variable that counted the presence of a series of material "goods" in the household, as a rough alternative estimate of household wealth. This index included the following "goods": house with electricity, house made of cement block, television, radio, bicycle, interior bathroom, refrigerator, truck, sewing machine, blender, car, and motorcycle.

b. Off-farm income refers to income earned in activities that lie within the agricultural sector, yet is not derived from direct sales of crops or livestock. Activities included in this survey were work as farm laborers, harvesting of aguamiel, sale of honey, and income earned through the renting of farm equipment.

c. Nonfarm activities were all the remaining income-earning activities outside the agricultural sector.

mules or donkeys dedicated these animals to draft power. Those households that could afford one or two pigs or goats ("medium animals") typically kept the animals for their own subsistence.

Off-farm income activities played a relatively strong role in household income across the livelihood groups (table 4.2). For the Subsistence Maize households, these activities consisted primarily of work as day laborers in the large irrigated fields in the Huamantla Valley and the collection and sale of aguamiel. For the three wealthier households (the Pulquero and the Livestock Specialists) this income originated from the commercialization of livestock products (goats and milk), tractor rental, and, to a lesser extent, pulque.

Nonfarm activities played a lesser role in household livelihoods but, according to interviews in the community, perhaps were increasing in importance. Many of the young men in the poorer households of Torres had begun a pattern of seasonal migration to the neighboring state of Puebla to work in cement block manufacturing in the late 1990s. Those who could not travel to Puebla (generally the older men and the younger women) found occasional supplemental wage income as carpenters or domestic servants in Huamantla. As is discussed in later chapters, although these patterns of nonfarm wage employment and migration offered partial compensation for the losses experienced from drought, these strategies entailed costs that contrasted sharply with those incurred by the few households in the community who were able to both enter into nonfarm employment and intensify on-farm economic activities in response to the new uncertainties they faced.

Plan de Ayala: Agrarian Revolutionaries among Rural Industry

Plan de Ayala is located approximately eleven kilometers north of Apizaco on a road that leads to the industrial city Xicohténcatl I, the state's largest planned industrial complex. The road from Apizaco is a steep two-lane road, climbing several hundred meters to an altitude of 2,540 m above sea level as it nears Plan de Ayala. The city of Xicohténcatl I and the chemical processing plants and other factories farther north toward the town of Tlaxco attract heavily burdened trucks that often slow traffic for kilometers on the steep hills.

Figure 4.2 A view north from Plan de Ayala's urban area with the ejido's barley fields in the distance.

The highway is also frequented by *combis*, the minivans that serve as public transportation among the villages and communities along the road to and from Apizaco.

The urban area of Plan de Ayala consists of a number of stone and cement-block houses located on a small grid of rutted dirt roads that climb the northern slopes of a large hill. In front of the village, to the north, are the ejido's plains: flat, high agricultural land dotted with trees and encompassing a watering hole, representing approximately two-thirds of the ejido's planted area. Here the soils are relatively fertile and deep and the terrain flat enough to support mechanized agriculture. Yet they are also clayey and drain slowly. Often after heavy rains the fields temporarily flood before the water infiltrates. It is in these fields that the ejidatarios tend to plant barley, oats, wheat, and, in years of ample rainfall, maize. Rainfall in the area is irregular, but averages between 700 and 800 mm annually (1961–98), just sufficient for rainfed maize.

The ejido extends two kilometers or so west along the road to Xicohténcatl I, where it is bordered by factories owned by the multinational companies Kimberly-Clark and Dow Chemical. Overlooking the Xicohténcatl I factories is the ejido's most prized land, the hill they called El Mirador. Not only are the soils of the hill lighter, better drained, and (once cleared of stones) more easily worked than those of the valley, but crops planted on the hill's slopes tend to withstand frost far better than those of the valley. All sides of El Mirador had been cleared and allocated for individual household cultivation at the time of the study except for the hill's peak, which remained communal land.

In addition to around 250 ha of cultivated land (titled by PROCEDE), the ejido's land is divided between the urban area (separated into individual properties, but in 2000 not yet titled by the PROCEDE program), communal pasture land on the east and southern sides of the village, and *malpais*, or "badlands," the pine forested slopes above the village, also for communal use. The Ministry of Agrarian Reform shows the total communal property of the ejido to be 359 ha. The ejido also contains a small gravel mine that brings in some revenue that is divided among the ejidatarios.

According to the 2000 National Population Census, Plan de Ayala has a total population of 325 individuals in sixty-four different households, but many of these households were the landless offspring of the founding ejidatarios of the community and did not farm or have rights as ejidatarios. I was told when I arrived in the village that there were thirty-two ejidatarios in the village, several of whom had married one another and thus were members of the same household. Sixteen of these ejidatario households were surveyed in June and July of 2000.

CONAPO rated Plan de Ayala as of "medium" marginality, given relatively high coverage of electricity and piped water and illiteracy rates of only 7 percent in the community. Despite the low illiteracy rates reported by CONAPO, none of the sixteen heads of households I surveyed in 2000 had had more than a primary school education, and nearly a third had had no schooling whatsoever. The education level of the total adult population was higher. Only 16 percent claimed not to have had any formal education, and almost a quarter had completed secondary school.

History of Plan de Ayala

The ejido was founded in 1975, during the last wave of land redistributions of the Echeverría administration. In 1972 a group of families from the ejido of Colonia Agrícola los Dolores invaded the neighboring hacienda, Piedras Negras, on which bulls were being raised for bullfighting. In the 1930s, the owner of Piedras Negras had been given a *certificado de inefectabilidad* by President Cárdenas to protect the hacienda from the land distribution process for a period of twenty-five years. By 1970 the certificate had expired, and the governor of the state conceded that the ranch was "excessively large" (Ramirez Rancaño 1990). After some aggressive mobilization, the smallholders eventually made claim to the land and were given 1,805 ha as the Ejido José Maria Morelos y Pavón. Very soon ideological differences involved the new ejido in conflict. Three of the invading families traveled to Mexico City to fight for an independent allocation of land. On February 24, 1975, Plan de Ayala formally was constituted as an independent ejido on 800 ha of the original allotment of 1,805 ha.

For several years, the three founding families and others who joined them camped out in very rudimentary conditions without any services. During this time, leftist students from the University of Chapingo in the state of Mexico lived with them, helping them with their petition for land and initiating what eventually became a strong relationship with the Partido del Trabajo, Mexico's labor party, and the affiliated regional peasant farmer organization, the National Independent and Revolutionary Worker and Farmer Coalition (Coordinación Nacional Obrera, Campesina, Independiente y Revolucionaria, CNOCIR).

Electricity arrived in the village in 1979 and piped water in 1981–82. By the early 1980s, the families of Plan de Ayala had begun to accumulate sufficient resources to improve their housing and community infrastructure. By 2000, the community had a kindergarten and primary school, and plans were being made to bring a *tele-secondaria* (a secondary school in which students are instructed through televised lectures, broadcast via satellite) to the community in the coming year.

When the farmers received the allocation of land from the hacienda, part of the ranch's property was also taken by the state of Tlaxcala for the construction of the industrial city of Xicohténcatl I. In 1982 the dirt road that transected the ejido became a paved two-lane highway to Apizaco, and traffic and public transportation increased.

It was then that the factories began opening for business in Xicoh-téncatl I, serving as a source of employment for the region as well as the ejido.

The ejido had support from BANRURAL in the initial years, in-cluding loans for production equipment and inputs, technical assis-tance, and even insurance. Over the first decade of production, the community planted various mixes of fava beans, black beans, barley, wheat, maize, and oats. In years of surplus, the ejidatarios sold their barley harvest to Impulsora Agrícola, a malt processor, via interme-diaries. They also sold surplus maize to CONASUPO until the grain-marketing agency closed in 1998. By the early 1980s, the ejidatarios were able to use bank credit and their harvest earnings to purchase some cattle for draft animal power, milk, and meat. These animals were traded as needed to finance the costs of construction and pro-duction in the early years.

Toward the end of the 1980s, the ejidatarios faced a dramatic change in their relationship with agricultural markets and service providers. As BANRURAL was reformed to focus on "commercially viable" farm systems (see chap. 3), the ejidatarios lost their access to BANRURAL's credit, technical assistance, and input support. The liberalization of Mexico's agricultural markets in the late 1980s and early 1990s also meant that Impulsora Agrícola was less interested in the quality and quantity of grain that the ejido could offer. By the mid-1990s, affected by the same series of droughts and frosts that had impacted the households in Torres, the Plan de Ayala farmers were also reevaluating their production and livelihood strategies in an attempt to find viable alternatives under increasingly competitive and risky production conditions.

Land and Agricultural Production

Initially the ejido worked as a collective. All land was farmed communally and the harvest shared equally. At the end of the 1980s the ejido was divided up into individual plots after some disagree-ments over the amount of resources each family was contributing to the production process. With only a few exceptions (two households that apparently were judged to have not contributed sufficiently to the struggle for the ejido in the 1970s), each of the thirty-one origi-nal ejidatarios was given an allocation of approximately ten hectares.

In the year 2000, households with landholdings that exceeded the ten hectares were those in which two of the original ejidatarios had married and thus combined their assets. Those farmers who were farming less than nine hectares in many cases were already sharing land with their adult offspring, or, in a few cases, had sold land after being given title through the PROCEDE program. Four of the households surveyed were sharecropping land (*a medias*, an arrangement in which the harvest is split between the landowner and sharecropper) in addition to their ejidal allotment.

All the households surveyed were self-identified farmers, and, in the year 2000, almost all of the households were planting their fields with some combination of maize, black beans, fava beans, barley, oats, and wheat (table 4.3). In addition to these crops, the ejido had twenty-seven hectares of nopal (commonly known as "prickly pear cactus" in English), planted as borders of the terraced fields of El Mirador. Unlike the other crops, these nopal plants were communal property. The plants were given to the community as a political gesture that, according to some, could be traced to President Carlos Salinas de Gotari. The ejido did not commercialize the nopal, perhaps in part because the plants were in the communal domain, but also because they believed that the plants were diseased from exposure to contaminants from the industries of Xicohténcatl I.

The farmers did most of the agricultural labor themselves with the help of their spouses and older children. As in Torres, maize was generally farmed with a yunta. Sixty-eight percent of the interviewed households owned their own draft animal power, and 19 percent rented the yunta. Barley and oats, however, were generally planted and harvested mechanically with a tractor. Once the field was mechanically tilled there was little more mechanical labor involved until harvest, when the grain was reaped with a combine and baled with a hay baler. Most farmers rented this equipment at the beginning and end of the production season. A small group of farmers had used money they earned when the ejido sold some of its communal land in 1997 to invest in a tractor that they owned and used cooperatively. They charged each other half of what they would be charged if they were to rent it from someone else, and this "rental" went toward paying gas and maintenance of the machinery.

Aside from the use of machinery, production was generally low

Table 4.3 Planted Area by Crop, Plan de Ayala (% of Total Area)

| | Year | | |
Crop	1998	1999	2000
Maize	29	36	36
Barley	40	35	41
Oats	16	22	18
Wheat	14	3	5
Bean (black and fava)	1	4	<1
Total	100	100	100

Source: Household survey data, 2000.

input. The majority of farmers retained maize seed from the harvest for planting the next season. In contrast, barley, oats, and wheat seed were often purchased annually, and farmers commonly employed an herbicide to keep down the weeds in the grain fields. Purchased fertilizers were not common; many of the farmers surveyed believed the land to be fertile and not in need of what they considered to be harsh chemical treatment.

Livelihood Groups

While rainfed grain agriculture was the primary focus of the ejido's identity, the community had begun to adjust to the challenges of the changing agricultural economy and new climatic risks in the 1990s. Unlike Torres, where the majority of households were pursuing a similar agricultural strategy, the livelihoods of Plan de Ayala households were diverse: ranging from households whose primary source of income was from nonfarm sources (Nonfarm households), to households with large livestock holdings in addition to income from a variety of sources (Livestock Specialists), to households with a relatively diversified livelihood portfolio, including a significant degree of off-farm activities (Income Diversified), to those who were mainly grain farmers (Maize Surplus) (table 4.4). The Maize Surplus household group was in many ways similar to the Maize Subsistence class identified in Torres: for both household groups, maize production was the

Table 4.4 Household Classes, Plan de Ayala (Standard Deviations in Parentheses)

	Income Diversified		Livestock Specialists		Nonfarm Specialists		Maize Surplus	
% of total sample	19.0	*	13.0	*	31.0	*	38.0	*
Households in class	3	*	2	*	5	*	6	*
Land per household member (ha)	1.2	(0.4)	2.3	(0.3)	1.4	(0.8)	4.8	(5.0)
Average ha	10.0	(0.8)	14.3	(5.3)	8.7	(3.2)	8.6	(4.3)
% ha lost to climate hazards	68.0	(21.0)	28.0	(26.0)	87.0	(6.0)	86.0	(9.0)
% of total ha in oats	35.0	(19.0)	42.0	(21.0)	15.0	(10.0)	11.0	(15.0)
% of total ha in maize	49.0	(20.0)	15.0	(6.0)	22.0	(11.0)	60.0	(22.0)
Average ha in maize	4.9	(2.3)	2.0	(0.0)	1.8	(0.6)	4.7	(2.4)
Number of crops planted	3.0	(1.0)	3.0	(0.0)	4.0	(0.8)	3.0	(1.0)
Number of large animals	9.0	(4.0)	11.0	(2.0)	2.0	(1.8)	2.0	(2.0)
Number of medium animals	3.0	(3.0)	5.0	(4.0)	3.0	(4.5)	8.0	(20.0)
Total average income (10^3 pesos)	50.3	(11.3)	29.8	(16.4)	38.4	(27.7)	11.7	(5.9)
Per capita income (10^3 pesos)	6.2	(2.7)	4.8	(1.6)	6.1	(4.8)	4.6	(4.5)
Avg. material goods index	7.0	(0.6)	7.0	(1.0)	7.0	(2.0)	5.0	(1.0)
% Off-farm income	22.0	(8.0)	13.0	(18.0)	0.0	(0.0)	3.0	(7.0)
% Nonfarm income	51.0	(13.0)	28.0	(40.0)	49.0	(23.0)	8.0	(12.0)
% Crop sale income	0.0	(0.0)	12.0	(11.0)	0.0	(0.0)	0.0	(2.0)
% Animal sale income	14.0	(5.0)	14.0	(19.0)	20.0	(31.0)	18.0	(21.0)
% Government transfers	13.0	(0.0)	33.0	(13.0)	27.0	(18.0)	61.0	(32.0)
% Pension funds	0.0	(0.0)	0.0	(0.0)	4.0	(10.0)	9.0	(22.0)

Source: Household survey data, 2000. For explanation of variables, see table 4.2. Data refer to 1999 unless otherwise indicated.

* No standard deviation for these variables.

primary form of livelihood. However, the Maize Surplus households of Plan de Ayala were distinguished by having double the land area to plant, more livestock (particularly goats, pigs, or sheep), and generally higher material wealth than their counterparts in Torres.

Livestock was an important part of the ejido's production system. Eighty-seven percent of the surveyed households had some small livestock (chickens, turkeys, and rabbits), and over half had at least one or two pigs, goats, or sheep. Large animals—milk cows, horses, mules, and donkeys—were also common, with over half of the households owning four or more such animals at the time of the survey. Income from animal sales was also a feature in the income profiles of all livelihood groups, including the Maize Surplus household class, the poorest farmers in the community. As I discuss in chapter 5, several households had sold livestock in 1999 in response to the heavy crop losses of the previous years.

The other distinguishing feature of the livelihood patterns in Plan de Ayala was the strong role of nonfarm income. Many of the original ejidatarios were in their twenties when they participated in the land invasion in 1972. In the year 2000, the community had expanded to incorporate the homes of the ejidatarios' grown children. As I discuss in chapter 9, the presence of a new generation of working adults within the ejido and the particular geographic characteristics of the community were providing most households, with the exception of the Maize Surplus group, with a basis for economic diversification despite heavy losses from climatic hazards. The community had gradually become more closely integrated into peri-urban and industrial wage activities. Some households were involved in petty commerce in Apizaco, or within the community itself (as general store owners). This process of "deagrarianization" was introducing a new dynamic into the community, mitigating, in part, its dependence on agriculture, yet exposing it to new risks associated with Mexico's project of rural industrialization.

Nazareno: Vegetable Farming in Central Puebla

The urban area of Nazareno is located at the eastern end of Puebla's central valley, on the south side of the new superhighway that connects Mexico City to the Veracruz coast and Oaxaca. Many farmers in the community actually have fields on the north side of the highway, and mule carts and pickup trucks laden with produce are a common sight on the small bridges over the superhighway. Nazareno is a few kilometers west of Palmar de Bravo, the "county seat," in a narrow valley between the Sierra de Soltepec in the south and the San Andrés hills (the foothills of El Pico de Orizaba, the highest volcanic peak in Mexico) to the north. I always enjoyed my drive to Nazareno, but particularly when the weather was clear and it was possible to see all four volcanoes—Popocatépetl, Iztaccíhuatl, La Malinche, and El Pico de Orizaba—from the entrance to the village.

The southern extension of the Sierra Madre Oriental and the shadow of El Pico de Orizaba deflect the humid easterlies in the summer, and, as a result, the climate of Nazareno is the most arid of the three communities. The meteorological stations of Tecamachalco and Palmar de Bravo, the closest to Nazareno, record average annual rainfall totals of 545 mm (1959–88) and 397 mm (1970–94), respectively. The aridity was notable not only in the dry slopes of the hills above the irrigated valley, but also in the sudden appearance of the arid-zone *izotl*, a form of yucca (*Yucca periculosa*).

In the 1950s, irrigation transformed the region from its colonial and post-independence identity as part of central Mexico's breadbasket into Puebla's primary center for vegetable production. The xerosols of the valley are well suited for agricultural production, and, with irrigation, vegetables gradually replaced grains in the valley floor. The rainfed grains were displaced onto the calciferous and infertile soils of the slopes above the valley, and, as a result, the crops are often stunted, with very low yields. Less than one-third of the total cultivated land in the municipio of Palmar de Bravo is irrigated, and thus there was considerable competition for access to this more productive land.

The 2000 National Population Census data report Nazareno's population to be 2,356 in 455 households. The population count is complicated by the fact that Nazareno blends almost imperceptibly into its sister community, San Miguel Xaltepec. Xaltepec's population is much larger—censused at 1,318 households—and the town offers many services that are unavailable in Nazareno. I surveyed a total of forty-four households in 2000, during the period in which the village successfully won administrative independence from Xaltepec.

Figure 4.3 A patchwork of irrigated fields prepared for planting near Nazareno at the start of the rainy season.

Nazareno is organized in rough blocks, with houses concentrated toward the center and north of the village. In marked contrast to the adobe houses of Torres, it is not uncommon in Nazareno for houses to be made of cement block. While in some cases (the most ostentatious two-story structures) the buildings were financed by remittances and successful vegetable sales, in many cases families had recently renovated part of their homes with support from a government program after many adobe homes collapsed or were severely damaged by earth tremors in the late 1990s.

CONAPO rated Nazareno as "highly marginal," given that 95 percent of households lacked sewage lines and potable water in 1995, and illiteracy was reportedly as high as 57 percent (CONAPO 1998). According to my survey data, almost 60 percent of Nazareno's adults had had either no schooling or had not finished primary school. In the smaller population of heads of households, a full third of those surveyed had had no schooling, and 46 percent had not finished primary school.

Although Nazareno had its own kindergarten and primary school, numerous general stores, two resident doctors, and several chapels and a church, residents turned to Xaltepec for many dry goods, for the secondary school, and for the weekly market. Transportation from both villages to Tecamachalco by combi is frequent, and it is also possible to take the second-class buses to the city of Puebla from the village entrance.

History of Nazareno

The hills that surround the valley of Palmar de Bravo are part of the larger Tehuacán region that was home to several pre-Hispanic ethnic groups, including the Olmec-Xicalanca, Toltec, and Chichimec peoples (Licate 1981). The Tepexi hills are a half-day's drive from Nazareno, where, hidden on a forested ridge, one can find the archaeological remains of an Aztec military garrison. Farmers in the valley reported that they frequently unearthed small clay figures of Olmec influence.

Beginning in the mid-1500s, the Spanish began to establish wheat and sheep farms in the valley and, in the process, resettled the valley's remaining indigenous population into centralized urban communities. Palmar de Bravo, San Miguel Xaltepec, Quecholac, and other communities neighboring Nazareno were created at this time (Licate 1981). Palmar de Bravo was part of the property of a large hacienda owned by the Spaniard Agustín Luna (Centro Estatal de Desarrollo Municipal 1987: 593). The settlement of Palmar, then known as San Agustín del Palmar, was a stopping point for travelers from Veracruz. Wheat was the most important crop in the valley during this period, and many of the households in Palmar specialized in baking bread for the colonial and Creole travelers.

According to one of the older members of the Nazareno community, Nazareno and its sister village, San Miguel Xaltepec, began an independent history in 1928, when the federal order came to divide up the five haciendas that controlled the land in the valley. In 1930, the ejido of Jesús Nazareno was officially created, with each ejidatario receiving approximately twelve hectares. Because the ejido was composed of allotments from five different haciendas, most of the ejidatarios' fields were scattered in different directions. In the early years they continued to plant the crops that had been traditionally grown on the haciendas: maize, beans, wheat, and barley.

In the 1940s, water from the Atoyac River arrived in Tecamach-alco, the large town southwest of Nazareno, through a new system of canals made possible by the construction of the Valsequillo Dam just south of the city of Puebla. By 1946 the canals were bringing irriga-tion to farmers in the Tecamachalco area, transforming agriculture in the region. The farmers of Nazareno did not have access to this wa-ter, but they were initially recruited to work on the irrigated lands in the Tecamachalco irrigation district. It was through this experience that Nazareno farmers were introduced to irrigated agriculture.

In the 1950s irrigation arrived in Nazareno, not from the ca-nals of the Atoyac River, but from wells drilled with public support into the aquifer that extended from the northeast into the Tecam-achalco Valley. Initially farmers planted the same basic grains they had planted in rainfed conditions and that were being planted in the Tecamachalco Valley. Then, according to local lore, a farmer who had gone to the United States to work (perhaps under the Bracero Program in the 1950s), returned with the ambition of planting car-rots. Soon others were copying his success, and the village diversi-fied into lettuce, cabbage, radish, beets, and other vegetables. They sold directly to buyers from Mexico City, where the demand for veg-etables was high.

According to an official at the National Water Commission (Comisión Nacional del Agua, CNA), the valley of Palmar de Bravo and the neighboring valleys of Los Reyes de Juárez and Quecholac today have more wells per square kilometer than any other part of the state of Puebla. One study reports that the area has at least 768 wells officially designated for agriculture (Aguirre Alvarez et al. 1999: 13). The CNA believes that there may be many more unregistered wells, perhaps bringing the total to over one thousand. Because of some evidence that the aquifer is being seriously overexploited, there is now a ban on the creation of new wells.

As irrigated production has expanded and prospered in the Bajío region west of Mexico City and in Mexico's northern states, and transport has improved all over Mexico, the production in the Tecamachalco region has become gradually less competitive. In 2000, most farmers were commercializing their goods through the region-al wholesale market of Huixcolotla, and the success of states such as Sinaloa and Guanajuato in supplying Mexico City and occasionally the United States with vegetables was restricting Tecamachalco farmers to the markets of southeastern Mexico.

Land and Agricultural Production

In 2000, Nazareno's irrigated fields were found within and immediately around the village, as well as in the plains on the other side of the Mexico-Oaxaca highway, in areas the villagers call San Bartólome and Santa Cruz after the haciendas that parted with that property in the 1930s. According to my survey data, just over one-third of the planted area was irrigated in 2000, and over three-quarters of the households had access to some irrigated land. There was an active market in water hours for those fields that were on the irrigation network, and some households without irrigation could sometimes access irrigated fields through tenant farming.

Sixty-one percent of the land of the surveyed farmers is ejidal, and the remainder is pequeña propiedad. The Nazareno ejido encompasses over one thousand hectares, and in the year 2000 there were 104 registered ejidatarios in the village. The ejido had not, at the time of the survey, completed the PROCEDE process, although the program was being discussed and debated within the community. Much of the ejidal property is not irrigated. These rainfed fields, called ven-turero—which translates roughly as land on which production is a gamble—were found on the slopes of the hills on either side of the valley in which Nazareno is located, on average over two kilometers from the households that tend to them.

In 2000, most of the irrigated land in Nazareno was under private title. As the value of irrigated production increased in the 1960s and 1970s, the cultivated land surrounding the original ejidal allotments was purchased by the ejidatarios and their relatives, so that soon there was more privately titled land managed by members of the community than there was ejidal property. The original ejidal allotments of twelve hectares were also gradually fragmented through inheritance, so that by 2000 many of those who claimed to be ejidatarios had only five or six hectares of the original allotment. The average landholding size of the surveyed households was 3.5 ha, and in general land was extremely scarce and in high demand. Approximately 25 percent of the planted area in 1999 was planted under tenant-farming arrangements, allowing some landless households to gain access to irrigated land.

The households of Nazareno grow a diversity of grains, vegetables, and even some fruit crops. Production in Nazareno is land-, labor-, and generally capital-intensive. Fields with irrigation are typically planted two or three times in one year, allowing for several different crops, or several harvests of the same crop, to be planted in the same field. In 1999, maize accounted for 42 percent of the 194 harvests of that calendar year and occupied almost half of the total area planted by the surveyed farmers. Most of the farmers' subsistence crops, maize and beans, are planted in the rainfed fields, but it is significant that in 1999 over a third of the irrigated area was planted in maize, despite the low market value of the crop and the scarcity of irrigated land in Nazareno (see chap. 6).

Seventeen other crops were planted in Nazareno in 1999, and all of these were irrigated vegetable crops. Green husk tomato (*tomate verde*, or tomatillo) was a particularly popular crop, covering 13 percent of the land planted in 1999. Other frequently planted crops were lettuce, cilantro, and carrot. Less frequently farmers planted flowers (primarily marigolds for the Day of the Dead celebrations), cabbage, onion, cucumber, radish, zucchini, beet, chili, mint, red tomato, parsley, and peaches.

As in Torres and Plan de Ayala, farmers in Nazareno plant their rainfed fields with the onset of the summer rains, typically in late April or early May. While irrigated crops can, theoretically, be planted year-round, the farmers plant most of their fields in spring, from March through June, after the risk of frost subsides. The most intensive harvest period is from September through November, when maize is harvested along with any vegetable crops maturing in that season.

Although hardly uncommon, the use of tractors for furrowing and tilling irrigated fields is not universal. In 1999, just over half of the households farming such fields reported using them, and the remainder relied principally on draft power. A third of households surveyed owned neither draft animals nor tractors, and thus were forced to rent one or the other, or both.

The irrigated crops typically involve heavy applications of fertilizer and pesticides. Chicken manure (*gallinaza*) is the most popular input, purchased by the truckload from the Bachoco egg factory in Tecamachalco. The vegetable seeds or, in many cases, the seedlings, are purchased from commercial input stores or from local nurseries. As crops mature, it is common for farmers to apply a variety of commercial pesticides and growth-stimulating fertilizers before harvesting. In contrast to the irrigated vegetable production, maize production in Nazareno is still, on the whole, a low-input activity, similar to the way it is produced in Plan de Ayala and Torres. Farmers typically plant maize from seed from their previous season's harvest, although (unlike in Plan de Ayala) they commonly purchase commercial fertilizers for their maize fields.

Livelihood Groups

Although Nazareno is a self-identified vegetable-producing community, the classification of household livelihood strategies illustrates that despite relatively widespread access to irrigated land, only 43 percent of the households reported substantial portions of their income coming from crop sales (i.e., the Large-scale Commercial and Small-scale Commercial groups in table 4.5). The remaining 57 percent of the surveyed households had either minimal irrigation (i.e., the Nonfarm specialists) or no irrigation (i.e., the Subsistence Maize class), but were nevertheless integrally linked to the fortunes and opportunities of the irrigated sector through the income activities in which they were engaged.

Those households classified as "Nonfarm" were those that tended to rely most heavily on income from activities such as carpentry, truck driving (taking the vegetable harvests to market), or petty commerce. These households, with landholdings averaging only two hectares, were unlikely to produce sufficient surplus to market their crops, even with some irrigated land. Their rainfed fields rarely achieved sufficient production for their subsistence, and, as a result, these households relied heavily on work as day laborers in the vegetable fields of their irrigated neighbors. As I show in chapter 9, the constraints faced by some of these poorer households were not very different from those of the subsistence-oriented households in Torres.

Unlike the ejidatarios of Plan de Ayala, the majority of households surveyed in Nazareno did not raise livestock as a significant

Table 4.5 Household Classes, Nazareno (Standard Deviations in Parentheses)

	Wealthy Outlier	Large-scale Commercial		Small-scale Commercial		Nonfarm Specialists		Maize Subsistence	
% of total sample	2.0	14.0	*	27.0	*	23.0	*	34.0	*
Households in class	1	6	*	12	*	10	*	15	*
Land per household member (ha)	5.0	1.2	(0.2)	0.5	(0.2)	0.3	(0.2)	0.9	(0.8)
Average ha	5.0	9.5	(2.7)	4.4	(1.7)	2.0	(1.3)	2.5	(1.3)
% ha irrigated	100.0	86.0	(20.0)	78.0	(23.0)	50.0	(40.0)	23.0	(36.0)
% ha lost to hazards	0.0	40.0	(13.0)	24.0	(22.0)	39.0	(26.0)	53.0	(40.0)
% of total ha in maize	20.0	18.0	(15.0)	37.0	(24.0)	78.0	(25.0)	83.0	(20.0)
Number of crops planted	3.0	6.0	(1.0)	4.0	(1.5)	2.0	(0.8)	2.0	(0.6)
Number of large animals	2.0	3.0	(1.0)	2.0	(1.7)	2.0	(3.0)	2.0	(1.8)
Number of medium animals	19.0	14.0	(14.0)	10.0	(9.5)	11.0	(21.0)	4.0	(6.3)
Total average income (10^3 pesos)	131.2	74.3	(48.9)	68.7	(94.4)	32.4	(18.3)	6.5	(8.0)
Per capita income (10^0 pesos)	131.2	12.3	(6.7)	10.2	(15.9)	5.3	(3.0)	2.3	(3.2)
Avg. material goods index	9.0	7.0	(1.0)	6.0	(1.2)	6.0	(2.0)	2.8	(1.3)
% Off-farm income	0.0	3.0	(8.0)	11.0	(29.0)	15.0	(28.0)	20.0	(37.0)
% Nonfarm income	0.0	0.0	(0.0)	7.0	(17.0)	66.0	(27.0)	9.0	(16.0)
% Crop sale income	98.0	90.0	(14.0)	63.0	(29.0)	0.0	(0.0)	2.0	(5.0)
% Animal sale income	2.0	6.0	(7.0)	9.0	(12.0)	16.0	(22.0)	40.0	(41.0)
% Government transfers	0.0	1.0	(0.0)	8.0	(18.0)	2.0	(4.0)	9.0	(26.0)

Source: Household survey data, 2000. For explanation of variables, see table 4.2. Data refer to 1999 unless otherwise indicated.

* No standard deviation for these variables.

economic activity, reflecting the resource constraints faced by many households as well as the particular land and labor demands of irrigation. Pigs and goats were perhaps the best suited for the conditions of production in Nazareno, given that the animals could consume the residues of vegetable harvests that were amply available in the village and did not require open pasture. The average numbers of "medium-size" animals in table 4.5 belie, however, considerable variability within each livelihood class. Just over 9 percent of the surveyed households together held 65 percent of the stock of pigs, goats, and sheep of the sample, and one-third of the households had no such animals. Large animals were also relatively scarce: again, one-third of the households had no large animals, and another third had only one or two. As in the other two communities, the percent of income coming from animal sales alone is not an accurate indicator of the household's commitment to livestock as an economic activity, given that the survey data reflected a year of poor production and high losses, during which many households sold the animals they had in an effort to recuperate lost revenues.

The Communities in Comparison

In a very general sense, the communities selected for this study were similar, reflecting common characteristics of rural communities all over central Mexico. Mexico's population is still growing quite rapidly, as illustrated by the young average age in the communities studied. Education is still a problem in rural areas, although in general the level of education is slowly improving with each generation. Basic services of water and sewage are still lacking, even in areas that one would characterize as being relatively close to larger urban areas.

The communities also illustrated the continuum of land-tenure arrangements that exist at the turn of the twenty-first century in Mexico. Plan de Ayala, a very recently constituted ejido, is almost completely composed of ejidal tenure. This does not mean that its land tenure is static: the presence of the industrial city on the eastern side of the ejido and the reform of article 27 are providing new opportunities for land sales. In contrast, Torres and Nazareno exhibit the mix of ejidal and pequeña propiedad landholdings that increasingly characterizes agricultural communities in Mexico as land markets are developed and institutionalized and the grown children of ejidatarios search for opportunities to farm.

Torres is the most subsistence oriented of the three communities, as indicated by the paucity of commercial grains or other crops grown in the village and the dominance of maize in the planted area. In Plan de Ayala farmers cultivate crops other than maize and beans and occasionally sell them as grain or forage. Nazareno, with 35 percent of its area irrigated, is the most commercially oriented of the three, producing a variety of vegetables for regional markets. Importantly, the crop production data in each community illustrate that maize production plays a large role in all three communities, regardless of its commercial orientation. Overall, however, the communities differ substantially in the diversity of ways in which households acquire their income (fig. 4.5).

Despite these very different relationships to agricultural markets, the recent histories of the three communities show that all the communities were being affected by processes of economic globalization and agricultural reform of the late 1990s, although in different ways. The majority of households of Torres were, at the turn of the twenty-first century, in a position of institutionalized marginalization. They were geographically isolated, relatively poorly educated, and facing a significant change in the social organization of their community. Aguamiel—their ancestors' connection to global markets through Mexico's pulque exports to Spain—had lost out to Corona beer and was no longer much help to their livelihoods. Now all but the largest landholders were being forced to look outside the community for support.

The ejidatarios of Plan de Ayala also experienced a shift in the internal economic organization of their community when the villagers decided in the early 1990s that they would no longer farm collectively. Unlike in Torres, the ejidatarios of Plan de Ayala had had a stronger historical dependence on federal agricultural services and support, as part of Mexico's "social sector." Thus it was not only shifts in external markets, such as the declining interest of Impulsora Agrícola in their crops, that had introduced new uncertainties

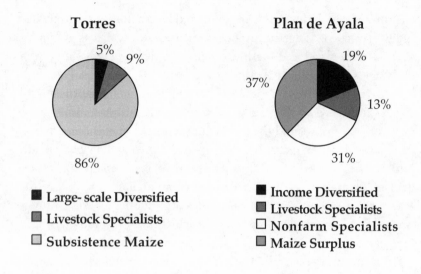

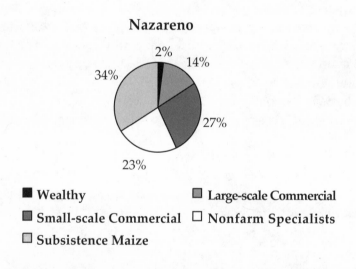

Figure 4.4 The livelihood groups in comparison. *Source*: Household survey data, 2000.

into their lives, but also important institutional changes marked by the restructuring of publicly subsidized credit and the closure of the grain marketing agency, CONASUPO.

In contrast, as a community of ejidatarios and pequeños propietarios whose members had for decades dedicated themselves to producing for commercial markets, the farmers of Nazareno had neither enjoyed the targeted services and support offered to Mexico's social sector nor been the targeted beneficiaries of the commercialization and research support that had been historically channeled to Mexico's largest farmers. Thus, in the year 2000, despite the community's commercial orientation, over half of the community reported incomes and livelihood strategies that reflected levels of economic marginalization characteristic of many households in Torres.

The household data from each community also illustrate significant variability in the livelihood patterns within each community, reflecting each community's collective history as well as the patterns of resource access and availability that structure internal relations within the villages. In Torres, landholding size is clearly associated with wealth and separates the households of the community into two distinct income classes that can be traced back to the nineteenth century. In Plan de Ayala, because of the ejido's recent formation, land is relatively equally distributed among the households, and average holdings are double that of Torres households. This obvious difference in the basic resource endowments of households in the two communities is not trivial. As I will argue in chapter 6, land limitations constrict the flexibility of decision making for households in Torres and inhibit their capacity to manage risk through economic diversification.

In Plan de Ayala no single livelihood strategy characterizes the community. Aside from the "Maize Surplus" households, none of the household groups in the community is clearly associated with significantly lower income or wealth. Yet the data do show substantial differences in average crop losses reported by the households in each group, illustrating that while different livelihood patterns might be similarly economically viable, they may not be equal in terms of effectively managing exposure to climatic risk.

In Nazareno, the most distinguishing attribute of the livelihood groups is not landholding size or income, but rather access to irrigation. Those households without irrigation were most comparable to the subsistence-oriented households of Torres: dependent on their own food production and the cash income they could acquire undertaking wage activities in agricultural labor markets. I quickly found out that while irrigation buffers Nazareno's farmers from some of the worst climate impacts, their risk profile is not simple and their vulnerability to climatic risk cannot be dismissed simply because of the community's access to irrigation (see chap. 8).

The ways in which households organize their livelihood activities, and the resources that they have available to them, largely determine how they cope with external shocks from climatic hazards, market volatility, or other sudden events. I turn to the idea of coping in the next chapter, where I discuss how households in each of the three communities differed in their responses to the droughts and frosts of 1998 and 1999, and illustrate that these climatic events were in fact only part of the stresses the households experienced in those years. In chapters 6 through 9, I take up four of the specific livelihood strategies identified in this chapter (subsistence maize farming, livestock specialization, commercial vegetable production, and nonfarm activities) to show how households' exposure and sensitivity to risk, as well as their adaptive capacity—the ability of households not only to cope with crisis, but to move forward toward greater resilience—differ according to the ways they make their livings. I hope that through this discussion it will be clear that adaptive capacity is deeply embedded in the specific environmental and socioeconomic meaning of "local," where households draw on a diversity of assets to respond to (and create) exogenous opportunities.

5 Climate Impacts and Household Coping Strategies

Drought, Frost, and Frustration

For three nights in July 2000, in the middle of one of the most critical months for maize development, temperatures in Tlaxcala suddenly plummeted and left fields burned by a black frost. At the time, officials estimated that 10,750 ha were completely destroyed and another 16,663 ha were partially affected. The fields of barley, wheat, and maize were singed yellow with frost damage.

The morning after the frost's most devastating impact, I visited Doña Judith, a strong and serious woman highly respected in Plan de Ayala. We drove out to her fields on the most protected area of the ejido, the slopes of the community's hill, El Mirador. The maize plants, now chest high (already stunted from earlier frosts that season), had brittle brown leaves and yellow stalks. The impact was not severe in all places—there were still patches of green among the yellow—but it was devastating all the same. Looking at her own fields, she seemed relieved. She said she was lucky; her fields were on a side of the hill that seemed to have been more protected and were also at a somewhat higher elevation than others. Those whose fields were lower on the hill or in the flat plains below the ejido's urban area were, by the look of it, heavily hit.

When I asked her what the other farmers would do about their losses, she shrugged. There wasn't much they could do besides reporting the area that had been affected to the agriculture ministry's office in the state capital. After a frost earlier that season, the agriculture ministry had provided bags of oat seed, but she thought they would deduct the seed from her PROCAMPO payment due at the end of the season. She did not think the seed would be much help given

Figure 5.1 Maize "burned" by frost, El Mirador, Plan de Ayala.

the going price for oats. Fingering the pale green color of the interior of some maize leaves, she thought perhaps some of the harvests would recover at least enough to provide some forage if not grain, provided it rained soon.

The midsummer frosts, so ruinous to production, had become all too commonplace for farmers in the Puebla-Tlaxcala Valley in the 1990s (see fig. 2.3). The rainy seasons of 1997 and 1999 were particularly poor for production in the valley, not only because of frost but because of irregularities in rainfall. In Puebla, aggregated rainfed maize losses for the state were nearly one-quarter of the area planted in both 1997 and 1999. Loss totals for the state of Tlaxcala were somewhat less in 1997 (12 percent) but identical to those in Puebla in 1999. While losses in 1998 were not quite so bad in either state, they still contributed to three straight years of poor production.

In 1997, after a relatively normal initiation of the rainy season, the rains suddenly became less consistent, and farmers in Tlaxcala began to complain of crop wilting after experiencing several long spells of dryness (Eakin 1998). Yields were low that year, and the drought's extension into the winter contributed to over four hundred devastating forest fires in eastern Tlaxcala in the spring of 1998 (Delgadillo Macías, Aguilar Ortega, and Rodríguez Velázquez 1999). The 1998 rainy season did not improve the situation much. Substantial rainfall did not arrive until mid-June, a month later than farmers expected. In August, the canícula entered "with water," but the poor rains at the start of the season had already affected yields.

The rains were again delayed in 1999, and at the end of the season, in October, farmers faced unusually heavy rainfall when most households were trying to dry their grain. More devastating than this rain and drought, however, were the frosts. In Tlaxcala and Puebla, households lost crops to both late (May and June) and early (September 11 and October 14 and 27) black frosts. The anomalous climatic patterns of the late 1990s have now been linked to the particularly strong ENSO events of those years (Magaña 1999).

We may never know whether the frequency and duration of the ENSO events of the 1990s were simply an unusual coincidence of extreme and anomalous events or a more disturbing signal of a marked shift in global climate patterns. Most farmers I interviewed tended to believe the latter. As one farmer argued, "We can't just talk about the poor weather of the last two years. Really in the twenty-five years we have been farming here we have had only about seven years of regular weather." The farmers in all three communities were remarkably consistent in their perceptions of local climate patterns, identifying the early 1980s as the point when conditions began to change. According to their observations, for the last fifteen to twenty years the rains have been arriving later, their crops are more frequently affected by heat waves and dry spells, and they have noted earlier frosts. Within this period of change, the climate events of 1998 and 1999 produced impacts that stood out in the farmers' narratives as particularly significant.

Impacts are a critical component of vulnerability analysis because they serve as a measure of exposure to risk. Yet the physiological sensitivity of the households' crops to climatic hazards does not, by itself, reflect the extent and character of vulnerability in the communities. Differences in land quality and use, cropping practices, and management all contribute to substantial changes in climate impacts from one season to the next, or between households in the same community farming in close proximity. How a farm household is affected by crop loss is ultimately a function of how it is able to manage climate risks and other stresses on its livelihood activities.

What Is a "Bad Year"?

Before reviewing in detail the particular events of 1998 and 1999 and the farmers' responses to them, I feel it is important to illustrate how the farmers themselves perceive a "bad year," *un año malo*, for their production and livelihoods. In order to gain some insight into the interaction of climatic hazards with other sorts of stress in farmers' lives, I asked the farmers who participated in the survey to define a bad year for me in their own words. Doing this allowed the farmers to characterize their vulnerability as they experienced it, whether from climate impacts on their crops or from other nonclimatic stresses.

Perhaps not surprisingly, climate impacts were most frequently mentioned as the underlying cause of farmers' bad years. Yet the particular climatic factors that appeared to be most threatening to households differed among the communities, despite the overall similarity in exposure to climatic events. In Plan de Ayala, farmers reported frost and hail events as the most damaging to their production and livelihoods. The flat plains that make up the majority of the ejido's land area are particularly exposed to frosts, yet the plains also accumulate runoff from the surrounding hills and thus are less susceptible to drought. As one of the more experienced farmers of Plan de Ayala patiently explained to me, frost and drought had very different impacts. "Frost is what affects us most because it kills everything at once, and doesn't leave anything. There aren't any parts of the land that aren't affected, except the hill [El Mirador]. Drought isn't as bad because it usually leaves something, at least some forage."

In Torres it was drought, not frost, that represented the greatest threat to harvests. Respondents explained that the high mesa on which Torres sits served to protect the crops from all but the most severe frosts, but that drought frequently caused declines in yields. Interestingly enough, drought was also named a strong contributor to "bad years" in Nazareno despite the fact that two-thirds of the community had access to irrigation. Their sensitivity to drought was in part owing to the general aridity of the environment of Nazareno and in part owing to the fact that the groundwater available to them was often not sufficient for the requirements of some vegetables. Farmers typically share a well with twenty to twenty-five other farmers, with the consequence that any one farmer will have an opportunity to irrigate only every twenty to twenty-five days. Should it not rain during that interval, the crops will be denied water for as much as three weeks, and inevitably the yield and quality will be affected. Farmers typically plant in the spring and summer months with the expectation that a portion of their crops' water needs will be met by rainfall. Thus in periods of drought, particularly during the summer rainy season, crops could fail despite the availability of groundwater irrigation.

While the farmers' responses indicate that climatic risk imposes a substantial negative impact on livelihoods, the nonclimatic factors volunteered by respondents as contributing factors to "bad years" illustrate the important differences in the sensitivity of their livelihoods as well as the particular requirements for livelihood success in the three communities. Approximately 20 percent of the factors defining "bad years" in each community were nonclimatic in nature (Eakin 2002: 207).

Family illness, a feature of "bad years" mentioned by many households, can necessitate not only unplanned expenditures that exacerbate economic losses from climatic hazards, but also result in a temporary loss in human capital and thus a decline in the capacity of a household to mitigate losses. One of the stories told to me by Don Martín, a young vegetable farmer, shows how easily a family illness can have larger repercussions. In 1991, Don Martín had three school-age children and was struggling to make ends meet from his irrigated plots without hiring any extra labor. His six-year-old boy had an accident—a piece of pencil got stuck in his cheek, became infected, and, because of a delayed diagnosis, the boy was sick for quite a while and needed an operation. Don Martín had to buy medicine and travel many times to Puebla, while trying to collect sufficient money for the operation. He had to borrow from moneylenders in another town, at an interest of 10 percent, compounded monthly. Because of his son's illness and the time he had to spend trying to cure him, he was unable to tend to his fields and weeds overtook his tomatillos. In the end he couldn't get a good price for them. He figured he lost the equivalent of 6,000 pesos for not taking care of his harvest, an amount that in those days was a good sum of money. And he fell into heavy debt. As Don Martín narrated his story, looking at his now teenage son, the emotion in his voice made the anxiety of that year palpable.

Farmers in each community highlighted a variety of other factors in addition to illness that contributed to a "bad year." Several households in Plan de Ayala mentioned the loss of livestock to disease, which affects households' financial liquidity at critical moments while increasing their expenditures. In Torres, many households mentioned migration as the most common nonclimatic factor, illustrating that for these households migration is a risky enterprise and can represent a significant impact on household security, particularly in terms of labor availability. In Nazareno, the commercial orientation of production exposes households not only to climatic risk but also to substantial market uncertainty and risk, and for this reason "poor prices" was a factor mentioned by almost 20 percent of households. Nazareno farmers explained that a drought alone or a severe frost was manageable, but when these events occurred at a time of family illness, or when the losses were combined with poor market prices or a sudden water supply problem from a water pump breakdown, the impact was magnified.

Hazard Impacts in 1998 and 1999

Regardless of the preferred definition of a bad year, over 80 percent of the surveyed farmers in Plan de Ayala and Torres, and 39 percent of respondents in Nazareno, identified 1999 as having been the worst year for their livelihoods in recent memory. In total, the surveyed households in Torres, Plan de Ayala, and Nazareno reported, respectively, 88 percent, 73 percent, and 38 percent of their planted areas affected. Maize yields were abysmally low, averaging only 200 kg/ha in Torres and 120 kg/ha in Plan de Ayala. In Nazareno, the yields of rainfed maize averaged 322 kg/ha, but with large variations from household to household.

Farmers in all three communities attributed most of their losses in 1999 to the midsummer frosts, and to a lesser extent to drought or some combination of the two hazards. One farmer in Plan de Ayala recalled having planted three hectares of maize and losing about 50 percent of the crop because it failed to germinate. Then his fields were hit by frost on June 23. He turned under his destroyed maize crop and planted barley and oats, but this crop was affected by a frost on July 14. He was able to salvage some of the oat for forage, and the barley had some grain but very low yield. He had no maize harvest at all.

Don Carlos, another farmer who had been planting in Plan de Ayala since the ejido was founded, had risked planting fava beans (*haba*), a crop particularly sensitive to low temperatures, and had to write off all three hectares he had planted because of both a partial frost in June and a total frost in early September. Like his neighbors he only recovered forage from his maize fields, no grain. He grumbled that he had not had a decent harvest in several years and was unsure now what to plant.

In fact, none of the surveyed households in the rainfed communities escaped losses in 1999, and only 20 percent did so in Nazareno, despite the widespread use of irrigation. Don Miguel, a particularly entrepreneurial Nazareno vegetable farmer, prided himself on never having completely lost a harvest until 1999. He reported having planted five times in succession in 1999, losing his seedlings each time to frost. He had never witnessed such a series of frosts, and when I spoke with him in 2000, he was beginning to doubt his luck. In general, respondents in Nazareno reported a greater diversity of causes of crop losses in 1999, including disease, wind damage, hail, mismanagement, poor market prices, or combinations of these factors.

The impact of the events of 1999 was probably exacerbated by the losses experienced by farmers in 1998. Although their losses then were less extensive than those of 1999, the households in Plan de Ayala and Torres still lost over half of their respective total planted areas. Drought and the late arrival of the summer rains (I was told in Plan de Ayala that the onset of the rainy season was as late as mid-July), followed by a midsummer frost, set back the maize crop and reduced yields. In Nazareno, the drought meant more problems with crop pests as well as increasing production costs, and the drought's impacts were complicated by the volatility of the vegetable markets in southeastern Mexico. Several vegetable farmers recalled that year in detail:

It didn't rain until the sixteenth of July and then it stopped raining until September. It was then that Chiapas was flooded. Without rain, the pests enter the vegetables. In 1998 the milpa was destroyed by such pests as *chupadores, pulgón, ácaro, araña roja*, and *la mosca blanca*. The plants were stressed, all of them without water. We had to irrigate more often, which meant buying water from neighbors. But then this caused problems of fungi because of the [irrigation]-saturated soils and the high temperatures. So we spent a lot of money on disease control and on pumping water, because in those conditions the cost of electricity goes up with the [increased] demand. And to top it all off, there was no market!

But what really surprised farmers was the unexpected heavy rainfall that occurred in August and September, when, if anything, they would have expected the midsummer drought. This event caused the odd report by farmers in Plan de Ayala of several fields that were affected by both drought and too much rain in a single season. As a result, maize yields in Torres and Plan de Ayala were quite low, averaging less than 500 kg/ha compared to expected yields in good years of 1,500–2,000 kg/ha. As will be discussed in the following sections, these losses affected seed stocks, grain reserves, livestock holdings, and households' labor allocation, making subsequent losses in 1999 more difficult to manage.

Mitigating Factors on Physical Impacts

Despite the fact that the households in the three communities were exposed to relatively similar patterns of precipitation and frost in 1998 and 1999, the events were differently experienced, partially as a result of local variations in climatic patterns between the three communities, but also because of differences in crop and land management. These differences are potentially quite important because they illustrate how impacts might conceivably be mitigated through changes in land use, crop choice, or crop management with the help of new technologies or perhaps climate forecasts (Eakin 2000). The relatively longer growing cycle of maize in comparison to barley and oats, for example, increases the likelihood that maize har vests will be affected by variability in the timing of the canícula or by anomalous frosts. If impacts are similar across a community *regardless* of crop choice, timing of planting, or other actions of farmers, then there is less hope that farmers will have the power to reduce the sensitivity of their production process to climatic hazards.

As it turned out, the different losses experienced by households in 1999 were not statistically associated with the month of planting or input use (Eakin 2002). Farmers' crop choices, however, appeared to have important influences over harvest outcomes. Maize is the primary food crop in both communities (and thus is highly valued for household consumption), but it has a longer growing season than wheat, oats, and barley and for this reason is more sensitive to late and early frost. The different climate sensitivities of the grain crops planted in Torres and Plan de Ayala are well known by the farmers, and they do their best to allocate their crops among their fields according to that knowledge.

In 1999, the fields that Plan de Ayala farmers planted in maize were six times more likely to have suffered from climate impacts than the fields planted in other grains. When they are concerned that their maize will not fully mature before the risk of frost rises in September, Plan de Ayala farmers try to protect their harvest by preferentially planting maize on the slopes of the hill, El Mirador, just to the east of the village. They then dedicate the more frost-prone plains in front of the village to shorter-cycle grains. But if the rains arrive on time, they typically can manage to harvest the maize in the lower fields before the first frosts in September. The problem has been the unexpected frosts in the middle of the growing season. In 1999 they planted only half their maize fields on the slopes of El Mirador and the other half in the plains and were hit by frosts in both June and September. As was evident by my visit to the frost-burned slopes of El Mirador in the summer of 2000, even planting more maize on the slopes was not a foolproof strategy.

Drought is also a problem for the slopes of El Mirador where the relatively fine soils tend to dry out more rapidly than the low-lying fields in front of the ejido. Thus farmers often have to gamble on the type of climate event that may affect them the most. In 1998, worried that the late arrival of the rains would mean their crops would not yet be fully mature when the first frosts arrived in September, farmers planted as much maize as they could on El Mirador. Yet drought was the predominant problem in 1998, and their maize, barley, and oats fields were all similarly affected.

In Torres, maize and beans were by far the most frequently planted crops by the surveyed households in both 1998 and 1999 (together covering 61 percent and 90 percent, respectively, of the total planted area in each year). Nevertheless, in both years the fields planted in oats suffered minimal losses in comparison to the relatively high losses to maize and beans. Farmers in Torres also said that their land was relatively homogenous in terms of topography and microclimate, and thus they were not able to exploit topographic features to buffer their crops from climate hazards as did farmers in Plan de Ayala.

Another factor that affects the sensitivity of a harvest to climatic variability is a household's management of crop diseases and pests. Crop diseases and pests are particularly a problem in the irrigated production of Nazareno, and in 1999 crop diseases accounted for 5 percent of the reported crop losses. The farmers interviewed in Nazareno identified a strong relationship between climatic variability and pest problems, attributing outbreaks of fungus, bacteria, or insects to damage to crops by hail, frost, or drought. Many other respondents asserted that one of the problems with drought, regardless of the amount of irrigation available, was dust—dust that they felt brought *chahuixtle*, a pest that was particularly associated with maize (*chahuixtle* is somewhat of a generic term for a variety of pests, but could be a manifestation of *Puccinia polysora* Undrew). Rain washed away the dust and kept chahuixtle under control. Araña roja, or "red spider" (*Polyphago tarsonemus*), is also associated with dry spells. One farmer claimed to have lost 50 percent of his maize and all his lettuce to this spider during the dry spring of 1998. The connection of disease and insect damage to climate is in urgent need of further research, particularly in relation to the possibility of climate forecasting and the ability of households to plan for input expenditures.

Of course, climate events are by no means the only or even the most important factor driving the incidence of crop diseases and pests. Farmers plant very intensively, rarely allowing their fields to lie fallow for a full year to kill off any persistent infestations. The close proximity of one household's fields to those of a neighbor's also inhibits effective disease control. Many farmers acknowledged in interviews that they were not experienced in identifying and diagnosing the pests in their plots. By not distinguishing between fungi and insects or between root and leaf pests, they sensed that they often fail to treat their crops effectively with the appropriate pesticides, allowing the pest to proliferate (see chap. 8).

Direct Economic Impacts of Crop Losses

Of course, yields and the extent of damage from climate events do not account for the full impact of the hazard on a household. The crop losses experienced in the three communities are compounded by the households' lost investments and earnings and their resulting increases in expenditures.

Understandably, few households with only rainfed fields produced sufficient grain in 1998 or 1999 to market their harvests. Although for most households maize is primarily a subsistence crop, it is also often exchanged as needed for cash, should a household have enough to spare. In 1998, slightly more than one-quarter of the surveyed households in Torres and a third of Plan de Ayala households managed to market some portion of their harvests. But in 1999, only the largest landholding household in Torres and a quarter of the households in Plan de Ayala reported selling part of their harvests. In both years in each community, one household accounted for the vast majority of the total marketed harvest value.

Even for those households that rarely, if ever, market their harvests, the crop losses of 1998 and 1999 represented a loss not just of a food and forage but of investment, if not of cash, then of time, seed, and family labor. Farmers' estimates of the cost of producing rainfed maize (excluding their own labor) average approximately 1,000 pesos per hectare (approximately US$108), reflecting the rental of draft animal power and/or fertilizer applications.

The investment losses of 1999 were also exacerbated by the fact that many households that typically did not purchase seed to plant were forced to do so in 1999 because of their poor harvests in the two preceding years. Almost 70 percent of households surveyed in Plan de Ayala, and 30 percent in Torres and Nazareno, reported having to purchase seed because of the loss of their seed stocks. Several

Plan de Ayala households, unable or unwilling to pay the 8 pesos/kilo (US$0.87) for the local uncertified seed sold in Apizaco, decided to plant the same grain they purchased to make their tortillas at 1.9 pesos/kilo (US$0.21). It was not only the cost of the seed that was problematic. Farmers also worried about the risks of using seed that was untested in their fields. When I asked where they found the seed they needed, I was told: "No one has seed or grain in the village. They have had to go outside [of Plan de Ayala] to buy it. Some farmers have gone to Tlaxcala [city], but we don't think this is a good idea because the [climate] conditions are different there and you cannot be sure that the maize will be successful."

In Nazareno, because almost all crops planted under irrigation are destined for commercial markets, losses also represent losses of potential earnings. In 1999, 10 percent of the total area planted in Nazareno was planted with crops that were intended for the market, but for various reasons—problems with prices, pests, and climate—did not result in any earnings for the household. According to data from the public extension service in Tecamachalco, a household could expect to lose anywhere from 5,000 to over 20,000 pesos from an unmarketable hectare of vegetables. Two of the more popular crops in Nazareno, tomatillos and zucchini, entailed investments of approximately 10,000 pesos. The production costs of beets and tomatoes exceeded 20,000 pesos. Even losses experienced early in the production cycle of a vegetable crop could be as much as half the total value of the crop, particularly if the farmers have purchased seedlings from a greenhouse rather than growing their own crops from seed.

For those households that were not expecting to market their harvests or that rarely achieved a surplus (such as the majority in Torres), the losses experienced were felt in greater consumption expenses. This was particularly the case in late 1998 and early 1999, as households began to deplete their grain stocks. In Torres, twenty of the twenty-two households surveyed (91 percent) reported having increased their maize purchases as a result of their losses to drought and frost. Most of these households had begun to buy maize in 1998 and 1999, although a few households began depending on purchased maize as early as 1997.

Because few households in Torres would be self-sufficient in maize even in a year of normal production (e.g., a year in which yields are at least 1,000 kg/ha), it is difficult to estimate exactly how much additional expenditure the losses of 1998 and 1999 caused the families. Although respondents reported a wide range of values, the median annual expenditure for maize in Torres was around 3,000 pesos (US$325), which in 2000 would have bought around 1,500 kg of maize grain or 750 kilos of ready-made tortillas. This figure is congruent with the findings of de Janvry, Gordillo, and Sadoulet (1997) who found that an average household in the 1994 national ejido survey kept 1,400 kg of maize grain for their own consumption and 1,200 kg for animal consumption.

Three-quarters of the surveyed population in Plan de Ayala reported making extraordinary maize purchases because of their losses in 1998 and 1999, but unlike those in Torres, most of these households (75 percent) began making these purchases only in 1999 and 2000, indicating that they either were able to extract some minimal harvest in 1999 or had a reserve of maize grain from previous years. As I talked with farmers in Plan de Ayala, it was clear to me that it was the cumulative effect of several years of poor harvests that was straining their food security strategies. One farmer commented to me: "We usually have a reserve of maize from year to year so that if the harvest is poor or we need extra, we have some in storage. That is what we did this past year [1999–2000], used a lot of our reserve maize. Now we have very little left. We don't know what we will do if the maize crop is poor this year. We can only hope for good rains."

In the summer of 2000, the extraordinary maize expenditures reported in Plan de Ayala ranged from only 200 pesos (US$21) (this family had just begun to purchase maize at the time of the interview) to one household that spent an estimated 8,000 pesos/year (US$870) (this latter figure also included expenditures on beans and was intended to feed a family of thirteen plus livestock). The median figure was around 3,000 pesos (US$325), as in Torres.

Coping Strategies

How households cope with the losses they experience, whether climate or nonclimate related, is another key element in understanding vulnerability (Blaikie et al. 1994; Downing, Watts, and Bohle 1996; Downing et al. 1999). Here I use the term "coping" to refer to *ex post*, short-term actions that households undertake to address unanticipated loss as distinguished from longer-term adaptive strategies that households may formulate to diminish anticipated future risks and uncertainties. Although short term in nature, coping strategies can illustrate a household's flexibility (through its access to key survival resources) in the face of a particular shock, and its resilience, that is, its ability to recuperate from loss. The coping strategies pursued by a household thus are also important as indications of longer-term adaptive capacity. Coping strategies that fail to enable a household to recuperate rapidly, that diminish resource stocks, or threaten future entitlements can have negative implications for the capacity of a household to adjust and adapt to shocks experienced in subsequent years, or to longer-term variability and change.

In the household surveys, the farmers and their families described the actions they implemented during the most recent "bad year" (which, in almost all cases, was either 1998 or 1999). The question was open ended, allowing respondents to name all actions they could remember as a response to the events they experienced. Respondents were only prompted to discuss changes in consumption patterns, livestock sales, maize purchases, off-farm employment, and equipment sales if they did not volunteer information about actions in these categories. While respondents reported similar types of actions in response to the losses they experienced, the number of households undertaking any particular response, and the range of responses reported in each community, varied considerably.

Torres

What is notable about the coping strategies of households in Torres is not which actions the households adopted, but what they did *not* do in response to their losses. Compared to Plan de Ayala, where the actual extent of the losses was less, Torres households reported a relatively narrow range of responses focused on participating in nonfarm employment and, to a lesser extent, livestock sales. Only 23 percent of households attempted replanting, no one reported taking out a loan, either from formal or informal sources, and very few received food rations (although almost every household interviewed reported having to purchase more maize than they would have normally because of their losses).

On the surface it would seem that perhaps the community was not so badly affected after all and that perhaps few households required any extraordinary measures to address their losses. However, given the extent of losses in 1998 and 1999, it is far more likely that the limited range of responses of the Torres households has more to do with their limited access to resources that could play critical roles in recuperating from climate impacts. Since the collapse of the pulque market in the early 1990s, there were few alternative income options in close proximity to the village. Increasingly, households had been relying on nonfarm activities, and they reported increasing their participation in these activities in response to their losses. The adult women who were not tending children frequently reported seeking temporary work in Huamantla as domestic servants, while the younger men had begun to migrate seasonally to the neighboring state of Puebla in search of employment. Of the seventeen adults who reported having migrated from the community at least once in their lifetimes, 76 percent of these had done so between 1997 and 2000, and all of them reported searching for work in the state of Puebla or the Federal District. No one reported leaving Mexico in search of work, although several indicated that they would have liked to do so but lacked the resources necessary to make the trip to and across the border.

Relatively few households reported selling animals in response to their losses, and those that did tended to sell a pig, goat, or sheep. Disturbingly, a few households reported selling their mules, their draft power. All the households that sold livestock in 1998 and 1999 in Torres said they did so out of urgent need for cash or an inability to support the animals. Perhaps in part because of these sales, only 36 percent of households owned a yunta at the time of the surveys in late 2000, and half of the surveyed population did not have any pigs, goats, or sheep.

Plan de Ayala

In contrast with Torres, a relatively large range of strategies was reported by farmers in Plan de Ayala, perhaps indicative of greater flexibility in resource use and access, or simply a greater diversity in the organization of livelihood activities in the community. For some households, nonfarm employment plays an important role in their management of crop losses. Other farmers like Don Carlos, who was older than many of the other ejidatarios, somewhat infirm, and living alone with his wife, felt that their lack of access to non-farm income put them at a disadvantage. He observed that the children of the ejidatarios who work are a help, saying, "There are only a few of us in my household now—all my children have left. It means fewer mouths to feed, but it also means less money coming in. Other households that have several members working in the factories have the resources. Sure, it can be tight, but together they can pull together what is needed."

The importance of the households' labor force in coping with crop losses was reiterated often in my conversations with farmers. In one group discussion, I was told that the key to surviving "bad years" was through "the whole family working together. . . . The wife has her activities; the head of the household is responsible for assuring there is enough food. If the children are less than fifteen years old, they can have problems because there isn't work for children that young. It is really tough. They have to think of other ways to get food into the household."

Livestock also played an important role in coping strategies in Plan de Ayala. Fifty and 69 percent of households sold livestock in 1998 and 1999, respectively, primarily calves and cows. After low yields in barley and oats in 1998 because of drought, few households had the forage in 1999 to support large herds, and many continued culling activities they had begun the year before. Aside from the impact of drought on the ejidatarios' cultivated crops, the natural pastures on the communal lands of the ejido were also affected.

Yet by the summer of 2000 the households that sold livestock in 1998 and 1999 still had, on average, larger stocks of animals than the average of the community. This fact suggests that the selling of livestock, even for reasons of cash scarcity and resource constraints, is not a sufficient indicator of vulnerability. To the contrary, the animal sales in Plan de Ayala may be more useful as an indicator of household resilience and robustness in face of loss.

Field replanting was also prominent in Plan de Ayala households' coping strategies. Replanting, however, requires valuable resources. Although households in Tlaxcala tend to keep their seed from one year to the next to plant, they may not have much seed in reserve, particularly after several years of poor harvests. Replanting in many cases thus can mean additional expenditures in seeds, field preparation, and labor. One of Plan de Ayala's younger farmers, a man in his forties with a young family of seven, had lost 1,500 pesos for each of his three hectares planted in maize in 1999. He decided to replant, but doing so required hiring a tractor twice to plow his fields, and increasing his costs by another 1,000 pesos for each hectare. When he told me this, he sighed. What he really lamented was the time he had invested: "What you lose is your own labor." And of course the harvest outcome is never assured. He harvested no grain in 1999.

Another household consisting of an older couple, two of their married daughters, and their grandchildren had a similar experience, although the support they had from their daughters' factory jobs had helped pay for some of the additional expenses. In 1999, they planted maize in April, but then in May lost the young crop to frost. They plowed the maize under and planted barley and a bit of oats instead. They estimated that they lost about 500 pesos per hectare (US$54) from planting the maize, and then invested about 500 pesos per hectare more in planting barley and oats. Because of the poor rainfall that season, their barley crop was "useless." There wasn't any grain, so they had to use it all as forage and were unable to commercialize any of it.

For these households, replanting in some senses increased their vulnerability by depleting their valuable cash resources without the compensation of a harvest at the end of the season. But the fact that these households, and the nine others who reported replanting, were able to find the resources to do so is also another indicator of a certain degree of resourcefulness and resilience that was not apparent in Torres.

Another important difference that distinguishes Plan de Ayala from the other case studies is the high percentage of households that reported receiving food rations from the government after the climate events of 1998 and 1999. Every household surveyed in Plan de Ayala received a few months of food rations, while very few households received such support in Nazareno, and none did in Torres. This discrepancy may reflect the fact that many households in Plan de Ayala are part of the campesino organization CNOCIR, which plays an active role in Tlaxcaltecan rural politics through its affiliation with the Partido del Trabajo and is one of the more vocal groups demanding rural benefits and services in the state. Plan de Ayala households were also offered temporary employment (twenty-two days of work at 27 pesos/day) in a public works program run by the state and federal government.

Like the households of Torres, households in Plan de Ayala also reported increasing their reliance on income from nonfarm sources, and for some households this involved the temporary migration of one or more household members. Of the nine adults in the survey population who reported having once migrated, six (66 percent) had done so between 1997 and 2000. Unlike in Torres, however, this migration was typically very local—either to the town of Tetla or the capital Tlaxcala—to work temporarily in construction sites.

Nazareno

Of the three communities, the coping strategies employed in Nazareno were perhaps the most complex. Households with several irrigated fields at different stages of production have the potential advantage of being able to recuperate the losses experienced with one harvest through the earnings from harvests in other fields. However, because the financial loss entailed is often high, crop losses in Nazareno often translate into an acute financial burden that can jeopardize future investments.

The labor-intensive and year-round nature of irrigated production also constrains the ways in which households can allocate their resources to recuperate from losses. Unlike the farmers of Plan de Ayala and Torres, vegetable farmers do not have the winter season to dedicate to alternative economic activities. On different occasions various farmers explained to me what seemed to be a standard sequence of coping activities, applied often in close succession and often in the course of a single year:

Don Martin: First, you sell off any animals you have to pay for household expenses. Second, you look for someone to share the risks. You plant vegetables a medias with the hope that you will get sufficient income to recuperate your losses. You can plant short-cycle crops because these will bring you income faster . . .

crops such as radish, kale, or zucchini. These all mature in about forty-five days. Third, you plant basic grains. You would migrate only when you are in debt and you can't think of any other way to get out of it. And if you migrate, migrate to the USA where you have the chance of recuperating your losses.

Don Jorge: First, you will borrow from friends and family, enough to invest in the next crop. Second, you will sell off animals to help pay for costs. Third, you will offer your land for sharecropping [a medias] to share the expenses with someone else. Fourth, you will rent out your land and work on someone else's land (or even your own land) as a laborer. Or you will work in some other job. Finally, if necessary, you will migrate.

Selling livestock is one of the most effective and secure ways of acquiring small amounts of cash. Sixty-four percent of respondents in Nazareno reported that they had sold livestock in 1999, principally to meet household expenses. As respondents in one group discussion said: "Everyone has animals, but in small quantities. Sheep, pigs, chickens, goats, turkey. We don't invest anything in these animals. We feed them what there is available. And sell them when the need arises."

After selling off livestock and still having only minimal cash reserves, a household might choose to plant a lower-investment crop or revert to a subsistence crop (maize, beans, or alfalfa) as a coping strategy. A rapid-growing, low-investment commercial crop (such as radish, green onions, parsley, or cilantro) with luck can bring a household a quick profit at low risk.

Planting subsistence crops in an irrigated plot enables the household to keep the land in production while boosting its self-sufficiency. I was told that the principal benefit from planting subsistence crops under irrigation, aside from having a harvest to consume, was that the crops have "stable prices and you can know if you will get a profit or not. This is the only way to recuperate losses. Planting vegetables, even those with very short cycles, is always risky because the prices change so constantly." That said, planting maize or other subsistence crops in irrigated fields entails a high opportunity cost. While a good yield of irrigated maize might be 4 to 5 tons/ha in Nazareno, providing a potential gross income of over 3,000 pesos (US$325) in 1999 (if all the harvest is sold), a hectare of cabbage (should all go well) *could* earn over 15,000 pesos (US$1,630).

For some households, even planting low-investment crops is economically unfeasible. Because of the narrow financial margin in which many Nazareno households operate, the economic impact of a harvest loss often extends far beyond the season of the loss, and prevents households from immediately recuperating their losses in another harvest. When I was interviewing farmers in the spring of 2000, several of them told me that they had not planted over the entire winter because of the debts they had incurred after losing their harvests to a frost in October 1999. One of these farmers had planted only a quarter hectare with marigolds for the Day of the Dead (November 2). But the loss amounted to 8,000 pesos, sufficient to put him in a critical financial situation. Another household recalled planting two hectares of lettuce on July 18, 1999, and then lost the entire area to the same October frost. They estimated their loss, not including their own time and labor, exceeded 14,000 pesos (US$1,521). Because of this loss, they were unable to find the resources to replant until the following May. Not only did they lose their investment in lettuce, but they also lost the potential income from the two hectares that were left unplanted from November until May. All their household investments—their oldest boy's education, their unfinished house, the new peach trees they had hoped to buy—were put on hold until they could once again manage to extract a surplus from their fields.

For these households, sharecropping is one of the last resorts before migrating. In Nazareno in 2000, 25 percent of the total area farmed by surveyed households was under some form of sharecropping, rental, or "lending" arrangement, compared to only 5 percent of the total area farmed in Torres and 6 percent of the farmed area in Plan de Ayala. Sharecropping arrangements typically involve committing a field and its water to another family to farm, in exchange for either half (a medias) or a third (*a terceras*) of the final harvest.

As an additional source of cash, many households turn to work as day laborers. Year-round production means there is no winter fallow period in which household members can leave the fields and search for alternative (and perhaps more secure) sources of income, as is the case with households in Plan de Ayala and Torres. Yet it also means that there is a year-round demand for labor for weeding, harvesting, and chemical applications, and this demand serves as a substantial, if low-paid, source of employment. Working as a day laborer in someone else's fields inevitably means that you devote less time to your own, which can again slow down the process of economic recovery.

Should these strategies still not stop the downward income spiral, the adult men of a household may opt for migration, leaving their fields to the remaining household members, to relatives, or to sharecroppers. Between 1998 and 2000, 34 percent of the households interviewed reported that at least one family member had migrated temporarily in search of work, and in half of these households the migrant had gone to the United States.

Comparing Coping Strategies

The impacts of the climate events of 1998 and 1999 in the Puebla-Tlaxcala Valley were significant. The interviewed households in the two rainfed communities in Tlaxcala reported extensive harvest losses in both years, essentially wiping out any expected harvest surpluses and in many cases forcing households to anomalous purchases of maize grain for their own consumption. The direct impacts of the events of 1999 were apparently more severe than those of 1998 and were undoubtedly exacerbated by two previous years of poor production.

The complexity expressed in farmers' definitions of a "bad year" illustrates the well-known lessons that have long been circulating in the literature of food insecurity and famine (FEWS 1999; Sen 1990; Watts and Bohle 1993): Households are not simply affected by declining yields or lost production volumes, but also (and often simultaneously) by entitlement failures such as loss of access to local employment, loss of human capital through illness, or losses in the exchange value of key resources such as livestock. It is clear that climate, while playing a critical role in production outcomes, is certainly not the only factor driving the vulnerability of the rural livelihoods in the three communities.

The importance of nonclimatic factors in production outcomes was particularly illustrated in the surveys and interviews in Nazareno, where farmers perceived a great diversity in the causes of their crop losses, ranging from hailstorms and winds to price volatility and management failures. While some events, family illnesses, for example, are unlikely to be related to direct climatic impacts, other events can have a synergistic effect on both the physical and economic consequences of a climatic event. Crop diseases and market failures for Nazareno's irrigated producers are two such examples. In fact, the involvement of Nazareno farmers in commercial vegetable markets significantly complicates any understanding of their vulnerability.

The analysis of the physical and economic impacts of the climate events of 1998 and 1999 highlights the differences in crop management and the particular requirements of production in household risk exposure, and it suggests that households may be able to mitigate some of the impact of climatic variability through management. The variability in physical exposure to frost offered by the protected slopes of El Mirador in Plan de Ayala, for example, gives farmers greater flexibility in managing frost risk. The differential sensitivities of oats, barley, and maize to frost and drought also offer the possibility that rainfed farmers may be able to minimize impacts through crop choice. These types of management adjustments can theoretically be facilitated with the provision of a reliable long-lead climate forecast, giving farmers the advance information they might need in order to make strategic crop and land-use decisions (Eakin 2000; Jones et al. 2000; Murphy et al. 2001).

As will be explored in detail in the chapters that follow, in practice, flexibility in crop and production management assumes problematically a diversity of, and access to, key physical, natural, and financial resources in central Mexico. Flexibility in crop choice depends in part on land availability, as well as on market opportunities and the availability of production technology. Flexibility in the timing of planting depends not only on the onset of the rainy season and the availability of planting and land preparation technologies, but also on how accommodating a household can be in its crop choice and on the inevitable constraints of soils and topography.

To cope with crop losses, households in the three communities tended to draw from similar resources: their livestock, their own seed and food reserves, and their labor in both off-farm (day laborers) and nonfarm activities. The particular types of coping strategies, and the sequence in which they are implemented, are quite similar to what has been observed in rural communities throughout the world (Batterbury 2001; Corbett 1988; Ellis 2000; Roncoli, Ingram, and Kirshen 2001). However, the differences in the number of different strategies households employed and the outcome of those strategies in terms of their resource stocks (land, livestock, seed, and grain) suggest that there were important differences in the resilience of households in the three communities. In Nazareno, household coping strategies are constrained by the financial and temporal requirements of irrigated production, yet are aided by the viability of wage labor in the local vegetable economy. Households in Plan de Ayala engaged in a diversity of strategies, including participating in government aid programs and nonfarm employment, but rather than indicating greater impact and vulnerability to hazards, this diversity most likely reflects the depth of human, financial, and sociopolitical resource stocks available in the community to recuperate from external shocks. In contrast, households in Torres reported a relatively narrow range of responses, although they reported high physical impacts from the climatic events of 1998 and 1999. The physical and economic marginality of this community appears to affect negatively the flexibility of their responses.

In the following chapters, the reasons behind these differences in coping strategies are explored in relation to the resources, opportunities, and constraining factors that frame the evolving livelihood strategies pursued by households in the three communities. It would be erroneous to believe that the ways in which households were coping with hazards in 1999 will be the way in which they will cope with them in 2010 or 2050. Yet by understanding how households are organizing their resources to manage uncertainty and by identifying the particular opportunities, entitlements, and institutions that are either facilitating or inhibiting these practices, we may shed some light on the critical elements of rural adaptive capacity as farmers face the new millennium.

6 Uncertainty with Limited Land

"Minifundismo" and Agricultural Choice

In the literature of natural hazards, poverty, resource inequality, and marginalization have all been put forward as important indicators of differences in vulnerability, following the logical argument that more impoverished households will have a narrower coping range, less flexible use of resources, and will be less empowered in their exchange relationships to acquire the assets they need for survival (Blaikie et al. 1994; Kelly and Adger 2000: 331). Yet among similarly poor populations, relative income and wealth data do not say very much about how the vulnerability and adaptive capacity of one household or community compares to another, nor do such data show how to formulate policy that might reduce vulnerability and enhance adaptive capacity. Identifying the particular endowments that enable households to acquire other strategic assets and determining how households organize these assets into "livelihood portfolios" that enhance resilience, flexibility, and adaptability over time are more useful in understanding differences in vulnerability (Scoones 1998: 8).

In this chapter I focus on the most basic of the strategies pursued by households in the three villages: subsistence maize farming. Subsistence production is a core element in *all* of the livelihood portfolios constructed by the farm households in the three communities, although it is the dominant form of production in the community of Torres. As will be discussed in the following chapters, for the majority of households in Plan de Ayala and Nazareno subsistence activities serve as an insurance policy that facilitates the households' engagement in more risky activities on- and off-farm. In contrast, for most of the households of Torres, their commitment to maize and bean production appears to *reduce* their range of choice and opportunity in responding flexibly to exogenous change. The key difference between the two roles of subsistence production, facilitating or restricting income diversification, revolves around access to land.

Access to land is the most basic entitlement required for agricultural production. In a highly variable and uncertain climate, households may lack the confidence that they will be able, in any give year, to produce sufficient food for their own consumption needs. This situation characterizes particularly those households classified in Mexico as *minifundios*, smallholders with so little land that they are unlikely, even in so-called good years, to meet their subsistence requirements (Cebreros 1990).

The problem of minifundismo in the Puebla-Tlaxcala Valley is compounded by the fact that agronomists have determined that maize is at best only marginally suitable to the climate and soils of the region, particularly in consideration of the high frequency of frost and the relatively short growing season (INIFAP 1998). As documented in the previous chapter, farmers in the three communities reported higher climatic impacts in maize than in other crops planted. Yet minifundio households face few alternatives. As long as market prices and wage opportunities do not assure households the capacity to purchase their food requirements and alternative land uses are equally unprofitable, households are likely to continue to plant maize, regardless of its climatic sensitivity. In other words, by necessity, minifundio households may be pursuing a strategy that is in some senses relatively maladaptive to climatic variability and extreme events because it represents their best available livelihood option.

Landholding Size and Maize Requirements

Under rainfed conditions, maize yields in the Puebla-Tlaxcala Valley in the 1980s and 1990s averaged between 1,200 kg/ha and 1,600 kg/ha. At an average household consumption of 1,500 kg/year, one hectare of rainfed maize might meet household food requirements. If one were to assume that self-sufficiency was a principal goal of smallholder production, additional land would be required to produce animal feed and seed and even more land would be necessary to assure sufficient grain for storage. According to the calculations of de Janvry, Gordillo, and Sadoulet, an average ejido household in Mexico would at minimum need 2,700–3,700 kg of maize to meet all these use requirements (e.g., human, animal, seed and storage) (de Janvry, Gordillo, and Sadoulet 1997), which, given the yields of Puebla and Tlaxcala, would mean having access to at least 2.0–2.5 ha. Given that the standard deviation of rainfed maize yields in Puebla and Tlaxcala is around 400 kg/ha, the actual amount of land a risk-adverse household would have to devote to maize production in order to assure self-sufficiency would be even greater (2.5–3.0 ha).

If these assumptions are correct, then one would naturally expect that households with small amounts of land would devote nearly all of their land to subsistence crops. Indeed, this is exactly what is happening in the Puebla-Tlaxcala Valley. The median area in maize planted by the households in 1999 was similar in the two rainfed communities (2.8 ha and 2.9 ha in Torres and Plan de Ayala, respectively) and appears to conform to the use requirement predictions of de Janvry, Gordillo, and Sadoulet described above (de Janvry, Gordillo, and Sadoulet 1997). Even the Nazareno households with access to irrigation tended to devote two hectares to maize.

Furthermore, among the households surveyed, the total area in maize increases with landholding size, to a threshold of approximately 3.5 ha, after which the correlation between maize area and total land area weakens. The positive correlation between total planted area and total maize area is evident not only in rainfed crops, but also among the subgroup of Nazareno households with irrigation, illustrating that even households with some irrigation but overall limited access to land tend to prioritize maize cultivation until their subsistence needs are satisfied. Indeed, no household in the three communities with less than 3.5 ha of land planted more than three different crops (fig. 6.1). With only a few exceptions, those crops tended to be maize, black beans, and fava beans, all subsistence crops.

This observed pattern of land use, where maize is the preferred crop up to a defined threshold of land area, is explained not only by household consumption needs, but also by the market for maize in Mexico. After the closure of CONASUPO in 1998 and the opening of Mexico's market to North American corn, profitably commercializing maize grain in the volumes produced by smallholder farmers has

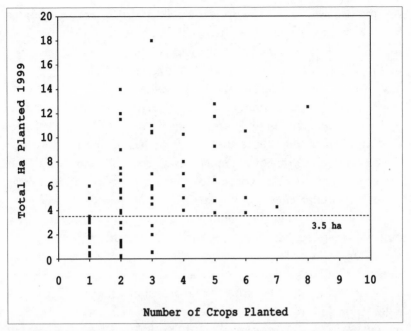

Figure 6.1 Landholding size and number of crops planted (Torres, Plan de Ayala, and Nazareno, 1999). *Source*: Household survey data, 2000.

become nearly impossible. One maize farmer in Nazareno lamented: "The problem is that the commercial grain houses, the tortilla makers, want only hybrid seed. This is why there is so much maize now from Argentina, Sinaloa, and the United States in the companies like Minsa. They would never buy my maize." His sentiment was echoed in Plan de Ayala, where farmers were directly aware of the competition: "We are importing maize from Canada and the United States that is for animals. It is yellow and poor quality. But they prefer that maize to make tortillas to what we can offer." And the farmers were not simply bemoaning the loss of buyers, but also the inequity in the resources available to farmers in Mexico compared to the United States. A farmer in Plan de Ayala who seemed to be always up to the minute on the latest political debates told me: "In the United States you can get eight tons of maize per hectare, pure forage maize. Because they have such large extensions the cost of production is really low, around 5,000 peso/ha. We don't have the water that they have in the United States. We can't compete. The maize from the United States is bankrupting us. Even our beans we can't sell. And they are charging us 8,500 pesos/ton to buy them [to eat]!" The households that are able to sell some maize now do so directly to neighbors or other residents in their community, or, in the case of Plan de Ayala, to landless households working at the industrial complex Xicohténcatl I.

Not only are the commercial opportunities for maize increasingly restricted, but, when I asked farmers to classify their crops according to their advantages and disadvantages, farmers widely perceived maize to be one of the most "risky" crops to plant because of its sensitivity to frost and drought—despite the fact that maize was planted by almost every household interviewed and surveyed.

In years of good yields, having maize in the household provides a buffer against rising consumer costs, unstable nonfarm employment, and, if the household is able to store a surplus, against future losses to climate hazards. Even in years when the maize field produces only a few kilos of grain, the *rastrojo*, the maize stalk and leaves, still provides valuable forage for livestock. Don Rudolfo, a vegetable farmer of Nazareno who every year planted maize in part of his irrigated fields, explained that a small area in irrigated maize produces quantities of rastrojo, enough to feed a cow and a couple of mules for a year. Although he said rastrojo is worth a lot in local markets, he felt it was worth keeping to support his yunta. Having his own mule and plow allows him to work his fields when and where he wants to instead of having to wait for his turn to rent a yunta or tractor.

Landholding Size, Crop Decisions, and Uncertainty

Given the uncertainty in rural wage markets and the lack of viable agricultural alternatives, one cannot argue with the logic of the "safety first" subsistence strategy described above. Yet for land-constrained households, the safety-first strategy necessarily limits the flexibility of both land use and crop choice. In other words, it would be unrealistic to expect such households to be willing to switch from maize to a shorter-cycle crop or to devote part of their land to an alternative activity that would reduce its climatic vulnerability *unless* the household's maize and bean use requirements could be assured from an alternative source.

The importance of subsistence for land-constrained households is illustrated by the differences in how crop and land-use decisions are made in the three communities. In Torres, subsistence requirements are what farmers most frequently mentioned as driving their crop choice (by 59 percent of households) and the amount of land they devoted to any particular crop (73 percent of households). I was told, "Maize is the principal crop because we don't have much land" and "We plant maize . . . because we have only a little bit of land, and we need maize [to eat]." Or, farmers' choice of crop is based on their crop-rotation schedule: "We don't have any other land so we have to plant maize . . . but we plan to rotate it with fava beans." Climate was considered in crop choices by only 9 percent of households.

In comparison, households in Plan de Ayala were far more likely to mention climatic variability (81 percent of households) as the determining factor in their crop choice and the microclimatic conditions of particular fields as the most important consideration in their crop allocation decisions (38 percent of households). Reflecting the commercial orientation of production, market viability, climate, and finances were mentioned by Nazareno farmers as the three most important factors in their choice of crops (30 percent, 28 percent, and 23 percent of households, respectively). Although fewer than 20 percent of farmers mentioned consumption requirements as a factor in their crop choices, the farmers in Nazareno tend to dedicate a substantial portion of their land to maize because of the economic insecurity stemming from involvement in vegetable markets. As I was told in one group meeting in the village: "We plant rainfed maize every year, regardless, but the yield is very variable. In the best years we get about 1.5 tons/ha . . . in the worst, as little as a couple hundred kilos. We can't count on it. So we typically plant some maize in the irrigated areas, so we can be *sure* to have some yield. This is what makes our lives secure. We produce vegetables only to get ahead."

Although their motivations for their crop decisions varied, the households in all three communities expressed an overwhelming commitment to planting at least some of their land each year in maize. The majority of the respondents in each community (two-thirds of the households surveyed in Torres, and over three-quarters of households in Plan de Ayala and Nazareno) reported that they *always* planted maize, often commenting, "If we don't plant maize, what would we eat?" However, a minority of households in each community said that there were some conditions under which they would not plant maize. In Torres, where the average landholding size is only four hectares, this reason was agronomic: the farmers felt the need to rotate their fields periodically with beans (another subsistence crop) in order to maintain soil fertility.

In Plan de Ayala, where households have on average double the land area of those in Torres, the reason was climatic: a few households said they sometimes would not plant maize if the rains were very late (e.g., June/July), with the argument that planting maize at that date would be fruitless. This was the perspective of one rather young grandmother in the community, who said that if it rained on time and sufficiently, she would plant as much as three hectares of maize, but in the summer of 2000, because "clavó mucho la seca" (the dryness set in), she was not planting any maize. The fact that she received income from her absent husband (a mechanic in Apizaco) and her son, a combi driver, undoubtedly also influenced her crop decisions.

In Nazareno, where farmers face a high opportunity cost in using their irrigated land for subsistence maize, market opportunities in vegetables were the primary motivating factor for not planting maize. And in these cases, the respondents explained that with irrigation they are often able to maintain a surplus of maize for a year in storage, and thus are able to free up their land for other crops while not affecting their subsistence supplies.

Uncertainty and the Minifundios of Torres and Nazareno

In the classification of livelihood groups, a majority of households in Torres (86 percent, or nineteen households) and a minority group of households in Nazareno (35 percent, or fifteen households) pursue livelihood strategies that epitomize the subsistence focus outlined above, and they are classified accordingly as Subsistence Maize households.

In both communities, the average landholding size of the Subsistence Maize household classes is less than three hectares, and, as would be expected, 80 percent to 90 percent of this land was dedicated to maize in 1999. Households in the Subsistence Maize groups also reported the highest crop losses in each of the respective communities, at an average of 53 percent of the planted area in Nazareno and an average of 84 percent in the Torres. These households are also the poorest in the two communities, with an estimated per capita cash inflow (gross monetary income) of only 2,300–3,600 pesos (US$250 to US$390) per year. Both groups face an urgent need to compensate for the limitations of agricultural production through income diversification. Migration to the United States, however, is not a feature of the strategies of the households in either of the communities, largely because they lack the resources to finance long-distance migration. Seasonal migration within the region, however, is a feature of some households' strategies.

Although the subsistence-oriented households in Torres and Nazareno share similar characteristics, the circumstances that structure their livelihood strategies are quite different, with consequently different implications for their vulnerability. In Torres, because the minifundios are the dominant class of farmers in the community, there are few resources within the community on which these households can draw in order to cope with loss, or adapt to change. With the collapse of the pulque industry, collection of aguamiel is less remunerative than previously, and the economic relationship between the smallholder subsistence households and the larger landholders has consequently weakened. With only a limited amount of land on which to meet their family's maize needs, these households also have very few animals—on average just the two mules for the yunta and one or two sheep or pigs for the household's consumption. These few animals can feed off the stubble of the maize fields without requiring the household to devote land to forage crops. Given their relative isolation from markets, it is not surprising that instead of selling their animals to cope with crop losses, these households tend to consume them.

The lack of economic activities within Torres forces these households to engage in external labor markets in order to cope with their losses. The households of the Subsistence Maize class are large, having on average seven members, and half of the household tend to be adults of working age, permitting the households to have a relatively diversified income base. In 2000, nonfarm income accounted for approximately a quarter of their total income, yet not one of the adults in the households of this group had a secondary school education, which limited their employment options. In the last half of the 1990s, the young men in the community began to seek employment in cement block manufacturing in the neighboring state of Puebla. This work requires them to live outside the community for several months of the year, returning only for the planting season. Although this work pays better than the more local nonfarm activities such as carpentry or construction assistants or, for the women, domestic work in Huamantla, the expense of living away from the farm for several months detracts from some of this economic gain.

On average just over half of the Subsistence Maize households' income came from sporadic participation in off-farm activities: working as day laborers in the fields of the larger farms in the Huamantla Valley and the continued collection of aguamiel for pulque. In order to access farm-wage employment from Torres, the adults (typically the young men of the households) are required to make the trip, often by foot, down into the valley below the village. Of course, as was shown by the definition of "bad years" by Torres households in the previous chapter, if the production in the valley is affected by hazards or market problems, the households can face a sudden contraction in the availability of work as day laborers.

Perhaps because off-farm and nonfarm employment is relatively less accessible and livestock are more difficult to maintain, the Subsistence Maize households of Torres tend to rely far more heavily on public welfare programs as a source of income than their counterparts in Nazareno. The average contribution of government transfers to total income was, at the time of the survey, 22 percent. The dependence of the Torres households on this source of income is new, a result of the households' engagement with new welfare programs implemented in the 1990s, as evident in the households' perceptions of the political and economic changes of that decade. In Torres, over two-thirds of the households perceived significant change in the policies of that decade, but not as much in agriculture as in welfare policy (table 6.1). This perception is not surprising given that as subsistence-oriented minifundios they had never benefited much from Mexico's agricultural policy and programs, and thus they had not individually been affected by the process of state retrenchment. In contrast, all but two of the households surveyed reported receiv-

Table 6.1 Perceptions of Institutional Change

	Torres % (#)	Plan de Ayala % (#)	Nazareno % (#)
No changed perceived	32 (7)	0 (0)	37 (16)
Change perceived	68 (15)	100 (16)	63 (25)
Total	100 (22)	100 (16)	100 (41)
Change perceived:*			
Negative	33 (5)	62 (13)	42 (14)
Less government help now	6 (1)	33 (7)	9 (3)
Prices have deteriorated	20 (3)	29 (6)	30 (10)
Increased competition	7 (1)	—	3 (1)
Positive	60 (9)	29 (6)	27 (9)
New programs; we are benefiting	60 (9)	24 (5)	6 (2)
Prices have improved	—	5 (1)	6 (2)
New crops now	—	—	3 (1)
New ideas, more open economy	—	—	3 (1)
New market opportunities	—	—	9 (3)
Mixed	7 (1)	9 (2)	30 (10)
New programs; we are not benefiting	7 (1)	9 (2)	30 (10)
Total	100 (15)	100 (21)	100 (33)

Source: Household survey data, 2000.
Note: The total response frequencies are greater than the number of respondents because several reported multiple results of policy changes.

ing funds from the new welfare programs instituted in the late 1990s (PROGRESA/Oportunidades).

In contrast, the Subsistence Maize households of Nazareno are in many ways a product of the dominant form of production in the community: irrigation. In the best of circumstances, the households of the Subsistence Maize class represent relatively young households in transition, awaiting the opportunity to purchase their own small piece of irrigated land. As part of a community defined by irrigation, these households also were not the beneficiaries of maize and basic-grain support programs in the 1970s. However, their welfare situation is also masked by their more prosperous vegetable-producing neighbors and their land tenure insecurity. In the worst cases, these are households of elderly residents who have never had access to irrigated land, and whose grown children are no longer near enough to support them. In both cases, it is the lack of access to and title of irrigated land, particularly given the arid climate and infertile soils of the rainfed production zone around Nazareno, that distinguishes this most impoverished livelihood group in Nazareno.

Despite their poverty, few households in this group were receiving support through PROGRESA, and 80 percent were not participating in PROCAMPO. As a result, their perspectives on institutional change were similar to the community as a whole and quite different from the majority of farmers in Torres (table 6.1). Of the 40 percent of households in this class who noted important changes in public sector support, half perceived these changes to be mixed or negative, resulting in more variable prices and inaccessible benefits.

Don Enrique is a characteristic farmer in the Subsistence Maize class in Nazareno. He is young, perhaps in his mid-twenties, and unmarried, living alone with his widowed mother. When I met him in the summer of 2000, his brother had recently left the household to try his luck in the United States, although the last they heard he had not made it there and was instead working in Baja California. Don Enrique was also contemplating leaving, hoping to be able to earn enough away from the community to start a family. But he was dismayed by the expense of migration: he heard that it cost at least 5,000 pesos to get to the border, plus more than US$600 for the *coyote* to take him across. He already had four other siblings, two married sisters and two brothers (and an uncle), in the United States.

When I asked whether he wanted to get out of farming, he explained that his family had only two hectares of rainfed land on which they planted maize and beans. Their yields were often just about 500 kg/ha. In the last few years they had lost a lot to both frost and drought. Normally he sold his maize, a kilo at a time, to neighbors in the village if he needed cash. For the previous four years he had also requested loans from neighbors. He was working as a day laborer in Nazareno, something that he had begun to do with greater frequency after his crop losses. He worked about three days a week for others, and three days in his family's fields. Each year he earned just enough to pay back the debt.

They did not own any livestock and had to rent draft animal power to plant. That summer he had been thinking about planting other crops such as nopal, but he believed that the market was too competitive and the price too low to make it worth it. When they could, they harvested wild nopal and palm fruit, and often neighbors with irrigation give them some vegetables. Despite his dispirited assessment of the productivity of his own land, he was interested in improving his production and was attending extension meetings offered by a regional farm and labor organization. He also was experimenting with improved maize seed and learning to make and use compost. I was impressed by his initiative, particularly when it was obvious that he did not have the land or time to make any dramatic improvements in his production.

Like their counterparts in Torres, these Nazareno households are also under considerable pressure to identify alternative sources of sustenance to compensate for the unreliable yields on rainfed land. Yet unlike with the Torres households, the relatively constant availability of work as vegetable harvesters in their neighbors' fields means that members of these households do not necessarily have to leave the community for extended periods in order to find wage income, although there are some households in the group with members working as construction assistants or domestic servants in the town of Tecamachalco. The wage opportunities within and outside Nazareno offer a greater diversity of employment options, although most of these opportunities are very low paid and temporary in nature. The dependence of many of the Subsistence Maize households on employment as day laborers in the vegetable fields also means that their fortunes are indirectly tied to the fluctuations in the vegetable markets. Unlike their counterparts in Torres, the Subsistence Maize households of Nazareno did not report significant income support from public welfare programs such as PROGRESA or from the agricultural subsidy, PROCAMPO.

In contrast to their counterparts in Torres, almost half of the Subsistence Maize households in Nazareno have some livestock, particularly medium-size animals. The greater prevalence of medium-size animals in Nazareno is perhaps partly a result of the fact that 23 percent of the households in this class have some irrigated land on which they could plant alfalfa, or at least increase their maize yields for animal forage. Vegetable residues to use as pig feed are also often readily available from neighbors, particularly after crop or market failures forced the vegetable farmers to abandon their harvests. Having some additional livestock to sell in periods of hardship can be a distinct advantage to affected households, as illustrated by the fact that an average of 40 percent of the income of the Subsistence Maize households came from animal sales in 1999 (compared to an average of only 4 percent in the Torres Subsistence Maize group).

According to the survey data, there were also significant differences in material wealth of the Subsistence Maize classes in the two communities. In Torres, almost 20 percent of households in this group lacked electricity, and just over 40 percent lacked televisions and radios. Aside from two households that owned bicycles, none of the households owned any form of transportation. Only one household of the group had a house made of concrete block. The Nazareno households appeared to be better off: All households had electricity, 40 percent of the households owned bicycles, nearly all households were made of concrete (in fact, more so than the average of the other groups of households in the community), a few households had interior bathrooms and refrigerators, and two households even had pickup trucks.

The frequency of concrete houses in Nazareno may be partly explained by the fact that an earthquake a few years earlier tumbled many of the adobe houses in the community, and Nazareno benefited from government support for reconstruction. Additionally, because of the degree to which fields are scattered in Nazareno (the average distance from the farm household to any given field is over three kilometers), bicycles are expensive but important tools for residents. One of the more common ways for households to acquire bicycles is through gifts given by appointed benefactors, *padrinos*, on the occasion of school graduations. As a way of facilitating the redistribution of wealth, households will typically try to select benefactors from wealthier friends and relatives who can afford to give the appropriate gift for the occasion. Unlike in Torres where all but three households were classified as Subsistence Maize, the mixture of income classes and the relatively inequitable distribution of wealth in Nazareno make such gift giving and wealth redistribution possible.

The Meaning of Maize

As with all households surveyed in the three communities, for the Subsistence Maize households in Torres and Nazareno maize means security. Farmers continue to devote significant areas of their landholdings to maize despite their frequent losses from frosts and drought and the crop's declining commercial value because they perceive their ability to secure their basic food requirements (namely maize and beans) through economic exchange as highly uncertain. However, for the land-constrained Subsistence Maize households, representing a majority in Torres, producing maize for subsistence is not simply a form of insurance but rather is central to their survival. Without additional land area to devote to forage or the yields and volume of maize to support livestock, these households are limited in their capacity to cope with extreme events. The low-skill wage employment they access tends to be within the agricultural sector and thus does not reduce the exposure of their livelihoods to shocks that may affect local agricultural production, or it requires seasonal migration and thus incurs costs.

Whether or not a particular type of livelihood strategy characterizes the majority of households, or only represents a fraction of households in a community, is important in interpreting the opportunities and constraints faced by the Subsistence Maize groups. As a subset of households within a community of irrigated producers, farmers like Don Enrique have relatively easy access to employment as day laborers, as well as the possibility of supporting some livestock with the vegetable residues of neighboring irrigated farms. Working as a day laborer does not pay well (a day's labor was worth 50 pesos, or approximately US$5 in 2000), nor is the work constant, but the costs of acquiring this employment are almost nothing and often an entire family will work. If they can pull together sufficient resources, these households also have the opportunity of sharecropping on a neighbor's irrigated landholdings. This gives them the occasional chance to increase their agricultural income and make some key investments in important amenities. Of course, these opportunities are not available to all—several households in the Subsistence Maize group in Nazareno consist of only the elderly or a single woman with children. These are the households with the fewest income opportunities and thus the least flexibility in coping with climate risk.

In Torres, not only are the Subsistence Maize households the dominant livelihood group in the community, but also, aside from the three households with the largest landholdings (the Livestock Specialist and Pulquero livelihood groups), the differences in livelihood activities and wealth between the community's households are small. With the contraction of pulque demand, there are few opportunities for income within the community to help households manage crop losses. Increasingly households are turning to temporary migration to Puebla. While this activity is perhaps the best option available to households, the material poverty of the Subsistence Maize households suggests that this strategy is not facilitating significant wealth accumulation, and as a result income from welfare programs is increasingly important in Torres. While this support is perceived as a positive change, it also suggests that the households may be developing a new vulnerability to sudden changes in social policy. Such sudden changes may be even more likely as the country embraces democratic reforms and decentralization and old forms of political patronage in the rural sector die out.

As will be illustrated in the next chapter, those households that have sufficient land to meet both their subsistence requirements *and* diversify into alternative crops have far greater flexibility in managing risk. Having land beyond what is required for subsistence not only permits greater flexibility and resilience in responding to climatic events, but also allows for income through livestock and livestock products and investment in both agricultural and human capital that, in turn, can improve the stability of rural livelihoods in the face of uncertainty. It is at the margins of their livelihood systems that households show the greatest adaptive capacity. Where livelihood margins are narrow—because of minifundismo, geographic isolation, or limited nonfarm opportunities—climate and economic uncertainty challenge the basis of subsistence, and adaptation may be particularly difficult.

7 From Maize to Milk

Plan de Ayala's Diversification into Livestock

Agricultural Diversification as Adaptation

One morning in August of 2000 I paid a visit to INIFAP, the branch of the National Institute for Forestry, Agriculture, and Livestock Research, in Tlaxcala, to discuss agricultural trends in the state with one of INIFAP's agronomists. He was particularly interested in climate issues and had been working on various ways of improving the availability of climate information to farmers in the state. He took a document off his shelf that he thought would interest me: "Productive Conversion in Rainfed Areas for the State of Tlaxcala." It turned out to be a technical document that INIFAP had prepared to support the state's crop conversion policy, a policy that he told me was being put in action in the late 1990s to reduce the state's sensitivity to climate hazards. I flipped open to the introduction and read "With the presence of [ENSO] in the country since the middle of 1997 . . . we must prepare the State for an alternative scenario . . . in which losses are minimized through crop species and varieties that ensure greater productivity than traditional crops." INIFAP was recommending "production systems with short-cycle species and/or varieties that require less water during the rainy season" (INIFAP 1998: 3, my translation).

I was curious. It was the first time I had seen articulated in Mexico support for a specific policy to adapt agriculture to a perceived change in climatic variability. (As of 2003, "crop conversion" is part of national policy, implemented through a new federal program called PIASRE [Programa Integral de Agricultura Sostenible y Reconversión Productiva en Zonas de Siniestralidad; Integral Program of Sustainable Agriculture and Productive Reconversion in Areas of Recurrent Loss].) I knew from a previous project that INIFAP had considerable interest in ENSO's effects on agriculture, and a few years previously I had actually participated with INIFAP in a project organized by the Center of Atmospheric Sciences (UNAM) on ENSO forecasting for farmers (Conde and Eakin 2003; Eakin 2000). But I did not know that INIFAP's interest had been translated into policy.

The agronomist explained the rationale for the government's policy. "The problem now is the frosts. They break the maize cycle; they come in May, June, August, and September. If the frost arrives in September it cuts the growing season to only 130 days. If the frosts are in July, there are losses in the middle of the season. It isn't possible to replant maize at that time for grain, only for forage. Even then it will be for subsistence only. The alternative is oats. It is a grain that serves commercially and is fodder as well. And it matures in 60–80 days. The state government has a program to convert farmers so that there will only be sixty thousand hectares of maize in the state."

Together with the state's agriculture ministry, INIFAP has developed crop suitability maps of the state to illustrate the optimal distribution of Tlaxcala's basic crops (wheat, barley, maize, and beans) on the basis of soil, topography, and climate conditions. With these maps as guidance, the conversion program aims to convince farmers who are planting crops considered inappropriate for their region to switch to another more appropriate grain. Much of this plan is oriented toward a redistribution of Tlaxcala's current principal crops, rather than toward the introduction and adoption of new crops. The ultimate goal is to reduce the area planted in maize by 91,200 ha by 2010. New crops are to be introduced only in those regions where none of the basic crops are suitable.

In the summer of 2000, the agricultural programs Kilo por Kilo and PROCAMPO were the primary vehicles for this transformation. They operated by partially subsidizing the cost of inputs to those farmers enrolled in these programs (certified hybrid seeds through Kilo por Kilo and fertilizers through PROCAMPO). After the severe frosts in July of 2000, I was told by state agriculture officials that oat seeds and fertilizer were also being distributed free in most heavily affected localities to encourage replanting, with the idea that the shorter growing season of oats would enable households to recuperate their losses.

The crop conversion program was ambitious, but not surprising.

One of the more obvious agricultural adaptations to climatic risk is through crop and cultivar choice. Furthermore, the analysis of agriculture areas in terms of "crop suitability," a process of matching crops to the environmental conditions most appropriate for their development, has long been a feature of Mexican agriculture, but perhaps was institutionalized during the Green Revolution when national agriculture research centers were established to guide agricultural development. In theory, farmers who have information on the crops or crop varieties most appropriate for anticipated or changing climatic conditions can mitigate climatic impacts while maintaining consistent agricultural productivity. Some of the more optimistic assessments of the capacity of agricultural systems to adapt to climatic change have been in part based on this expectation (e.g., Crosson 1993; Kaiser et al. 1993).

Farmers' annual crop decisions also theoretically can be optimized through the use of climate forecasts that give them sufficient advance warning to choose the right crop for the forecasted climate conditions (Hammer et al. 2001; Mjelde, Harvey, and Griffith 1998). In the best-case scenarios, farmers are already familiar with the appropriate range of alternative crops, and the adjustment to climate essentially consists of making more efficient annual crop-mix decisions in terms of expected yields and anticipated economic gain.

Crop and seed selection as a strategy to mitigate climate risk is not a new concept to Mexico's smallholders. Although there has been very little academic discussion of farmers' diversification into barley and oats in response to climatic stress, earlier accounts of crop and seed selection among smallholders in Central Mexico found that sensitivity to climatic hazards is a feature in farmers' decisions about maize varieties and maize-bean intercropping (Altieri and Trujillo 1987; Bellon 1991).

Yet climatic risk is not the only factor driving crop choice. One has only to recall the widely documented effort to extend the Green Revolution benefits to small-scale maize producers in the Plan Puebla experiment of the 1960s and 1970s to find evidence that farmers' crop and input choices are based on complex cultural, economic, and social preferences, which new "improved" crop varieties often cannot fully satisfy (González López 1990; Redclift 1983). Farmers participating in the Plan Puebla experiment proved to be very reluctant to make the substantial investments in fertilizers and hybrid maize seed required of them, in part because of their perception that there was a high risk that they would lose their investment to drought (Redclift 1983). As any farmer in Torres would tell you, the cultural and subsistence value of a crop that you are very familiar with, particularly in the context of unfavorable producer and consumer markets, may easily exceed the benefits of higher yields from switching to a crop of unknown performance or that you cannot eat.

Data have already been presented that suggest that crop switching and diversification may be a viable adaptation strategy to climatic risk in the three communities studied. Households in Plan de Ayala that planted oats reported significantly fewer losses in 1999 than those that did not, suggesting that oats may offer climatic advantage over maize in years where similar climatic patterns are expected. The Plan de Ayala ejidatarios I interviewed are quite aware of these advantages, ranking oats (and, in some cases, barley as well) consistently as the most "rapid" of the five common crops grown in their communities (wheat, barley, oats, maize, and beans), the least sensitive to drought, and the most resistant to frost damage. Yet despite these noted advantages, in 1999 oats averaged less than 20 percent of the total planted area in Plan de Ayala. In fact, although oats were gaining popularity in Tlaxcala as a whole, the crop occupied only 1 percent of Tlaxcala's area planted in annual crops in 1999 (INEGI 2000b).

This chapter explores the role crop choice and diversification play in the livelihood strategies of farmers growing rainfed crops in Plan de Ayala, discussing both the limitations of crop diversification as an end in itself and the apparent advantages of a diversified crop base for facilitating households' access to a series of alternative activities, namely those involving investment in livestock. The chapter focuses on three of the four household groups in Plan de Ayala (the Maize Surplus households, the Livestock Specialists, and the Income Diversified household). All the households in these groups have access to sufficient land on which to diversify away from a pure subsistence livelihood strategy. Yet, as the following sections will illustrate, even these households face a variety of economic, social, and cultural incentives and disincentives that complicate decisions about crop diversification. The Maize Surplus households, for example, face market, financial, and human resource constraints that limit the potential contribution of crop diversification to their livelihoods. However, for the Livestock Specialist and Income Diversified households, crop diversification, instead of being an end in itself, serves as the foundation of an alternative livelihood strategy, based on livestock raising and livestock products. For these households, their maize-forage-livestock strategy not only addresses serious obstacles to participating in commercial crop markets but also appears to enhance their resilience to climatic variability and extreme events.

The discussion in this chapter will extend to a small group of households in Torres, the Livestock Specialists, that also follow strategies based on crop diversification. These households have significantly larger landholdings than the majority of households in Torres. Although the history and context of their diversification strategies are different, they share many of the production and human resource characteristics of the Plan de Ayala households. With their larger landholdings, diversification into forage and medium-size livestock is a means of surviving not only the lack of market for basic grains but also the collapse of the pulque market. These households are those that have historically dominated the economic activity of the community and thus are in a particularly advantageous position to alter the nature of their livelihoods.

Advantages of Crop Diversification for Managing Climatic Risk

The ejidatarios of Plan de Ayala each have on average nine hectares of land on which they plant an average of three to four crops, double that of the land-constrained households of Torres. During the last three years of the 1990s, on average a third of the total area cultivated by the surveyed households was planted in maize, 39 percent in barley, 18 percent in oats, and the remainder in wheat and beans. Of the five crops commonly planted in the ejido, maize and wheat were the crops with the longest growing cycle (130 to 160 days) and thus needed to be planted as soon as the ground was moist enough (after a few days of good rainfall) and when the risk of frost appeared to be low. In the best circumstances, this period falls in early or mid-April. Planting any later than the end of May considerably raises the risk that the crops will be damaged both by the timing of the canícula and the onset of frosts in the fall. Thus if the rains are delayed, as they were in 1997, 1998, and 1999, maize is less viable in comparison with barley (120–130 days), oats (80 days), or beans (90–120 days). These latter crops can be planted as late as June and July and still mature before the first frosts in the fall. As described in chapter 5, the farmers of Plan de Ayala employ this knowledge annually in their planting decisions, selecting the most appropriate crops to coincide with their assessment of the climate risks of the season and their particular household consumption needs.

The households also exploit their knowledge of subtle differences in different seed varieties in order to improve their harvest prospects. Many also still intercrop maize and beans to mitigate risks. One farmer said, "We know about five or six varieties of maize. We usually plant white maize, a *criolla*. Sometimes we chose a faster variety, such as *xocoyol*, *maíz negro*, or *rojo*. When the weather demands it. These varieties mature in four months." When I asked about the benefits of intercropping, I was told it wasn't simply intercropping that diminished climate risks (see also Trujillo 1990), but also the type of beans intercropped with maize. Don Carlos explained: "There are two varieties of beans you can plant around the maize plant: *enrededor*, which climbs the maize plant, and *peruana*, which is low lying. In good years it is better to plant the climbing beans, although it makes the harvest more difficult (you have to separate it from the maize), because it yields more. But in bad years, it is better to have the peruana because it is better under freezing conditions. This year we will plant the peruana because it is more *violente* [rapid/hardy]. Last year we planted the other kind and it was affected by frost."

Farmers are not only adjusting to seasonal changes in rainfall and temperature but responding to what they perceive as a shift in climate patterns. With a growing season comparable to that of maize, but with no use for domestic consumption, wheat became much less popular as the ejidatarios began to plan for the type of climatic events they experienced in the late 1990s. One farmer explained his crop choice this way:

This year I plan to plant wheat if the rains arrive. Wheat takes five months and so there is still time to plant it if it rains enough.

. . . So far, maize is the only thing I've planted. I am planting less wheat than before because of the past two years of poor rains. More than two years ago we planted wheat, but now it doesn't yield. There isn't sufficient rain. It didn't rain last year until June, and so we had to turn under the wheat crop and plant oats. The wheat was also hit by frost. Of all the crops, barley is what usually does best. Here it is the fastest growing, followed by wheat and fava beans, and then by maize. We can plant only a little maize here because of the cold and frost. We have frost in spring, and now in summer, and then the first frosts arrive in fall.

Each ejidatario has been allocated one or two hectares on the hill in addition to their fields in the plains in front of the village. Having this land available to protect maize, the crop that is most valued for their subsistence, gives them greater flexibility in the use of the remaining fields. In fact, in anticipation of continued adverse climatic conditions (particularly frosts) in the summer of 2000, the ejido began to demarcate the remaining uncleared land on El Mirador in an attempt to expand this relatively protected area for planting. In general, the households surveyed reported that they tend to decide the amount of land they dedicate to any crop on the basis of both observed and anticipated climatic patterns, the particular exposure of their available fields (mentioned by 38 percent of households), their consumption requirements (25 percent), and their judgment of each particular crop's sensitivity to climatic stress (19 percent).

Several households reported that their strategy is to expand their maize area by two to three hectares in "good years" into the flat fields in front of the village, and in "bad years," when the rains arrive late, plant these fields in barley or oats. In other words, as Doña Marta explained to me, because maize is preferred, but is the most sensitive crop planted in the ejido, the amount of land that (given climate conditions) can be devoted to maize determines the amount of remaining land that would be allocated to alternative crops. "If it rains on time and sufficiently," she said, "I will sometimes plant as much as three hectares of maize, but if it doesn't rain enough I won't plant it at all." I asked what she had done the previous year. "In 1999 we planted three hectares of oats (in the valley) and five of barley at the beginning of June. It was too dry for maize. Some risked [planting maize in the valley], but then they were exposed to frosts in the fall or earlier and had to replant. We planted barley and oats because these crops aren't as slow as maize."

Market Obstacles to Diversification

The premise of the crop conversion policy in Tlaxcala is that the alternative crops to maize would not only be better suited in terms of climatic variability but also viable economic options for smallholders (INIFAP 1998). Crop diversification as a strategy for mitigating climate risk is of limited benefit if the selected alternative crops are not of any utility for the household, for either consumption or exchange. The director of Puebla's branch of the national farmers' organization, Fundación Produce AC, described the problem of diversification in these words: "Maize no longer pays to produce . . . so farmers are diversifying, without stopping to plant maize because they need to eat and maize is what they eat. They need commercial alternatives that are not only good in face of climatic hazards but are good economically. Oats are not economical . . . the price is too low, there is no market, and farmers can't eat it."

Despite the fact that the ejidatarios of Plan de Ayala plant a diversity of crops besides maize, my interviews with the farmers revealed that in general they see little commercial benefit in marketing their harvests of these alternative crops. One of the primary obstacles is getting access to the correct inputs. In order to be able to meet the quality standards of the commercial flour, malt, and even feed markets, the farmers understand that they would need to invest in the commercial seeds and fertilizers required by the industries. Theoretically, Tlaxcala's smallholders have access to these inputs via the government programs Kilo por Kilo and PROCAMPO. However, as the Plan de Ayala farmers explained, while the Kilo por Kilo program offers seed at a discount of 60–80 percent off the commercial price, acquiring the seed from the state's agriculture offices requires transportation costs, time, and, despite the discount, a considerable outlay of money for the purchase of the seed.

Normally most farmers save seed from each year's harvest, and thus are accustomed to negligible seed expenses. Furthermore, farmers explained that they would need to purchase hybrid seeds annually to achieve the consistent high yields and quality products demanded by the industries, and this is a financial commitment that few households are prepared to make, particularly if the harvest is not guaranteed. For example, Doña Judith had been considering planting hybrid seed and had attended a demonstration of one of the maize varieties from Asgrow. She told me "One sack of seed costs 700 pesos. And that is only 16 kilos. It is such a high investment and it doesn't serve to replant for a second generation. They say that the yield will decline every year. And it requires lots of chemicals. That is expensive, and it is also not good for the soils." She told me that three farmers in the community had experimented with the seed in 1999, after attending the demonstration. But she had not been convinced, and, along with the rest of the ejido, the three farmers had lost their harvests to frost in September.

Perhaps she was right to be cautious. According to one of the government's extension agents in Tlaxcala, Kilo por Kilo offered only three or four seed varieties, and, contrary to the program's intention, these were not targeted specifically to different agro-climatic regions of Tlaxcala. Farmers were not always informed about the appropriateness of the seed for their region, and thus they were reluctant, given the heavy losses to climate hazards in recent years, to experiment with something that they were not sure would yield. As one farmer emphatically said, "If I am not sure I am going to harvest, I am not going to go into debt by purchasing seeds and fertilizers."

As of 1999 there had been only two applications in all of Tlaxcala to use PROCAMPO funds to switch from basic grains to alternative crops (SEFOA 2000). More farmers in the state were participating in the Fertilizer Program, in which farmers could "cede their rights" to their PROCAMPO payments in exchange for fertilizer from one of the commercial distributors in the state. Three households in Plan de Ayala participated in this program, but many others expressed their skepticism about the appropriateness of the products offered for their area. The *comisario ejidal* of Plan de Ayala complained: "There isn't a choice . . . only *triple* [triple super phosphate] and urea, and what if they aren't right for these soils? Or perhaps we don't even need either of them?"

While PROCAMPO was apparently not facilitating the adoption of new crops in Plan de Ayala, it was playing a critical role in supporting the general production costs associated with planting oats, barley, and wheat. All of these grains required a combine to reap the grain, and, if the crop was to be harvested as hay, a hay baler was also needed. According to the households surveyed in the community, the cost of renting the tractor for these services averaged 51 percent of the production costs for oats and 49 percent of the production costs for barley, at a price of approximately 600 to 700 pesos per hectare in 1999. This cost was approximately equivalent to the amount of the per-hectare PROCAMPO payment in 1999. Many ejidatarios use the promise of the arrival of the PROCAMPO checks to contract the services of the tractor on credit. When the payment arrives in September, the farmers are already in debt, and the checks are typically written directly over to the tractor-service provider. Given the lack of alternative sources of finance, without PROCAMPO it is unlikely that the farmers could afford the tractor's services. One particularly cynical farmer told me, "PROCAMPO is to silence the campesinos, keep us from complaining." He added, "It doesn't arrive in time for preparing the fields, and so we fall behind in our work. As a result we have to borrow from [informal] lenders or neighbors knowing that we will have PROCAMPO in the fall. We look for where there are people who have ranches or industries and ask for loans there. For example, there is one lender who owns a line of trucks in Apizaco. He charges about 40 percent per month in interest. And if we have to ask for 2,000 pesos, and PROCAMPO is only 700 pesos, it isn't enough. But we pass [our PROCAMPO checks] on directly to the lender anyway."

The economic risk farmers face by experimenting with commercial seeds and inputs is exacerbated by the lack of crop insurance. In the 1970s, when the ejido had just been founded and was receiving BANRURAL financial support, crop insurance was a mandatory part of every crop technology package extended to the farmers. Most of the ejidatarios interviewed did not think the program had offered sufficient compensation for their losses, and their negative experience left them extremely skeptical about the value of the service. Thus when the Tlaxcaltecan government offered a 1,500 pesos/ha insurance package to all smallholders enrolled in the PROCAMPO program for the 2000 season, none of ejidatarios of Plan de Ayala participated.

Even if the farmers can be persuaded of the benefits of investing in the improved inputs, they are not convinced that they will be able to find a viable market for their harvests. When Plan de Ayala first started production as an ejido, some of the ejidatarios regularly sold their barley harvest to Impulsora Agrícola via intermediaries that came to their fields with trucks. By 1996 they had lost access to Impulsora Agrícola as a result of poor yields, repeated years of poor quality grain from frost damage, and increased competition from imported grain.

According to the coordinator of the federal extension service in Tlaxcala, PEAT, although Impulsora Agrícola regularly publishes its purchasing prices, those prices are seldom offered to farmers because the company always finds some reason to "discount" on the basis of poor grain quality. Even farmers who purchase inputs on credit directly from Impulsora Agrícola typically do not have a written contract from the company guaranteeing them a purchasing price. The extension agent estimated that under optimal production conditions, the state's malt plants might buy as much as 26 percent of their barley from Tlaxcaltecan farmers. The perpetual problem of frost damage in the barley harvests, however, means that typically only 2–3 percent of the plants' demand is met by Tlaxcaltecan harvests.

The liberalization of both input and producers' prices in the 1990s makes the ejidatarios' production even less competitive. The exasperation of the ejidatarios at their situation was palpable. When I asked Don Apolonio why he had not planted a few of his fields in the summer of 2000, he exclaimed, "There isn't any way for us to get a fair price. We can't sell directly; we have to work through intermediaries . . . the prices just don't make ends meet. Last year they were offering .80 to .90 centavos per kilo. It's nothing." He pointed north toward the sierra. "There is a ranch across the highway where the fields are all yellow now with flowering barley. They get high yields, use lots of chemicals and tractors, and fill whole trucks with the grain. And so they get a better price. It is hard to sell in small quantities at the quality they want. It isn't worth it for me to invest in lots of chemicals when I can't be sure I will even have a harvest in the end." Without access to the industrial markets for barley, oats, and wheat, the ejidatarios who wish to commercialize these crops are forced to do so in small quantities through intermediaries and local merchants, or, in many cases, directly to neighbors who need animal feed or fodder.

The farmers associated the changes they observed in their market opportunities directly with the federal government's international trade agreements: "Before NAFTA there was a guaranteed price for barley, but not now. The government thinks we will do better with NAFTA, but we haven't. Now we are completely at the mercy of the intermediaries and the buyers. They always pay very little."

The prices in these markets were dismally low for all grains for several years, often barely exceeding 1 peso/kilo, and in real terms, farm gate prices had actually declined during the 1990s (fig. 7.1). One ejidatario complained: "We aren't appreciated. You say that they give us inputs for free . . . well, it's nothing. The costs of everything are so high, and they keep the prices for our products so low that we can hardly make a go of it. And it is we that carry the weight of the nation in grain. *'Llevamos el peso de la nación en granos básicos.'*"

According to local merchants, the price in 1999 for oats is particularly low, ranging from .60 to 1.00 pesos per kilo of grain, or 8.00 pesos per bale of hay. In Plan de Ayala in 1999, households estimated their yields at only 1.00–3.5 tons/ha, when they managed to get grain at all. Many households simply harvested their oat crop as hay.

The market for oat hay is also highly variable, although potentially profitable. For those farmers who purchased hay during the dry season, prices per bale can be as high as twenty pesos. According to an INIFAP representative, prices of hay in "bad years" are sometimes ten times that of "good years," providing a substantial profit to households with surplus production. Yet typically in the months after harvest, prices decline to only six or eight pesos per bale, which barely covers the baling cost of four to seven pesos per bale.

One of the households interviewed in Plan de Ayala planted oats in 1999 on the basis of the Tlaxcaltecan government's recommendations. Unable to sell their oat hay because of lack of demand, and without the means to consume it themselves, the hay bales were rotting at the entrance to the community through the summer of 2000. The farmer told me that he hoped the bales would eventually make good compost. He had calculated that it cost him five pesos to make each bale of hay, and it would cost an additional two pesos per bale to take the hay to market. At the going price of eight pesos per bale it was not worth the effort. Don Antonio, a farmer who was considering investing more in livestock, told me that he doesn't normally sell

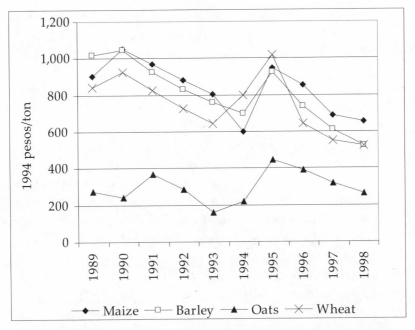

Figure 7.1 Farm gate grain prices, Tlaxcala (adjusted for inflation). *Source*: Elaborated from data from the Sistema de Información Agrícola de Consulta (SIACON) database, Sistema Integral de Información Agroalimentaria y Pesquera (SIAP), Secretaria de Agricultura, Ganadería y Desarrollo Rural (SAGARPA).

oats; the crop sells too cheaply, at about sixty centavos per kilo. When he buys oat seed, as he did in 1998 when he first planted it, it cost three to six pesos per kilo. He complained: "The *coyotes* get the profit; they can charge us what they like. They buy low and sell high."

Other households in Plan de Ayala were equally frustrated with the crop. Doña Marta, the young grandmother who, in the summer of 2000, decided not to plant any maize because of drought, described how six years previously she had tried to commercialize her oat harvest without success, and since then had decided to plant barley on the slopes of El Mirador: "This is because barley is a little more commercial than oats and it is worth protecting it. Six years ago we tried to sell a sack of oats to pay for milk for the baby, but no one would buy it. We had to return from Apizaco with the oats and no milk." Her neighbor, Don Diego, told me that "despite the advantages of oats, we won't plant it this year . . . the seed is very expensive, about four to six pesos per kilo, and we would need 150 kilos for one hectare. And we lack the machinery to bale the hay, and if there is a delay in getting the machinery, we risk losing the crop to rot. You either need to own the machinery yourself, or have a lot of animals that can use the oats as forage."

Not surprisingly, in the face of the discouraging economic prospects for their crops, the households surveyed in Plan de Ayala are generally very negative about the institutional changes they have observed in the last decade (see table 6.1). All but one household perceived substantial changes in agricultural policy in the 1990s, particularly in relation to rising input costs, declining producer prices, and lack of public support. This view contrasts sharply with the perceptions of the farmers of Torres, who, as beneficiaries of new welfare programs such as PROGRESA are far more positive about the impacts of the changes they have observed.

From Forage to Milk to Markets

Given the obstacles they face in commercializing their barley and oat grain and hay, the farmers in Plan de Ayala need to convert their harvests into a product that they can either consume or sell more readily in local markets. For a number of the households, the solution to this problem is livestock. In areas as densely populated as Tlaxcala, open pasture is limited and the cost of buying forage and animal feed is prohibitive for small-scale operations. However, households with more than a minimal amount of land (e.g., more than three hectares) can afford to plant forage crops in addition to maize, and in doing so can also support livestock. In 2000, a majority of households in Plan de Ayala had more than three large animals, and a quarter had more than five, even after the heavy crop losses of 1998 and 1999. In comparison, in Torres, where landholdings averaged only four hectares, most households had only one or two mules for the yunta, and some lacked even that.

Although in the year of the survey two-thirds of the households in Plan de Ayala were owners of one or more cows, horses, mules, or donkeys, the animals play different roles in the households' livelihoods, depending on the land, labor, and alternative income sources available to the household. Almost a third of the households of Plan de Ayala, classified as Nonfarm Specialists in this study, are pursuing a strategy in which livestock plays only a minor role. The role of livestock in the remaining three groups ranges from an investment to a source of income. The Maize Surplus households invest in medium-size animals (pigs, sheep, and goats) as a form of household economic security. For the Livestock Specialist and Income Diversified households, raising livestock is not only a form of insurance but also a source of off-farm income through the sale of milk, and, over the long term, a means of diversifying into high-skilled nonfarm activities.

Farmers in all three communities reported that raising cows and calves is a better long-term investment than raising pigs or goats, but the latter are less expensive to maintain, matured rapidly, and are easily sold or eaten, providing households with some income or food within relatively short periods of time. According to livestock experts in the state agriculture ministry, the market for beef in Tlaxcala is poorly developed, so the most economically viable use for cows is in raising them for milk production.

The two households in Plan de Ayala with the largest landholdings have the highest number of large animals. These Livestock Specialist households are each headed by two ejidatarios who had married each other and thus had combined their ejidal allocations to create an average of fourteen hectares, five to six hectares more than the average amount of land available to other households. These households not only had double the amount of protected land on El Mirador, but they also tend to plant proportionally more land with oats. Not surprisingly, these households are also those that reported the lowest crop losses to climatic hazards among all the households in the community (see table 4.4).

Although the price of milk is low, averaging only two pesos per liter (less than US$0.20 per liter), and has to be sold daily because of a lack of refrigerated storage, the income from milk sales offers the advantage of a steady weekly allowance that can cover many small household expenses while keeping the focus of household labor on the farm. One milk cow can bring a household 16 pesos a day, equivalent to a family's daily consumption of tortillas.

Perhaps more importantly, interviews with farmers indicated that this income is often used to finance the daily transportation and expenses associated with school attendance. Households in Plan de Ayala identified the most financially difficult times of the year as the times of school entry and exit, in September and June. A mother of five in one of the poorest households in Plan de Ayala told me she was going to pull her son out of secondary school because of the costs, what she estimates to be nearly 500 pesos a month. Another woman told me: "Here in Plan de Ayala we have a primary school. For secondary school you have to go to Apizaco. And for the high school, you have to go to Tlaxcala. All this travel requires capital. The combis on the highway charge more than usual because of the factories. It costs about four pesos to go to Apizaco—that's eight pesos a day for each child to go to the secondary school. If you went all the way to Tlaxcala for the high school, it would cost about twenty pesos a day, just for transportation. On top of that there is the uniform, the books, and other costs. It is too much."

The Livestock Specialist and Income Diversified households of Plan de Ayala are also the most educated households in the community. It is quite likely that the income from livestock contributed initially to giving these households access to secondary school education, with the result that in the year 2000, they were benefiting from involvement in remunerative nonfarm activities, as well as from remittances sent from gainfully employed relatives.

Both of the Livestock Specialist households also have strong social ties through which they access resources: one has close personal links to CNOCIR, a campesino political organization in Apizaco associated with the national Labor Party (Partido del Trabajo), and the other is one of the leaders of a small group of eight households in Plan de Ayala that share the use of a tractor. According to interviews with some members of the community, the connection with CNOCIR and the Labor Party facilitates access to special credits and public agricultural programs.

For all these reasons, together the Livestock Specialist and Income Diversified households report the highest monetary incomes in the community. These households also have similar levels of material wealth, suggesting that their incomes offer sufficient stability to enable them to accumulate wealth over time.

Doña María, the head of one of the Livestock Specialist households, is a case in point. She is an older ejidataria who, after all her father's property had been given to one of her brothers, decided to join the others of Plan de Ayala in their fight for land in the 1970s. She began life on the ejido with nothing, as did the other ejidatarios. She worked weekends in Apizaco as a domestic worker and weekdays in the ejido. Eventually she was able to invest in 150 goats that were fed off the ejido's natural pastures. With this herd, she raised sufficient money to send all of her ten children to secondary school and to help build her two-story cement house.

As her children grew up, she began to lack the labor to tend goats or sheep in pasture (this task was often done by younger children), and as more land was brought into cultivation, she also recognized that there was insufficient natural pasture to support such an activity. Instead, she decided to raise milk cows, earning in the summer of 2000 about 600 to 900 pesos a month depending on how many of her cows were producing milk at any given time. In 1998, she had to sell three of her cows to pay for some household expenses. Eight of her children, now adults with technical positions (e.g., a railroad engineer, a merchant, factory workers), live outside the community and regularly send part of their earnings back to her. She used these remittances in 1999 to replant her frost-affected fields with oats. In 2000 she had four cows and seven calves, and, aside from being tearful over the prolonged absence of one of her younger sons from the village (he had joined the army), considered herself to be quite lucky.

Having surplus land (beyond what is necessary for subsistence purposes) and planting oats is not the only key to a successful milk-cow operation. Tending cows is labor intensive and requires a long-term financial investment. With children attending school, adults often undertake this labor. The Livestock Specialist and Income Diversified households are large, averaging six and nine people, respectively, with an average of five adults per household.

In contrast, the Maize Surplus households average five members, with only two adults. Women head half of these households (two widows and one with an infirm husband), and the remaining households consist of single men living alone and an elderly couple. In terms of total income, these households are on average the poorest of the community, with a relatively undiversified income base and a high dependence on government subsidies through the PROGRESA and PROCAMPO programs.

Perhaps because of a lack of adult labor, the Maize Surplus house-holds tend to specialize in pigs, sheep, and/or goats, rather than milk cows, not unlike many of the poorer households in Nazareno (see chap. 6). In small numbers, ungulates and other livestock such as pigs can be fed with household vegetable wastes and the available forage on the ejido's common pastures. Without the human resources for alternative sources of income, the Maize Surplus households tend to focus their production strategies on food security, planting on aver-age over 70 percent of their average eight hectares in maize. Surplus maize not only buffers them against interannual variability in yields, but also provides them with sufficient grain and rastrojo to support a small number of animals for both their own consumption and for sale in the case of economic necessity.

Adapting to Change with Livestock

If one compares the incomes and strategies of the house-holds of Plan de Ayala with the majority of those in Torres discussed in the previous chapter, in relative terms, the maize-oats-livestock strategies of many of the ejidatarios of Plan de Ayala are not only more successful in buffering them against some of the worst liveli-hood impacts of the climate events of 1998 and 1999, but are also addressing the lack of profitability in local grain markets. Almost half (47 percent) of the households surveyed in Plan de Ayala indicated that their livestock activities had become more important to them in the last five years, suggesting that for these households, investing in livestock was one way they were adapting to the new environmental and institutional uncertainties they faced.

In order to convert their domestic livestock into something more than a fallback activity, the Maize Surplus households need to overcome investment constraints, shortages in family labor, and considerable un-certainties related to the sources of technical assistance and finance. That said, there is some evidence that households in Plan de Ayala and Torres that have sufficient land are beginning to organize themselves to address these uncertainties and to maximize the benefits of livestock management despite the institutional challenges of the agricultural sector. In all of these cases, the households' efforts are facilitated by their active participation in existing social relationships and their previous experience with acquiring resources from public institutions.

The benefits of such relationships were evident in the subset of households in the Maize Surplus group that had organized themselves to jointly purchase a tractor. For these households, the costs of mechanical inputs to production were cut in half, freeing up resources for other investments. Owning a tractor also gave them greater flexibility in the timing of their agricultural activities and provides them with additional off-farm income through equipment rental. Independently, each of these households lacked the labor to manage large herds of livestock; however, in 2000 they had begun to discuss the possibility of pooling a portion of their individual landholdings as well as their labor to invest seriously in livestock as a "way out" of repeated crop losses to hazards and unfavorable grain prices. They sought out the advice of an extension agent in Tlaxcala who came to discuss various financial, legal, and technical options for accessing support for a livestock corral and machinery necessary to clear land for oats and forage-maize development. After the agent described various legal options they might consider in order to transform their group into a formal organization, he asked them what sort of production activities they were interested in. One farmer in the group commented: "Here oats are the only thing worth the effort. It is what works out best because of its short cycle. But we forget that, and we continue to fail."

While the leader of the group was skeptical about the new democratization of Mexico under President Fox, he was also serious about seeing what they could gain from the process, noting that "Fox has capitalist proposals for campesinos, and if we organize ourselves we can take advantage of them." After weighing the costs and benefits of various options, the group decided to avoid formal bank loans and instead incorporate their group as a small enterprise and apply for whatever support was available under the federal program Alianza para el Campo. They were determined to depend as little as possible on government support in order to assure their production would be economically viable.

One of the households in Torres with substantial landholdings also decided to pursue a similar strategy, but in this case relied not

Figure 7.2 Don Miguel Leal Hernández with pulque ready for sale in the Huamantla Valley. Pulque sales have diminished to almost nothing for his family.

on the collaboration of neighbors but on family. The Fernández family, one of the two households in the Torres Livestock Specialist class, was a relative newcomer to livestock. They were one of the original pulque processors, but with the collapse of the pulque market in the 1990s and a heavy debt burden after the peso devaluation of 1994, they had suffered hard times. Only in 1999 had they been able to finish paying off their debt. Through the help of a rural development nongovernmental organization (DEPAC), they acquired a new loan from the public credit agency, FONAES, for the purchase of sixty goats. With twelve hectares cultivated and eight additional hectares available as pasture, they meet the implicit scale requirements of a "commercially viable" agricultural enterprise. Like the livestock owners of Plan de Ayala, they hope to meet almost all the feed requirements of the goats with their own forage production.

To acquire the loan, they traveled around the state and even to Puebla in order to obtain "letters of commitment to buy" from dairy processors and accurate price information by visiting the regional livestock market. Their careful financial plan commits them first to selling goat milk and eventually to the commercialization of cheese as a family enterprise. There were seven adults in the household at the time of the interviews (four with secondary education) and only two children, and all the adults were committed to helping with the family business. In this case livestock is not the activity that has facilitated higher education; rather, it was the households' previous earnings from pulque that opened educational opportunities and, through this experience, important contacts with sources of external finance. Eventually the Fernández family hopes to be able to employ some of the community in their cheese-making enterprise, in an attempt both to compensate for the loss of income the community has suffered as a result of the collapse of the pulque industry and to revitalize the community's internal economy.

Lessons for Adaptive Capacity

The apparent success of the oats-livestock strategies pursued by the Livestock Specialist and Income Diversified households in Plan de Ayala and the Livestock Specialist and Pulquero households in Torres offers some important insights about adaptive capacity. First, although Tlaxcala's crop-conversion policy can be criticized for being unrealistic about the feasibility of small-scale households' participation in commercial grain markets, the policy is interesting in its recognition of the sensitivity of current cropping practices to climatic risk and also for its identification of theoretically viable alternatives in short-cycle crops. In this sense it may be one of the first programs in Mexico to address adaptation to perceived climate changes explicitly.

To engage successfully in a maize-oats-livestock strategy, households need land. The INIFAP agronomist with whom I discussed Tlaxcala's crop-conversion program at length told me that he thought the best strategy for a farmer is to plant "two to three hectares of maize, two to three hectares of beans, two to three hectares of fruit trees, and two to three hectares of forage for livestock. This would satisfy their domestic needs without any government help." The eight to twelve hectares necessary to implement this strategy are simply not available to most of Tlaxcala's farmers. Yet with an average of nine hectares, the ejidatarios of Plan de Ayala are beginning to move in that direction. Because oats are less sensitive to the climate events that in recent years have devastated the ejido's barley, wheat, and maize crops, households that planted oats in 1999 found that their harvests were relatively unaffected. Although all of the households in the Livestock Specialist and Income Diversified classes in Plan de Ayala sold a few animals in 1998 and 1999, they were able to keep enough animals to maintain a low but stable income from the sale of milk, and in this way they resisted the economic impacts that so disrupted households with smaller landholdings and less diversified strategies.

In Plan de Ayala, access to frost-protected land on El Mirador is particularly advantageous. By planting their household requirement maize on the slopes of the hill, households can risk diversifying into alternative crops. It is also likely that a livestock strategy is more viable for households with the right mix of household labor, although I was not able to determine from the survey data what such an ideal mix might be. In some interviews with households in Plan de Ayala, farmers commented on the advantage of having younger children who can assist in tending the livestock in pasture. The survey data, however, revealed that the households with larger numbers of livestock were those with more adults, perhaps because school tends to detract from children's labor time, but also because more adults in the household means greater flexibility in allocating labor into both livestock raising and other nonfarm economic pursuits, and both kinds of activities tend to be mutually supportive in the context of the household economy.

The planning processes of the households that are intending to enter livestock production as a primary economic activity illustrate the importance of technical support, planning, and finance in transforming what would otherwise be a basic coping strategy into a successful economic activity. The fact that some households in Plan de Ayala and Torres are managing to organize themselves to take advantage of the available opportunities and technical support shows that the "institutional vacuum" that was created by the policy trans-formations of the 1990s is not impossible to navigate, particularly for those households that already have established a strong basis for collaboration either within their own household (as in the case of the Fernández Family) or with their relatives and neighbors.

The other important element in the maize-oats-livestock strat-egy is education. All the households that have invested in livestock activities tend to be those with higher education. It is difficult to know whether livestock ownership is what facilitates these higher educational levels or vice versa, or perhaps the two developments are the result of other unconsidered variables. In other circumstances, households might rely largely on maize sales for financing school costs, but with the closure of CONASUPO, poor yields, and poor maize prices, milk is now a more attractive alternative. Thus it is not surprising that the few adults in each community who have higher educations are concentrated in the households with larger livestock assets.

In short, crop diversification is working as an adaptive strategy for a significant number of households in Plan de Ayala, but largely as a strategy that facilitates investment in livestock. The households that are able to participate in this strategy have relatively larger landholdings, giving them the flexibility to respond to climatic sig-nals without compromising their subsistence needs. And, from the material wealth indicators of these households, it appears that the strategy they were pursuing is permitting a reasonable amount of material security that the majority of the smaller-scale households in Torres presented in the previous chapter are unable to achieve. In the next chapter, crop diversification is explored again, but this time in the context of the irrigated vegetable producers of Nazareno, where, ironically, their mode of production appears to be heightening their insecurity.

8   Market Exposure, Irrigation, and Constraints on Adaptation

Don Miguel had planted his crop of zucchini a medias in a distant field on the other side of the Puebla-Oaxaca freeway. It was his field, but because his neighbor was contributing the seed, fertilizer, and herbicides in the sharecropping arrangement, he had not argued over the choice of crop. But as I set out with his family in a borrowed pickup truck to help pick and package the crop, he expressed his concern. This was the second picking, but the price had been low all week. The zucchini could not wait. He had already postponed the harvest that he had planned for Friday to Saturday so that his children could help and he wouldn't have to hire any labor. The field was only about one hectare, but in order to get the crop picked by the afternoon there were at least ten of us working, including Don Miguel's family, myself, and his neighbor's family. I worked with the women and younger children picking, while the men carried the laden baskets of zucchini to the edge of the field. There they washed and packed the squash in layers of newspaper in wooden crates to prevent bruising, each box carefully covered with a special brown paper bought especially for this purpose. By dusk we had harvested just two-thirds of the field.

A week later when I was in Nazareno, Don Miguel told me that they were going to try to sell another picking from the same field; so I abandoned what I was doing and took off with him to Huixcolotla, the location of the regional wholesale market. When we arrived around 6:30 p.m. the market was calm. There was an orderly line of twenty or so parked pickups and trucks, with the farmers milling around, talking, eating peanuts, and waiting. "Waiting for a price." We walked over to one of the farmers and asked how the situation

Figure 8.1 Harvesting tomatillos, Nazareno.

was. He shrugged and told us, "They aren't buying." The buyers were obvious: men in starched white shirts, polished shoes, and big belt buckles. I watched as one such skeptical man peddled up on a bicycle and asked to see the contents of a farmer's crates. The man eagerly peeled back the paper on the top and revealed what looked to me like perfectly sized fresh young zucchini in neat rows. The buyer seemed utterly disinterested but asked to see another box further back in the truck, suspecting that the farmer had perhaps buried the less attractive samples of his harvests at the back of his truck. The farmer silently obliged, seeming almost to be holding his breath. Then the tension broke. The buyer shrugged and frowned and said he didn't like it and wasn't buying. Not even for ten pesos a crate. He turned his back and peddled off. That evening there was no market.

From my initial meetings with the vegetable farmers of Nazareno I had heard how volatile the market was and how little control they felt they had over the outcomes of their harvests. While they often laughed at themselves and the unpredictability of their fortunes, beneath their resignation was an underlying anxiety. More than anything, they compared their production decisions to games of dice and luck. Planting, they told me, is like the lottery. "You plant but you never know."

Having expected that because of their access to irrigation the farmers of Nazareno would be substantially better off both materially and in terms of their capacity to manage risk, I was at first surprised by their depiction of the insecurity of their livelihoods. Irrigation is one of the oldest methods employed by societies to adapt agriculture to otherwise inhospitable climatic conditions. Theoretically, access to irrigation, particularly from groundwater sources, can substantially reduce the sensitivity of the farm system to unpredictable and variable rainfall. Irrigation can also mitigate irregularities in the distribution of rainfall, preventing water stress at key points in a crop's development, and providing consistent levels of soil moisture in irrigated fields may make crops slightly less sensitive to hard frosts than comparable soils under rainfed conditions.

On the semiarid and subhumid highlands of Mexico, irrigation may also facilitate farmers' entry into commercial markets where they may have better opportunities for profit than those who are limited to rainfed crops. This opportunity is particularly important in the current context of rapid agricultural change and market liberalization in Mexico. When Mexico entered into NAFTA, there was some expectation that those farmers specializing in nontraditional crops or high-value alternatives to maize would be able to compete in specialized export markets (de Janvry, Sadoulet, and Gordillo 1995; Marsh and Runsten 1998; Nadal 1999). Indeed, vegetable production has increased gradually over the last decade, in part because of better access to markets in the United States and Europe (de Grammont et al. 1999; Marsh and Runsten 1998).

The farmers of irrigated vegetable in Nazareno thus should theoretically represent farmers who are pursuing a "win-win" strategy at the turn of the twenty-first century—protected by irrigation from the climatic shocks and hazards that are affecting the farmers of Torres and Plan de Ayala, and participating in more promising agricultural markets in the new era of NAFTA and other international trade agreements. Yet I found that the farmers using irrigation in Nazareno were neither exempt from climatic risk nor necessarily more economically secure than their counterparts in Plan de Ayala, and in many cases, the instability and inflexibility of their livelihoods makes their vulnerability comparable to the resource-scarce households of Torres.

Climatic and Market Uncertainty in Irrigated Production

Vegetable farmers in Puebla's eastern valley produce largely for the market of southeastern Mexico: Chiapas, Oaxaca, and the Yucatan. They commercialize their harvests principally through the regional wholesale market of Huixcolotla, located thirty minutes from Nazareno outside of the commercial town, Tecamachalco. Less often, the farmers send their produce to the wholesale market of Mexico City.

Nazareno farmers compete in the Huixcolotla market with produce from the states of Michoacán, Guerrero, Hidalgo, and Mexico. Vegetable prices in the Huixcolotla and Mexico City markets are extremely variable. In periods of high supply, the vegetable brokers in Huixcolotla and Mexico City often fill their contracts within a few hours, causing sudden drops in vegetable prices as demand dwindles. Some farmers, who have access to a telephone, call their "coyote," or broker, before harvesting to get an estimate of the going market prices and a recommendation for the appropriate timing for commercialization, but the progressive maturation of their crops in the field considerably limits their ability to delay or accelerate harvest activities. Even if the price appears viable the morning the household sets out to harvest its crop, by the time the produce has been cleaned and packaged for sale (at least a half a day's work for most crops) the price has often dropped. It is not uncommon for farmers to be unable to sell their crop at all because "there was no market"—no one was buying at any price.

Approximately one-quarter of the households surveyed reported plowing under the crop of at least one field each year, principally because the going price did not justify the cost of harvesting. In these cases, the households generally let the crop rot in the field until they can pull together the resources to replant. Less frequently, farmers will plow under a crop because of climatic hazards or crop disease. Climatic hazards and crop diseases often have only a partial impact on a field, allowing for the possibility of crop recovery with either chemical treatment or change in the weather. Often it is the combination of poor prices, climate variability, and uncontrolled pest problems that causes the most damage to farmers' incomes. Crops affected by light frosts, high temperatures, or water deficits are often more susceptible to disease, and both climate and crop disease affect the quality of the harvest and thus its commercial value in very competitive markets.

Explanations of Price Variability

Like the barley farmers of Plan de Ayala, many of the vegetable farmers look north to lay the blame for the market volatility they experience. Despite the physical distance of Nazareno from the international border and the fact that very few farmers export directly to the United States, the inelasticity in demand for fresh produce makes it impossible for the vegetable farmers of Nazareno *not* to be affected by the variability in both the domestic and international vegetable markets. This volatility in prices translated into a largely negative perception of institutional change over the last decade by the surveyed households (see table 6.1)

The farmers explained to me that when their competitors in high-volume vegetable-producing regions such as the Bajío (Guanajuato and Michoacán) or Sinaloa faced problems in exporting their vegetables, they turned to the domestic market to commercialize their harvests. This drives down prices for the farmers in the Puebla Valley, who, as producers of lower-quality products in smaller volumes, have nowhere else to turn to sell their products. Many of the villagers I spoke with believed that this type of behavior was becoming increasingly prevalent.

Some farmers also hypothesize that both local climatic events and hazards occurring in competing vegetable-producing regions are increasing the variability of the prices they receive. In a discussion I had with a group of farmers in Nazareno, a farmer commented, "There are times when there are *siniestros* [climate impacts] in the United States, and there is greater demand here and the prices rise. This is because there are other regions in Mexico that are big vegetable producers . . . like the Bajío. So when there is demand in the U.S., they sell abroad and export everything, leaving the domestic market to producers in Puebla. But if there isn't demand abroad, then those farmers sell domestically and the price crashes for Puebla farmers. *Aquí es pura suerte.* [Here it's pure luck]."

By listening to the gossip in the wholesale markets, farmers have acquired very specific knowledge about these price-climate relationships. In a mapping exercise in which I asked several farmers to identify competing vegetable-producing regions, the farmers not only pointed out the specific localities that they felt were their strongest competitors for specific crops, but also the hazard that most frequently affected production in that region and the season or month in which that area was most likely to be affected (fig. 8.2). They also knew that heavy rains or mudslides in southeastern Mexico can obstruct transport and thus prevent the commercialization of their crops. One farmer even reported trying to anticipate particular climatic patterns in competing regions in choosing his crops in the hope of second-guessing market fluctuations. Apparently he was not very successful. "I planted carrots last year to coincide with the summer season," he told me. "In June and July there are often floods in Guanajuato and the price of carrots can go up because the farmers in Guanajuato can't enter their fields to harvest. But this didn't happen. I have also planted lettuce to be ready in October when there are Pacific coast cyclones that also can affect Guanajuato."

It was not clear from the survey data whether farmers' perceptions of price variability and market risk have changed since Mexico's entry into NAFTA and the beginning of an increasingly open trade regime. Data on prices of key vegetables sold in Mexico City's wholesale market suggest that for some crops grown in Nazareno there has been a negative trend in real prices since the mid-1990s. One retired vegetable producer in Nazareno, Don Fernando, recalled the difficulty of production conditions during the economic crisis following the devaluation of 1994: "Everyone planted but left most of the harvest in the field because there weren't any prices. People were traveling to Mexico [City] with their harvests, but the buyers were only offering the price of the packing and the trip, nothing for the harvest itself."

Another farmer felt that 1991 had begun a downward trend in prices. He told me that after 1991 "there has been no profit in vegetables. It's pure luck now." In 1991 he had done well with a carrot harvest and bought a pickup truck. But now, he told me, "It would be impossible." When I asked what he thought had triggered the change, he said he thought that perhaps it was because it is drier now. He had heard that in regions that were formerly completely rainfed, farmers had begun to put in wells to grow irrigated crops, and this was increasing the competition for his own harvests. The perception that the area under irrigation had expanded in Mexico as a national response both to market opportunities and to repeated drought was common in the community.

In the group interviews, farmers also commented that their costs of production were increasingly unviable in face of the rising prices of imported inputs in Mexico's liberalized markets. The farmers noted that the price of seed, pesticides, and fertilizers fluctuated with international exchange rates for the U.S. dollar, causing significant uncertainty in their estimations of their investment requirements. They laughed with frustration when I asked them how they planned for their production expenditures: "Plan? Last year I bought a pound of seed for lettuce in May. I called [the store] when I was thinking about buying it and they told me it cost 1,300 pesos per pound. And then later, when I had put the money together, it cost double! Double! Because of the exchange rate."

This uncertainty is also exacerbated by the households' dependency on private sector input distributors to diagnose and treat the crop diseases they observe. A representative survey of vegetable farmers in the entire Tecamachalco irrigation district conducted by the Colegio de Postgraduados found that over half of farmers were turning to input stores as their primary source of technical advice (Aguirre Alvarez et al. 1999). These farmers are aware that the motive of the store is to sell them chemicals and that they often were advised to purchase more than they needed, or something that perhaps was not appropriate for their problem. In the words of the Colegio de Postgraduados study, farmers "undertake an indiscriminant use of chemical products, applying true pesticide 'bombs' motivated by their ignorance of pests and disease vectors and the management of chemicals, under the total influence of the commercial agrochemical houses which, in order to increase their profits, promote the use and abuse of chemical products" (Aguirre Alvarez et al. 1999: 32, my translation). The authors of the study found that farmers associate the power of the input stores in part with the lack of an agricultural ex-

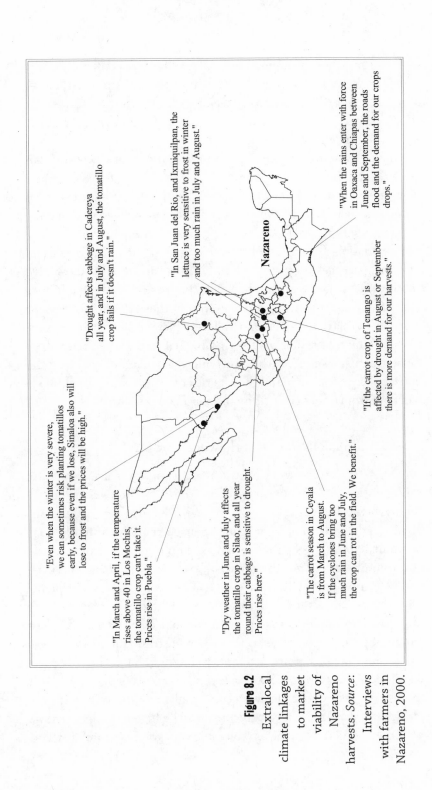

"In March and April, if the temperature rises above 40 in Los Mochis, the tomatillo crop can't take it. Prices rise in Puebla."

"Even when the winter is very severe, we can sometimes risk planting tomatillos early, because even if we lose, Sinaloa also will lose to frost and the prices will be high."

"Drought affects cabbage in Cadereya all year, and in July and August, the tomatillo crop fails if it doesn't rain."

"In San Juan del Rio, and Ixmiquilpan, the lettuce is very sensitive to frost in winter and too much rain in July and August."

"When the rains enter with force in Oaxaca and Chiapas between June and September, the roads flood and the demand for our crops drops."

Nazareno

"Dry weather in June and July affects the tomatillo crop in Silao, and all year round their cabbage is sensitive to drought. Prices rise here."

"The carrot season in Ceyala is from March to August. If the cyclones bring too much rain in June and July, the crop can rot in the field. We benefit."

"If the carrot crop of Tenango is affected by drought in August or September there is more demand for our harvests."

Figure 8.2 Extralocal climate linkages to market viability of Nazareno harvests. *Source:* Interviews with farmers in Nazareno, 2000.

tension service in the region. This perspective was confirmed in my own interviews in Nazareno. Of the two-thirds of surveyed households that reported occasionally seeking technical advice, 42 percent relied primarily on input stores for this help. Another 38 percent asked their neighbors or relatives for advice.

In contrast to the farmers of rainfed land interviewed in Plan de Ayala and Torres, who expressed considerable confidence in their knowledge of their production processes (and little use for technical advice), farmers in Nazareno expressed a peculiar helplessness or powerlessness with regard to their input choices and application. By their own admission, they often had trouble reading the fine print on the chemical packages they purchased, and they lacked basic knowledge about the application of the chemicals that they bought. One farmer speculated that the input stores often sold them at least 50 percent more chemicals than necessary to address their problem. Local agronomists think that rather than saving the harvest, this practice often causes further damage to the crop while considerably increasing the household's investment and thus its risk of significant economic loss and debt from either climatic impacts or market failures.

The Shaky Promise of the Vegetable Market

As is the case with most farmers who face seasonal climatic constraints and competitive markets, the crop-choice decisions of the irrigated producers of Nazareno are the outcome of their constant weighing of climatic risk and their perceptions of market opportunity. Some choose their crop based on their assessment of the crops no one else is planting. Others try to second-guess the market by planting crops that have higher prices at the time of planting (with the expectation that the price will hold to harvest), or low prices at the time of planting (with the expectation that the price will rise by harvest because everyone would stop planting that crop). The farmers laughed at my attempts to understand the logic of their decisions. After going over several hypothetical examples, they put it to me this way: "Cabbage is very cheap right now, so we go with the idea that if we plant it again the price will be high again by the time of harvest. And if the price of cabbage is very good, we think perhaps our luck will hold and we plant the crop again, but twice as much of it. This is the 'Great Illusion of the Campesino!'"

Still others try to second-guess the market by planting particular crops for seasonal markets: "For carrots, we expect the best prices in June, and in January and February, so we try to plant in January and September to hit those markets. For romaine lettuce, we plant in April and May to hit the markets in July and August, and in August to hit the market demand at Christmas. The problem is that everyone is doing the same, so there is a high risk that the price will collapse before we have had a chance to sell our harvest." Or, as another farmer explained, "The price of lettuce is variable, but there are seasons of best prices. The most favorable conditions are when you plant in September, to harvest at Christmas when people eat more lettuce. And to plant in May to harvest in August, before the price drops in September. This is because the school season begins in September, and the price falls because families have to spend so much on school fees and supplies that there is no demand. When the price is high, it is about one peso per head; when it is low it is about 50 centavos per head."

In fact, the available price data from the Mexico City vegetable wholesale market generally do not support the farmers' perceptions of market demand (fig. 8.3). Interannual variability in seasonal crop prices can be considerable, defying any farmer's ability to plan for seasons of high prices. And while there are apparently periods of high demand for particular crops (e.g., marigolds for the Day of the Dead market, or lettuce for Christmas dinner), without an organized system of gauging market demand and supply, the farmers of Nazareno often find their strategies fail to bring them the earnings they expected.

Complicating their market strategies are the limits that climatic factors place on their crop choices, as well as their decisions about when to plant. Despite the general access to irrigation, climatic hazards still feature prominently in households' definitions of "bad years" and account for three-quarters of the crop losses they experienced in 1999. In part, this climatic sensitivity is a function of the instability of the farmers' irrigation supply. Farmers report areas, particularly where there are a large number of well users, where the

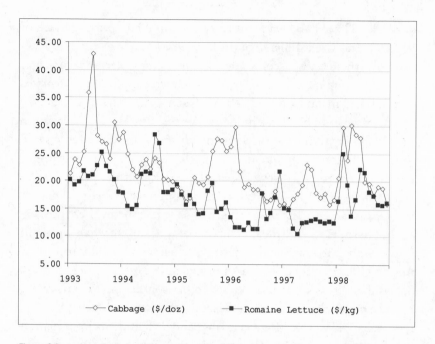

Figure 8.3 Average monthly prices of romaine lettuce and cabbage in the Mexico City wholesale market 1993–98 (prices adjusted for inflation). *Source*: Apoyos y Servicios a la Comercialización Agropecuaria (ASERCA), Secretaria de Agricultura, Ganadería y Desarrollo Rural (SAGARPA).

irrigation provided by the wells is no longer sufficient for the crops of higher water consumption. Thus, their crop choice depends not only on the expected rainfall of the weeks following planting, but also on the crops' water requirements and the availability of irrigation, particularly the possibility of "renting" irrigation rights from other well members who are not intending to plant that cycle.

Frost damage is another threat to production, prohibiting farmers from planting crops sensitive to low temperatures during the cooler months. Tomatillos and zucchini, some of the more popular crops in Nazareno, are particularly susceptible to frost in the late winter, although farmers who risk planting in winter tend to receive higher prices for their harvests. Ultimately the choice of what and when one plants is an inevitable gamble, as Don Rudolfo explained:

Those who plant *tomate* [tomatillos] in late December or January are in competition with Sinaloa, but not with other farmers in the region since most won't plant until the risk of frost is lower. Everyone gains if Sinaloa has problems with its harvest because the price rises for the produce in Puebla. And when the weather is good in Morelos, the Puebla farmers also lose because the markets are full. The problem is, if you planted in December, you would be most likely to lose to frost. About 1,500 to 2,000 pesos [per hectare]. Most would turn the crop under and plant tomatillos again, or another inexpensive crop that has high returns. It is much safer, despite the disadvantages of price, to plant in mid- or late February.

Within the constraints of seasonal climatic variability and perceived market opportunity, households face significant financial obstacles to pursuing a consistent commercial production strategy. Almost a quarter of the households reported that financial considerations have a strong influence in their crop choices. In addition to the significant costs of labor, seeds, fertilizer, gallinaza (chicken manure), and machinery, households also face a monthly electricity bill for their portion of the use of the irrigation pump. In Nazareno, all but three of the community's well associations require that their members pay a minimum portion of this electric bill, which averages 200 to 300 pesos (US$22–US$33) per irrigation turn, even if they do not use the water. To make irrigation profitable, they need to get at least two harvests from each irrigated field, although the frequency of crop losses means that households are not always able to pull together the resources required to do so.

Not only are households that experience a series of crop losses often in debt from their investments, but unlike their rainfed counterparts, they do not have the opportunity of the winter fallow period to recuperate these losses in nonagricultural activities. As a result, it is possible for households to find themselves in a rapid downward spiral of increasing economic crisis within the span of a single calendar year. For some households, the only way out of such a crisis is through temporary migration to the United States, in the hope that they will be able to recuperate sufficient funds to begin replanting again.

Nazareno Households' Management of Risks and Uncertainties

Although over three-quarters of the surveyed Nazareno population has access to some irrigated land, not all households are dedicated to vegetable production as their primary economic activity. Approximately 43 percent of the households surveyed in Nazareno are principally producers of irrigated vegetables, according to their income profiles and the diversity of crops they plant. These households were featured in primarily two livelihood groups, the Large-scale Commercial and Small-scale Commercial households. The Large-scale Commercial households have landholdings averaging nine hectares, with on average 86 percent of this area irrigated. The average landholding size of the Small-scale Commercial households is only half that of the Large-scale producers, although this land tends also to be mostly irrigated. With irrigation, both household groups plant a variety of vegetable crops in addition to maize and beans, and they are able to support relatively large numbers of medium-size livestock (see table 4.5).

Despite the significant differences in landholding size, the average incomes and the level of material wealth of the households are similar. However, there are differences in the sensitivity of the households to climate hazards. In 1999, losses of the Large-scale Commercial household group averaged 40 percent of their planted area, while the losses for the Small-scale Commercial households were nearly half that amount (two-thirds of the households reported losses of less than 30 percent). The Large-scale Commercial households also reported having had to turn under their harvests more frequently than the smaller-scale vegetable producers in the previous three years, either because of climatic impacts, crop disease, or market failures.

In part this difference may relate to the proportion of the farmers' total area devoted to maize. Although the household groups each planted on average almost two hectares of land in maize, this allotment represents 37 percent of the Small-scale Commercial households' total land area, while only 18 percent of the Large-scale Commercial households' landholdings. Much of this maize was irrigated, and irrigated maize, even slightly damaged by frost, would probably satisfy the consumption requirements of an average household, while similar damage on a lettuce field would make the harvest unmarketable. With a larger proportion of land dedicated to high-investment and highly sensitive vegetables, the larger-scale vegetable farmers are more likely to report frequent and extensive crop losses.

Managing Risk through Reducing Costs

Although the vegetable-producing households of Nazareno believe they have no control over the volatility of the market, or the vagaries of the weather, to some extent they can control their input costs and agricultural investments. Through these expenditures many households try to manage uncertainty and minimize the economic impact of frequent losses. In cases where the household is already in debt, managing input expenses means planting low-cost crops such as radish or cilantro, or maize, as described above. However, there were some households interviewed that were attacking the problem of their risk exposure more proactively, through managing the amount they invested in purchased inputs and labor. Instead of focusing solely on monitoring costs as they arose in the process of production, these farmers were interested in cutting their investments significantly from the start, by educating themselves to prevent and diagnose their own crop ailments, by investing in organic fertilizers made from the compost of their fields, and even by producing their own seeds for planting.

Approximately fifteen households, all of them in the Small-scale Commercial group, were participating in weekly extension meetings, which they had solicited from a local nongovernmental organization, ICTAPEC. The service was contracted through a producer organization, Asociación de Productores de Oriente del Estado de Puebla (Eastern Puebla Farmers' Association), which is associated with the Partido Revolucionario Institucional-affiliated labor union FROC-CROC. Importantly, the ICTAPEC is not linked to any commercial input supplier and thus provides relatively objective advice. The extension agent focused his lessons on the management of crop diseases and pests, educating the farmers on identifying what was affecting their crops and on how to apply only the appropriate types of chemicals.

These farmers also attended a demonstration on organic composting, and several subsequently experimented with the technique in their own fields with positive results. The cost of gallinaza was expensive, averaging over 2,000 pesos per hectare, and often gallinaza was applied in combination with other chemical fertilizers. Given these costs, producing one's own fertilizer from vegetable and crop residues and manure represents a considerable savings. Don José, a quiet and thoughtful farmer who attended the composting demonstrations, told me that by using organic compost made from animal manure and vegetable residues he had actually managed to cut his expenses in half.

Don José's case is particularly intriguing because he is one of the few farmers I interviewed who claimed that he has never had to plow under a field because of poor prices or climatic problems, and he has never experienced significant crop losses. I spent some time with him trying to understand what made his fortunes so different from his neighbors. He told me that although he had only 2.5 ha of irrigated land, in discontinuous fields, all of his property is a relatively short distance from his house. When I talked to him in 2000, he was hoping someday to purchase more land. He told me that his expansion plans were not held back by a lack of resources, but rather that there has not been any land available in the immediate area around the village and he was not interested in land farther out because of the expense of getting to and from the fields.

When he has the resources, Don José expands his prospects through sharecropping additional irrigated land that others are not able, or do not wish, to plant. He and his wife count on the help of three of their five children in the fields (two are too young to help) and in tending their twenty sheep, their few pigs, and their cow after school. They hire labor only for the harvests. He always plants some maize from seed that he personally selects for high yields (which he estimated were around 5,000 kg/ha under irrigation), but only just enough for the family. Because of the high yields, he doesn't need to plant more than half a hectare. No one in his household has any source of income other than from the crop sales.

When I asked why he thought that he has suffered fewer losses than other farmers, Don José admitted that he is lucky. But he also replied that he thinks it a myth that there is no demand for the vegetable crops. He is convinced that if his harvest is of good quality, it will sell. His philosophy is to never invest more than the minimum he might get for the crop. He does not purchase seedlings for planting as other farmers do, preferring to harvest and plant his own seed, thus avoiding the high costs of transplants. He was also concerned about the inefficiencies in water use in the community, and hoped soon to be able to receive a loan to install drip irrigation, although he thought that the loan would be difficult to get because of the small size of his property. He belongs to one of only three well associations in which the water users pay only for pumping the water they actually use. This also reduces his costs.

Don José tries to time his planting and harvesting so that the crops are not at a vulnerable stage of development when there is a high risk of frost. He often observes the experiences of others and avoids planting crops that are particularly high risk (e.g., flowers for the Day of the Dead market). Instead, he tends to specialize in just a few vegetables. And, although he does not recognize it as such, it was clear he had an advantage over many other households: a relative is a vegetable trader with a stall in the regional market of Huixcolotla, and also has a small truck to transport Don José's harvest to the market. Through this connection he never had problems selling.

Don José is clearly an "innovative farmer" who is willing to experiment with new approaches to production to mitigate the risks he faced (Richards 1985). Not only is he investing considerable time and energy into controlling the economic risks he faces through organic inputs and even by producing his own seed, but he also has important connections in the local market that make better market prices more accessible.

Most households I interviewed were not as innovative or fortunate. For most, particularly the Small-scale Commercial farmers, the cost of labor in vegetable production means that such farming remains a family enterprise in which all family members, even the smallest children, are involved in the required labors. Labor-intensive activities such as harvesting, irrigation, weeding, or planting are reserved for times when the children are not attending school and can help in the fields. Even so, often the market prices are so low that they do not justify even the material costs (the packaging materials and transport) of harvesting.

The way in which the community of Nazareno was founded also

means that, unlike with Don José, few households have fields concentrated in one location. In fact, many fields are quite far from the
village, and thus the time required for monitoring and supervision is
also problematic. The mean distance between any given household
and its fields is over 3,000 m. Fields that are not regularly monitored
can quickly fall prey to insect infestations, weeds, or fungi. Those
households with fields near to their homes are at an advantage, while
those who have acquired fields at random as they have become available are more likely to have to travel long distances by bike or on
foot to work. This distance not only makes bicycles critical household
assets, but also limits the capacity of a single household to manage
several fields at once.

The field distances and costs of labor may be why the incomes of
the two groups of vegetable producers do not differ substantially, and
why the larger-scale household group also reports higher crop losses.
The labor-intensive nature of irrigated production on nine hectares
may well exceed the capacity of an average family to manage alone,
and the cost of employing labor would increase costs in relation to
possible gains from larger volumes.

Income Diversification and Agricultural Intensification

Finally, one of the more obvious differences between the two
vegetable-producing household groups is the degree to which they
have diversified into a variety of economic activities. The Small-scale
Commercial households have relatively more diversified income portfolios, with comparatively more income coming from tractor rental,
honey production, greenhouse work, and occasional work as day laborers in neighbors' fields (all sources of off-farm income). They also
benefit to a lesser extent from nonfarm income (representing on average about 7 percent of their total income) contributed by household members working as construction assistants or as other low-
wage laborers. Although these activities can make the households
susceptible to changes in local agricultural economy, both nonfarm
and off-farm income tend to complement rather than compete with
the human and physical resources needed for vegetable production.
In contrast, the Large-scale Commercial households rely almost completely on their vegetable production for income (representing on av-

erage 90 percent of their total income), putting them at considerable risk because of volatility in the vegetable markets.

For some households, diversification and agricultural intensification are ongoing and highly experimental processes. In face of the constant uncertainty of the vegetable market, some households are considering changing the nature of their strategies entirely in an attempt to find the right balance of activities and investments that will provide the economic security and advancement they desire.

For example, a group of farmers has decided that fruit trees may offer better economic returns than vegetables, and they have formed an official business association in order to receive credit for the purchase of peach trees. They hope that when the trees are well established they will be able to pass on grafts from their trees to others who desire to join their association. They think that the peaches will bring a more stable income to complement their vegetables, because there is less competition for peaches in the region. Because of the risk of hail damage, they are training their trees to grow so that the highest branches shelter the fruit on the branches below. Frost is also a problem for peaches, tending to affect the interior branches that are most protected from hail. However, since the project's inception the greatest threat to the harvest has been theft from neighbors and a plague of beetles that consumes the ripest fruit just before it is ready for harvest. They have yet to commercialize the fruit.

In another case very similar to the maize-oats-livestock strategies of farmers in Plan de Ayala, a small group of vegetable farmers—brothers—considered raising high-quality sheep instead of vegetables. One of the farmers told me that he had had enough of vegetable production. He had not realized a profit since 1992. He and his partners planned to use part of their land as a corral and part for producing irrigated alfalfa, sorghum, soy, and maize to feed their herds and their own families. Concerned about anticipated water shortages, the farmers hoped that their forage crops would be less water intensive than vegetable crops. They thought they would process the animal manure into compost to sell to their vegetable-producing neighbors as an alternative to the expensive gallinaza. As with the Fernández family in Torres, these households applied for a loan from FIRA, and they hoped to commercialize their sheep as meat for the Mexican restaurant chain Sanborn's through a production contract. With this strategy, the farmers believed that they would be engaging in a more secure, higher-paying market for meat while escaping the persistent problems of frost, crop disease, and competition in the vegetable market. The project, however, did not meet the bank's approval and as of 2005 had not materialized.

"Playing the Lottery" in Nazareno

Given the declining market for maize and the other grains that are produced under rainfed conditions in central Mexico, one would think that the vegetable farmers of Nazareno would have far more opportunities and benefits under neoliberalism. They have irrigation, enabling them to enter into competitive agricultural markets; they are already (relatively speaking) mechanized and "modern" in the sense that they use tractors, purchased seeds, and fertilizers; and they have been integrated into regional markets for decades. Yet, although the total average household income reported to me by households in the two groups was in the range of 70,000 pesos in 1999, and thus well above Mexico's poverty line of two minimum salaries (approximately 20,000 pesos/year), their material possessions were at that time relatively few, fewer in fact than the more economically diversified households in Plan de Ayala and Torres.

The inability of many of Nazareno's vegetable farmers to accumulate wealth has its roots in their commitment to uncertain and risky processes of production and the difficulty households face in diversifying their economic activities to mitigate risk and compete in the vegetable trade. Their relatively small production volumes and the low quality of their produce largely excludes them from more profitable export markets and commercial contracts, although they are highly sensitive to changes in the demand of those markets.

Although it is evident from the surveys that market uncertainty plays a central role in structuring their production decisions, it is also clear that these decisions are essentially made "in the dark" without the wider knowledge of regional market trends that might facilitate planning. The farmers' economic risks are also compounded by their dependence on chemical inputs without the accompanying knowledge to manage that dependence effectively. This lack of information increases their vulnerability to variability in the macroeconomy (through changes in input prices) in addition to increasing the economic impact of crop losses.

Water, the farmers' fundamental source of capital, is also increasingly unreliable and scarce, exposing them to the variability in rainfall and dry climate of the region and to inevitable increases in energy costs as they draw water from greater depths. In 2000, very few farmers in Nazareno were even considering investing in drip or pressurized irrigation systems. Although most farmers acknowledge the inefficiencies in their water use, they lack the incentives and finances to improve their system. At the end of the year 2000, the office of the National Water Commission (CNA, or CONAGUA as it is known in Mexico) in Puebla was planning to implement an "austerity" water-use plan in which meters would be placed on every well to limit the withdrawal of water to only seven hours per day. This effort, combined with small programs run by the CNA and Alianza para el Campo to improve irrigation efficiency, may push some households to modernize their irrigation systems, although because each well is managed collectively by twenty-five or so well association members, there is considerable social inertia to change, particularly if such change requires financial commitments from each member.

The fact that those households that appear to be the most committed to vegetable production, the Large-scale Commercial households, are not substantially wealthier than other vegetable producers in the community, and that their losses tend to be higher, suggests that their commitment to irrigation comes at the expense of their capacity to diversify economically and manage their labor, time, and chemical inputs effectively to mitigate risk.

In contrast, the Small-scale Commercial households appeared to manage the variability in their livelihoods by straddling both commercial and subsistence strategies. Like the Subsistence Maize households described in chapter 6, the Small-scale Commercial vegetable producers are also committed to planting maize for their own subsistence, and their strategies involve periodic forced retreats from vegetable production to the security of subsistence crops, facilitated by the land and water markets of the community and the relatively constant demand for agricultural wage labor. In essence, the strategies of these farmers reflect a rational response of smallholders to the dual demands of commodity and consumption production (Netting 1993; Turner and Brush 1987). This strategy enables the survival of households as agriculturalists in the valley, although it is not uncommon for farmers who have slipped rapidly and progressively into substantial debt to find themselves suddenly without any recourse but migration.

In an environment in which households liken their production strategies to "playing the lottery," surprisingly few households—Don José is one exception—are focusing on what they can control: their input costs, the allocation of their limited labor, and the intensity of their land use. Those who have found a way to manage the risky markets effectively tend also to be those who have organized themselves to access scarce institutional resources from FIRA or alternative financial institutions. Yet these households also face considerable obstacles. Those farmers who are experimenting in organics, for example, as yet have not found a market for their crops, and thus while they may be able to reduce some of their input costs by avoiding some purchased chemicals, they do not yet have access to the niche markets that provide further economic incentives for this strategy. Despite their proximity to the middle-class consumers of Mexico City, the domestic markets for organic or gourmet vegetables are still poorly developed.

Contract farming with vegetable brokers might address some of the problem of price volatility and market risk, yet in 2000 this type of arrangement was unheard of in the area. According to the extension agents with DEPAC (a nongovernmental organization operating in Puebla that helps finance rural initiatives), contracts with buyers are difficult given the small production volumes of the farmers. The households would need to organize themselves formally into larger groups in order to produce the consistent volumes needed in contract arrangements. For contracts to work, many commercial buyers—for example, hotel and restaurant chains and supermarkets—also need a paper trail of receipts, requiring farmers to apply for recognition as a private business, cooperative, or formal producers association. This step, in turn, implies paying taxes, something few farmers in Nazareno were willing to do. Thus, without production contracts or market insurance, the small-scale producers, not the buyers, bear the burden of market risk. Without more formal arrangements such as contract farming, the success of Nazareno's more adventurous farmers depends on their ability to create among themselves relationships of trust and collaboration that can improve their chances of accessing formal support.

Despite these challenges, some farmers are optimistic about the community's future. Don Fernando, a farmer with a long history in the community commented: "Nazareno is changing. Now *ingenieros* are coming to help the farmers. There are about three or four groups of farmers who are working with the técnicos, looking for benefits. There is more education: now the village has its own satellite secondary school, and its own teachers. And the children are growing up to be ingenieros too. There are people, the youth, who are leaving and returning with money. And they are building houses. But there are few opportunities here in the village. You can work a medias, but there is no land available. And one can't live on the salary of a day laborer, yet some people have to. Because of the generally poor prices, people are leaving to look for work."

In the year 2000, Nazareno became incorporated as an independent town, and sewer lines were laid down across the urban center. The ejidatarios of the community were organizing to protest their lack of access to the Huixcolotla market, in the hope that they would be able to counteract the control of the *caciques* [local bosses] there and sell directly to warehouse owners rather than through intermediaries. And the news of the state's plans to have a segment of the Plan Puebla-Panama highway pass through Tecamachalco initiated rumors of land sales to foreign factories and possible changes in the future of agriculture in the region as well as new nonfarm opportunities. Some of these rumors have proven to be true: In 2004, the Mexican cement processor Cruz Azul purchased three hundred hectares from an ejido in Palmar de Bravo to build a cement factory, at an estimated cost of US$307 million. The construction apparently promises employment for some 2,500 workers (*Latin American News Digest*, 30 Sept. 2004). As the next chapter will detail, the locating of such industries in rural areas leads to important household choices about labor allocation and livelihood, with different consequences for risk exposure.

9 Rural Industrialization and Risk Management

Deagrarianization and Livelihood Security

I had arranged to interview Don Diego a week earlier, after chatting briefly with him in the main street of Plan de Ayala. When I walked up to his home on a chilly and gray day in May, I noticed that one of the buildings around his concrete patio housed a small store, supplied mainly with packages of chips and candy. It was unmanned, but I assumed there was always someone keeping an eye out for customers. Don Diego had not returned from a trip to Apizaco when I arrived. His two daughters and his sons-in-law invited me in to wait and partake in the dinner that they had prepared. Sitting around the wooden table in a room that looked as if it also served as a bedroom and kitchen, they talked about their work and the family's farm. Don Diego's daughters were both employed sporadically in the factories down the highway. They complained that the jobs were not stable and the salary was poor. One of his sons-in-law worked as a carpenter, traveling to Apizaco or wherever his talents were needed. He also complained that the work was very irregular.

When Don Diego and his wife Doña Gaby joined us, the conversation became very animated. Doña Gaby told many stories about their struggles to survive in the initial years of the ejido without water and electricity. They had nothing when they began. They lived in one room, with a laminated roof that frequently became covered with ice on the inside in the winter. Their children were always sick with one thing or another, and once one of their daughters had been hospitalized.

Now that their children are grown and they have the help of the incomes of their two youngest daughters and sons-in-laws, things have improved. In 1994 they renovated their house and built it all in concrete block. Doña Gaby said that they now depend far more on their daughters' salaries than previously, because of the problems they have had with their harvests in recent years. She and her daughters were quick to clarify that neither their wages nor the farm's production was sufficient to live on. Don Diego told me that they have nine hectares, and they always plant at least one hectare of maize for their own consumption. In a pinch they sell maize for cash. When I mentioned I had also seen the store, Doña Gaby laughed and said that it was good to have because when things got tight, she could always "borrow" from her store. They have a car, which helps to get provisions for the store from Apizaco.

While appreciating the income from the factories, Doña Gaby was critical. These factories are all foreign, she said. Mexicans do not have the money to invest. Mexico exports all the best quality products and leaves the second quality for domestic use. She told me that her daughters had to sew on clothing labels saying "made in the USA" when it is not true; the clothes are made here. "And then they export the clothing and re-import it," she exclaimed. "They sell it at a 'quality' price when we know it was made here."

Those who research the impact of climate hazards have long recognized the importance of nonfarm activities and rural-urban migration as coping strategies (Corbett 1988; McCabe 1990; Scoones 1996). Nonfarm income, by definition, offers the advantage of being relatively independent of the variability that affects productivity in agriculture, whether from climatic shocks or other exogenous stresses (Adger 1999). It is now also accepted that off-farm and nonfarm wage employment play integral roles in the livelihoods of households traditionally viewed as "peasant," whether in Africa, Asia, Europe, or Latin America (Bryceson 1996, 2002; de Janvry and Sadoulet 2001; Ellis 2000; Yúnez-Naude and Taylor 2001). Over the last decade, the participation of rural households in nonfarm wage activity has surged. Some analysts believe that the growth of nonfarm wage activity in rural life represents not simply a means of coping with isolated crises in the rural sector, but rather a defined shift in the orientation of livelihoods toward a far more diversified income base (Bryceson 2002; Ellis 2000; Reardon, Berdegué, and Escobar 2001).

According to a recent analysis by de Janvry and Sadoulet, nonfarm wage income accounts for an average of 55 percent of rural income in Mexico, surpassing self-employment income, agricultural wage income, and remittances (de Janvry and Sadoulet 2001). In Latin America, as part of the opening of national economies to foreign investment, increasingly nonfarm activities include wage employment in factories and rural industries (Reardon, Berdegué, and Escobar 2001). Although the consequences of this trend are not yet clear, most recent studies have argued that in general nonfarm income activities have significant positive impacts on rural poverty and productivity, and that policies that facilitate such livelihood diversification may substantially contribute to rural development (Bryceson 2002; Reardon, Berdegué, and Escobar 2001; Yúnez-Naude and Taylor 2001).

Surprisingly, income diversification is not often considered as part of *agricultural* adaptations to climate variability and/or change, despite recent research showing how nonfarm income is increasingly an essential part of households' risk-management strategies. The tendency has been to sectoralize research so that the process and potential for adaptation to climatic risk is explored within the narrow, and often artificial, boundaries of what constitutes agricultural activity. However, if one approaches an analysis of adaptation by documenting what rural households are actually doing to manage uncertainty, then nonfarm income is impossible to ignore.

While diversification into nonfarm activities may not, in and of itself, satisfy the need to identify *agricultural* adaptations to climatic risk and change, such diversification does imply *livelihood* adaptation, and thus leads to a very real characterization of trends and future vulnerabilities of rural households. If farm households are not simply relying on occasional employment in nonfarm activities to cope with sudden agricultural crises, but rather are diversifying from an agricultural base into nonfarm activities in a more permanent manner, this shift will not only mitigate the sensitivity of household income to hazard impacts but may also enable households to continue agricultural activities that otherwise would be unviable. In other words, nonfarm activities may indeed form part of adaptation strategies *in agriculture*. Measures of households' capacities to diversify into nonfarm activities and the overall stability of these sources of income thus may be important indicators of the flexibility of households to respond to repeated or rising frequency of climatic shocks.

In this chapter I discuss household involvement in nonfarm activities, focusing on the consequences of rural industrialization for adaptation and risk management. I focus on the households of Plan de Ayala, where diversification into nonfarm activities appears to be not only a response to the fragility of agricultural production in the late 1990s but also a direct response to new economic opportunities represented by rural industrialization.

Growth of Nonfarm Opportunities in Tlaxcala and Puebla

Mexico entered NAFTA with the expectation of increased foreign investment, new jobs, and better salaries for Mexican workers (de Janvry, Sadoulet, and Gordillo 1995; Dussel Peters 2000; Gerber and Kerr 1995). While these jobs and salaries were not directly linked to rural development in the negotiation of NAFTA, there was official recognition of the need to decentralize economic activities and create "new poles of development" in areas that have been traditionally neglected (INEGI 1999b). During the 1990s, these development poles have materialized into industrial parks and corridors not only at the U.S.–Mexico border but also throughout Mexico as states began to compete for some of the benefits of the foreign investment (Dussel Peters 2000).

The 1998 national economic census reported a total of 381 industrial parks in the country. Although almost half were at the U.S.–Mexico border, there are a growing number of such sites much farther south. Tlaxcala reported six industrial sites, and Puebla had thirteen, together representing 5 percent of all such sites in Mexico (INEGI 1999b). These industrial zones house everything from large chemical and technology industries to relatively small *maquilas*. *Maquila* is the term for the export assembly plants that constitute a significant proportion of the manufacturing sector. Their location in Mexico is based on the availability of one primary input: cheap labor. Whether the product is automobiles, electronics, or clothing, the inputs and parts are typically imported. According to INEGI data for Tlaxcala,

97 percent of the inputs purchased by the maquilas in that state were imported, and domestic inputs (excluding labor) constituted only 10 percent of the total aggregated output value in the subsector (INEGI 2001b). The finished product is then exported, benefiting from low tariffs mandated under NAFTA.

According to a study commissioned by CEPAL, in the 1990s the maquilas became one of Mexico's most dynamic exporting subsectors. Between 1994 and 1998, maquilas accounted for 41.49 percent of total exports from Mexico and, by 1999, 25 percent of total direct foreign investment (DFI) in Mexico (Dussel Peters 2000). These figures are in marked contrast to direct foreign investment in agriculture, which averaged only 0.16 percent of total DFI between 1994 and 1998 (Dussel Peters 2000).

The states of Puebla and Tlaxcala have both emphasized this type of industrial development since the 1970s. In 2000, Puebla was home to a number of long-established industries that were major regional employers of technically qualified workers. The automobile company Volkswagen has one of its largest plants outside Germany in Puebla (Sánchez Daza 1998). In March 2000, Tlaxcala had over three hundred industries in the state located in its six industrial parks, corridors, and cities along key transportation routes in its central valley (Industrial Development Ministry 2000). In both states, maquilas have played a strong role in leading the growth in manufacturing. The growth of this sector was most dramatic between 1995 and 1998, when the total value of production of the maquila subsector grew by almost 300 percent. By 1999, there were 3,297 maquila establishments in Tlaxcala, more than double the number in 1990.

In Tlaxcala, Xicohténcatl I, the industrial city just a couple of kilometers east of Plan de Ayala, is one of state's largest industrial complexes, containing thirty-three industries employing almost seven thousand people in 2000 (Industrial Development Ministry 2000). Among the industries in Xicohténcatl I in the year 2000 were Dow AgroSciences and Dow Chemical, Kimberly-Clark, Grammer Automotive, Haas Automotive, Olivetti-Lexicon, and a variety of other chemical, plastics, metals, and clothing manufacturers.

The community of Torres is also not far from another industrial park, Xicohténcatl II, located on the highway from Huamantla to Torres. Xicohténcatl II is relatively new, and only nineteen of the thirty-four factory sites were occupied at the start of the year 2000. Most of the industries entered the park in 1998 or 1999. In 2000, daily minimum wages in the industrial parks were advertised in promotional materials as being equivalent to US$3.27 plus benefits (amounting to a total of US$4.12/day), or approximately 45 pesos per day (Industrial Development Ministry 2000).

Nazareno is not directly adjacent to an official industrial zone, although the town of Tehuacán, about 100 km east of Nazareno, is the site of numerous textile maquilas and small industries. Although official data at the municipal level were not available, a local labor union organizer estimated that there were at least twenty small-scale clothing maquilas in the Tecamachalco district alone. At the time of my research in Nazareno, there were rumors that the regional employment situation would soon change. Various labor organizations and developers were lobbying the state government to put Tecamachalco on the path of the Plan Puebla-Panama (PPP) development initiative. The PPP, which is being promoted by the Fox administration in collaboration with the Inter-American Development Bank, the World Bank, International Monetary Fund, and United Nations Development Program, involves the development of a large transport and industrial corridor from Panama through Central America and southern Mexico to Puebla (Flynn 2001). The objective of Plan Puebla-Panama is to extend the type of economic growth and development that has taken place on Mexico's northern border to the impoverished south, while simultaneously strengthening the economic linkages between Mexico and its southern neighbors.

Household Participation in Nonfarm Activities

Of the three communities, households in Plan de Ayala are the most widely engaged in nonfarm activities. Three-quarters of the households surveyed reported receiving contributions of nonfarm income, and this income on average contributed to almost a third of their total income. In contrast, 45 percent and 38 percent of the households surveyed in Torres and Nazareno, respectively, reported receiving income from nonfarm sources. The average contribution of such income to these households was not only less than in Plan de Ayala (averaging around 20 percent) but also more variable from household to household.

The seasonality of rainfed agriculture allows for greater participation of the heads of farm households in secondary-income earning activities in Plan de Ayala and Torres than in Nazareno, where production is year-round and allows little time for income diversification. In Plan de Ayala and Torres, the majority of heads of households reported having secondary occupations, and approximately a third in each community are involved in nonfarm activities. These rates are comparable to de Janvry and Sadoulet's finding that nationally 32 percent of rural heads of households are engaged in nonfarm activities as secondary occupations (de Janvry and Sadoulet 2001). In contrast, only 36 percent of the heads of households surveyed in Nazareno reported having secondary occupations, and only 16 percent of these were engaged in nonfarm activities.

Because diversification into nonfarm activities requires a reallocation of labor, agricultural households will tend to pursue nonfarm activities only when the returns from nonfarm labor exceed those from agriculture, or when nonfarm activities can be pursued without detracting from agricultural production (Ellis 2000). For this reason, the economic activities of all the adults in a household are likely to be a better measure of diversification than simply those of the heads of households. Thirty percent of adults in the surveyed households in Plan de Ayala reported nonfarm activities as their primary occupation compared to only 9 percent of the adult population in Torres and Nazareno. This difference not only suggests a greater availability and access to nonfarm opportunities in Plan de Ayala, but also that nonfarm activities are being developed as a central part of farm-household strategies rather than as an alternative livelihood.

The type of nonfarm activities in which the households were engaged also differed substantially between Plan de Ayala and the other two communities. In Plan de Ayala, nonfarm jobs range from traditional types of temporary manual labor (e.g., construction assistants, drivers, carpentry assistants) to jobs that require some formal training and/or formal education (e.g., factory workers, musicians, teachers, electrical engineers). At the time of the survey, two-thirds of the adults with nonfarm employment in Plan de Ayala worked in these latter types of jobs that tended to require formal education, and of these, half were working in factories. These occupations do not always pay more than agricultural wage work; in fact, the minimum factory wage of thirty-five pesos a day plus benefits in 2000 was less than the agricultural wage of forty-five to fifty pesos a day, but working conditions are often considered more pleasant than in agriculture. In contrast, the majority of the adults with nonfarm wages in Torres and Nazareno tended to be involved in activities that required less formal training and were temporary in nature.

Education, age, and physical location have been identified as important determinants of the importance of nonfarm employment for rural livelihoods (Berdegué, Reardon, and Escobar 2001; de Janvry and Sadoulet 2001; Yúnez-Naude and Taylor 2001). It is quite likely that some of the observed differences among the three communities can be explained in part by these variables, particularly the lack of participation in skilled employment of Torres households. Employment in factories and manufacturing typically requires at least a secondary school education, and often this type of employment is only available to individuals between the ages of eighteen and thirty-two. Without easy access to a secondary school, the households of Torres have the lowest average education levels of the three communities (see chap. 4) (table 9.1).

In one group discussion, I asked the farmers in Torres why no one was working in the factories in the Huamantla Valley. I was told that once a representative from one of the factories of Xicohténcatl II came to Torres and tried to recruit some of the village youth for work. They would be given a training course and then evaluated for jobs. But no one went. When I asked why they had not responded, the farmers shrugged and looked glumly at their feet. The *presidente auxiliar* (the village administrator) volunteered the opinion that the community was lazy and unambitious. He said no one in the community had more than a primary school education, and it was doubtful there were jobs for them. No one contradicted him.

Aside from the presidente auxiliar, in 2000 the four members of the community of Torres with relatively skilled employment were self-employed: two storekeepers, a nurse, and a mule-cart maker. The primary source of nonfarm income for the remainder of the households was from seasonal labor in construction sites or in cement-

Table 9.1 Education and Nonfarm Employment

	Plan de Ayala %	Torres %	Nazareno %
Households with nonfarm income	75	45	38
Heads of household with secondary occupations	75	64	36
Adults in households with secondary school completed	27	7	15

Source: Household survey data, 2000.

block making, both activities that require temporary migration from the community during the dry season.

Differences in education levels are not as sharp between the adults of Plan de Ayala and those of Nazareno, and in general access to education and employment is similar for households in the two communities. In Plan de Ayala, households are aware that the higher-wage jobs of the industrial zone require at least a secondary education, and this knowledge provides an additional motivation for ensuring that their children attend school. I was particularly impressed at how adamant the women are that their girls attend secondary school. Several women commented that they are convinced that families now need two incomes, and that it is really difficult for girls to get a job without a secondary school education.

Despite similar overall education levels, participation in nonfarm activities is far more widespread across households in Plan de Ayala than in Nazareno, and the adult members of farm households in Plan de Ayala have more skilled positions than those of Nazareno. This difference suggests that it is not necessarily education or location that accounts for the differences in nonfarm employment between the communities, but rather the nature of their respective production processes. The next section explores the role of nonfarm income in addressing livelihood risks and uncertainties in these latter two communities, focusing on a subset of households in each community that specialize in nonfarm activities.

Nonfarm Income and Agricultural Risk Management

In Plan de Ayala, the Nonfarm Specialists household group is so named on the basis of the households' *relative* specialization of income in nonfarm activities (representing 49 percent of their total income). As described above, nonfarm activities are important across all households in Plan de Ayala, and, in fact, those households classified as Income Diversified have an average of 51 percent of their income from nonfarm sources. The difference between these households and those labeled Nonfarm Specialists is the lack of diversification into alternative agricultural or off-farm activities of the latter group. The nonfarm economic activities of the Nonfarm Specialists include factory and carpentry employment of some of the younger adult members of the households, with additional income from store management and metalworking.

In Nazareno, the group that is identified in the livelihood classification as Nonfarm Specialists is even less diversified than its counterpart in Plan de Ayala: nonfarm activities contribute on average 66 percent of the total income of the households in this group. For these ten households, their nonfarm activities consist of work as storekeepers, drivers for vegetable trucks, domestic servants, carpenters, or (in one case) a factory worker. Unlike the Plan de Ayala Nonfarm Specialists, the households in Nazareno also tend to report some income from off-farm activities, namely work as day laborers in neighbors' vegetable fields. And, unlike those in Plan de Ayala, Nazareno households' nonfarm activities are almost exclusively the domain of the Nonfarm Specialist households. The contribution of nonfarm activities to the average total income of the other household groups in Nazareno ranges from 0 percent in the class of Large-scale Commercial vegetable producers to 20 percent in the Subsistence Maize households.

Nonfarm Specialists in Plan de Ayala

In Plan de Ayala, specializing in nonfarm activities can be interpreted as representing an alternative—and in many ways, economically equivalent—strategy to the oats and livestock strategy of the Livestock Specialist households discussed in chapter 7. The Nonfarm Specialist households have landholdings that are sufficiently large to allow them to diversify away from maize but perhaps not big enough to support large numbers of livestock (see table 4.4). Yet in terms of the numbers of available working adults and material wealth, the Nonfarm Specialist households are comparable to the Livestock Specialist and Income Diversified household groups, both of which also rely to some extent on nonfarm income. In face of the same constraints of unviable grain markets and frequent crop losses to frost, instead of investing in milk cows, the Nonfarm Specialist households take advantage of the availability of adult labor and the proximity of peri-urban and urban areas to engage in nonagricultural activities.

For example, it is clear that Don Diego benefits from the continued participation of his daughters, now adults with children of their own, in the household's economy, even at the expense of having to share the agricultural harvest with the extended family. Don Diego and other ejidatarios interviewed in Plan de Ayala commented that the income of their working children has been particularly important in paying for their agricultural investments and cash needs during the years of heavy frost losses.

Yet, as is evident in Doña Gaby´s comments and the remarks of others interviewed in the village, the wage income from factory work is not particularly high, and the additional security offered by the factory work is regarded with some ambivalence. Doña Gaby complained: "My daughters work really long hours for little pay—about 45 pesos/day, plus some benefits, but these aren't as good as before. The pay is hardly enough to buy the products they are making. In one of the clothing factories they make women's lingerie. It costs 25 to 30 pesos for a lingerie set. You can hardly buy one set for a day's salary!"

Don Antonio also recognized the symbiotic relationship between the households' agricultural production and nonfarm activities, but was not entirely convinced the outcome was all beneficial. His son has been working in a factory making Wesson auto parts for nearly fifteen years, since he was sixteen. While admitting that the pay is generally low, Don Antonio explained that now that his son has experience and knowledge he has a higher position and the pay is better. And, until there was a change in management, they received generous Christmas bonuses, including rice, sugar, tea, flour, and blankets (Don Antonio's wife brought me a very nice wool blanket from a bed in the next room for me to admire). But then, surprisingly, Don Antonio reflected that it has not really helped to have the factories nearby. "Our lives have gotten worse since they opened," he said. He noted that the cost of transportation has risen. He told me: "Yes, our children can work there, and they do contribute to the household. But it isn't enough money, really. If they had to live on their own, paying rent, taxes, electricity, gas, it wouldn't be enough. They can only work there because they live at home. They don't have to buy or rent land, and they can eat the maize, eggs, meat . . . what we get from the fields. In the cities you have to pay taxes on the land you have, and if our children had to invest in their own land and houses they wouldn't be able to on the salary they are getting. They are paid thirty-three pesos a day. The factories pollute, they don't invest in the land, and they don't pay well."

Like Don Antonio's son, many of the ejido's younger generations tend to remain within the household of their parents while engaging in factory work. The proximity of the factories means that migration is not necessary in order to find employment. This living arrangement not only permits the ejidatario household to benefit from nonagricultural income, but also allows the younger generations to enjoy the benefit of the agricultural harvest. During periods of good harvests, the income from nonfarm activities can be invested in household improvements, equipment, transport, or luxury items. Similarly, the agricultural harvest in many ways subsidizes the factory wages, allowing the factory workers to survive on otherwise minimal pay. During years of poor harvests, the households increase their reliance on the nonfarm income for covering basic household necessities and food.

The relatively easy access of Plan de Ayala households to nonfarm employment contrasts with the experience of Torres households, whose involvement in nonfarm wage labor typically involves seasonal migration and thus transport and living expenses and long absences from the farm. Because of these expenses, the salaries they earn in cement-block manufacturing in the state of Puebla are often sufficient only to ensure the household's survival through the next season. In other words, these farmers were simply "getting by" rather than "getting on" (Davies 1996), illustrating that similar economic activities can have quite different livelihood outcomes depending on the location of a community and the resources available to households (Batterbury 2001; Carswell 2000). The Torres households also lose the benefit of having additional labor available on the farm for planting or other agricultural investments and improvements.

Although heavy reliance on nonfarm income may help households address the economic impact of their losses, it does not necessarily reduce their exposure to climatic hazards. The crop losses of the Nonfarm Specialist households in Plan de Ayala are almost identical to the Maize Surplus households, averaging over 80 percent of their total planted area. Without a large investment in livestock, the Nonfarm Specialists plant, on average, only 15 percent of their total area in oats and the remainder in maize for subsistence, barley, and beans or wheat or both.

It is also possible that the dedication of these households to nonfarm activities may detract somewhat from their investment in agriculture and thus exacerbate their losses. Some of the ejidatarios interviewed, particularly those who had chosen a livestock strategy as the "way forward," were critical of those who were dedicating themselves to alternative, nonagricultural activities. They commented that climate was not the cause of the heaviest crop losses but rather "lack of work" and the failure of households to perform their agricultural labors on time. Some of the strongest criticism came from an elderly ejidatario who, after suffering an eye and foot injury in 1998, has been unable to work in his fields. His son now helps him. "In the years since 1990, there have been some good years," Don Ezequiel told me. "It depends on how you invest and work the land . . . those who don't work hard enough are hit by the climate events. This is what makes the difference. People envy our production, because we work hard and don't have so many problems." Regardless of the underlying cause of the sensitivity of the Nonfarm Specialist households to hazards, it is clear that these households have an advantage over their Maize Surplus neighbors in that they had a source of income relatively insensitive to climate that can help mitigate the economic impact and livelihood disruption of crop losses.

Nonfarm Specialists in Nazareno

The Nonfarm Specialists of Nazareno are households that, like the Subsistence Maize households of the community, lack sufficient irrigated land for participation in commercial vegetable markets (see table 4.5). Although they have nearly double the amount of irrigated land as the households who are dedicated solely to subsistence farming, their total landholdings still averaged less than two hectares, and they tend to devote nearly all of this land to maize and beans. As in Plan de Ayala, it is the availability of at least some adult labor in the household that allows them to enhance their income base. With four to five adults of working age in the Nazareno Nonfarm Specialist households, they have double the adult labor of the Subsistence Maize households.

Although the estimated average income of the Nonfarm Specialist households is at best only half that of the Small-scale Commercial households, in terms of material possessions the household groups are more or less equal. This discrepancy suggests that while the total monetary income of the Nonfarm Specialist household is lower, its livelihood strategy may offer more stability to households (and hence the capacity to accumulate some possessions) than irrigated vegetable production.

One of the challenges for households that are involved in nonfarm activities is integrating these activities into strategies that are otherwise agricultural. In contrast to the situation in Plan de Ayala, where the seasonality of rainfed agriculture and the proximity of factory or peri-urban employment permits a diversification of livelihoods to incorporate both farm and nonfarm activities, in Nazareno nonfarm and farm activities are almost mutually exclusive. The year-round, labor-intensive nature of irrigated production puts considerable demands on the allocation of household labor. Despite the uncertainties and frequent losses experienced by the vegetable-producing households, they cannot afford to spare family members for nonagricultural activities. The expense of hiring labor to replace the family's efforts would make their cost of production soar and their production entirely noncompetitive.

Inevitably, the households that attempt to undertake both commercial agriculture and nonfarm activities run into problems. On a tour of the Nazareno ejido with the comisario ejidal, we saw several fields that appeared to have been abandoned midway through the crop's development. The comisario ejidal attributed the abandoned fields to people in the community with other jobs. "Many are truck drivers or have other sources of income that keep them away from their fields," he said; so they "do not invest as much and sometimes they lose a lot to weeds." But he also reflected that perhaps they don't mind as much because they have another source of income. He shrugged as if to indicate that he found it difficult to criticize them. He said that some farmers are working in order to find a way to get money to invest in their land, and then, because they are working, are too busy to care for it. Thus, because of conflicting demands for labor and time, those households that engage in nonfarm activities tend to be truly "specialists": their nonfarm activities exclude alternative agricultural investments and strategies such as sharecropping (unless they are owners of irrigated land and are able to find others to farm the land for them).

Another significant difference between the participation of Plan de Ayala and Nazareno households in nonfarm activities is the relation of those activities to the local agricultural economy. In Nazareno, 44 percent of the surveyed adults with nonfarm employment reported that they work as either vegetable-truck drivers or village shopkeepers. Both these activities, particularly chauffeuring vegetable trucks, depend on the vitality of the vegetable business in the community. In comparison, few of the adults with nonfarm employment in Plan de Ayala are working in activities that are directly dependent on the agricultural economy or the general prosperity of the village.

At the time of the interviews in 2000, the availability of nonfarm opportunities was changing for Nazareno. The Eastern Puebla Farmers' Association (APOEP), which has strong links to some of the farmers in Nazareno, was participating in the negotiations of the development programs associated with Plan Puebla-Panama in Tecamachalco. According to a spokesperson for APOEP, the rainfed lands of an ejido just a few kilometers from Nazareno were to be purchased for the construction of both the new Plan Puebla-Panama highway and for an associated industrial park. It was hoped by APOEP leaders that the park would provide a source of employment for the youth in the Tecamachalco area and allow the ejidatarios whose land was to be purchased a viable economic alternative. APOEP had contacted a private Israeli firm as a consultant on the park's development in order to promote the use of the park's effluent as irrigation for the remaining ejidal property. Although this park never materialized, in 2005 a large cement factory sprung up in the dusty foothills of an ejido southwest of Nazareno.

Although in 2000, when neither the industrial park nor the cement factory were yet real possibilities, the farmers interviewed were generally positive about the development of industries in their municipio, but unsure how they would directly benefit. In the survey, only one household reported having income from factory employment; however, in independent interviews I discovered there were a few households in which women were employed in maquilas, but these households were typically those that did not have any irrigated land. As in Plan de Ayala, the households in Nazareno expressed some ambivalence about the factory work.

Don Alfonso´s household was a case in point. Don Alfonso's wife, Josefa, and daughter, Juana, were both working in a maquila in the nearby town of Quecholac. Don Alfonso does not have any land of his own and typically sharecrops, if he gets the opportunity. He also runs a small greenhouse in the patio of his house, producing seedlings for transplanting at 10 to 16 pesos per tray. Juana told me that the maquila where they were working was not very good. They were paid very little, about 350 pesos a week for an 11.5-hour day. They sew and have special tasks in the factory. Juana and her mother recounted many stories of maltreatment: people being dismissed without pay, promises of raises that are not kept, and forced overtime. They said that most of the maquilas are foreign owned, although managed by Mexicans. The majority of their fellow workers are women, "even children twelve or fourteen years old."

Even with this critical perspective on their jobs, Juana and Josefa needed the work. They had heard that a new factory was going to open down the road and was going to pay as much as five hundred pesos a week, including the cost of transportation to the factory. They were thinking of switching to that factory, particularly because of the help with transportation costs. Juana was also trying to increase her chances for better employment by attending a high-school equivalency course on Saturdays. On the weekends, when not working in the factories, Juana and her mother help out in the fields her father sharecrops, applying pesticides and weeding.

When I mentioned the possibility of maquila work in interviews with farmers that owned irrigated land, interviewees cited transportation costs to and from Nazareno and the time away from the demands of farming as primary deterrents. After all, I was told, most households can find temporary wage employment in the fields in the immediate vicinity of Nazareno for fifty pesos a day, a wage that some farmers think has been driven up by the presence of maquilas. This upward pressure on the cost of labor makes the contributions of unpaid family members even more valuable.

The vegetable farming households in Nazareno thus face a difficult dilemma. Because of the economic uncertainty of irrigated production and the scarcity of irrigated land, many farmers hope their children will be able to find occupations in nonagricultural activities. Yet in order to finance the education of the next generation and provide them with the full range of opportunities on- and off-farm, they need the full participation of all household members in the daily practice of irrigated agriculture. Thus, while nonfarm income is a way for land-scarce families like Don Alonso's to find economic security, it does not appear to be a viable alternative for those households that are embroiled in the uncertainties and volatility of the vegetable markets.

"Getting on" through Farm and Factory

According to the literature, there are two general motivations for a household's diversification into nonfarm labor. A household may diversify out of necessity in response to "push factors" such as economic crises related to production failures, illness, or other sudden problems, or nonfarm income may be a household's response to the prospects of investment and the proximity of new nonfarm economic opportunities (Carswell 2000; Davies 1996; Hussein and Nelson 1998). Traditionally, in vulnerability analysis, the concern has been with "push factors," the climatic disasters that have driven households to diversify their livelihoods, either temporarily or permanently, into alternative activities. The process of "deagrarianization," as identified by Bryceson, de Janvry and Sadoulet, and others (Bryceson 2002; de Janvry and Sadoulet 2001; Ellis 2000), suggests that understanding the "pull factors"—the changes in the broader economy that provide new opportunities for diversification—may be equally important in understanding the future vulnerability of rural populations.

Mexico's previous two administrations were committed to a maquila model of economic development, a model that has had a transformative effect on the rural landscape. New industrial zones and corridors have improved roads and services to rural areas and offered, for those with the appropriate level of education, a new decentralized source of employment. Despite the uncontrolled population growth along the border states, problems in maintaining standards in working conditions, and accusations of environmental contamination, the Fox administration maintained its faith in the maquila model and with its plan to extend the perceived benefits of this model of development to the more depressed areas of central and southern Mexico through the Plan Puebla-Panama project.

In view of the sensitivity of the rural population to climatic shocks and the seemingly fragile prospects for agriculture in the new liberalized economy, this model can be perceived as providing a way forward for Mexico's campesino households. The capacity of campesino households to survive as farmers increasingly appears to depend on the contribution of nonfarm activities to their livelihoods. This finding is supported by a number of studies that have shown that income diversification from agriculture is not only a response to broader economic reforms that have reduced the profitability of agriculture (Bryceson 2002), but also a means by which households can acquire the resources to continue production (Berdegué, Reardon, and Escobar 2001; Carswell 2000; de Janvry and Sadoulet 2001; Ramírez Juárez 1999). As Batterbury comments on the diversification strategies of Zarma farmers in Niger, "Voluntary diversification . . . can therefore be seen as a way to spread risks, but also to enlarge opportunities for economic gain through juggling different forms of 'capital'" (Batterbury 2001: 441).

The welfare benefits of nonfarm income, however, are not automatic, but rather depend on a household's education levels, access to transportation and sources of employment, and even the productive resources (land, tractors, and water) available to the household. As research in both Africa and Latin America has shown, households with limited landholdings, poor access to sources of employment, and low levels of education are also the least likely to enjoy substantial welfare gains from nonfarm or off-farm employment, although such income may constitute a relatively large proportion of their total incomes (Carswell 2000; Corral and Reardon 2001; de Janvry and Sadoulet 2001; Yúnez-Naude and Taylor 2001). As Carswell argues in her study of Ethiopian rural livelihoods, income diversification as a livelihood *choice* (rather than a necessity for survival) may require a certain degree of security and stability in the household's "mainstay base activity" (Carswell 2000).

In Torres, necessity is driving income diversification, yet socioeconomic marginalization is limiting the capacity of households to gain from their activities. The logistics of committing to regular nonfarm employment from the isolated community of Torres are difficult and costly. Education is an even greater obstacle. In Torres, where 71 percent of adults had no more than a primary school education, a factory job is difficult to obtain. Even in Nazareno, the twelve to fifteen pesos per day for transportation to and from the neighboring towns where the newer maquilas are located is often prohibitive, particularly in relation to the average daily wage of thirty-five to fifty pesos. The greatest obstacle to participation in maquila work in Nazareno, however, is the fact that nonfarm employment competes directly with the intense labor requirements of irrigated production.

In contrast, in Plan de Ayala, it is not simply the Nonfarm Specialists who are acquiring nonfarm income, but rather all households that have the labor to spare for such activities. This income is providing not only a means of year-to-year survival as in Torres but also apparently sufficient stability in income so that the households can begin to accumulate wealth. And it also appears that the presence of the factories is providing new incentives for education in general, and for girls' education in particular.

It is impossible from this study to say how typical the situation is around the industrial zones of Tlaxcala, yet the Plan de Ayala case alone appears to be an example of what de Janvry has called "a modern embodiment of the concept of functional dualism" (de Janvry, Gordillo, and Sadoulet 1997: 204). According to this interpretation of Latin American rural development, the location of factories in semirural locations not only takes advantage of a relatively unskilled, and thus low-wage, working population, but also relies on the fact that this population will most likely have strong links to agricultural communities, which then can partially subsidize the industrial wages through the production and sharing of subsistence crops.

In its current form, the ultimate "functionality" of this dualistic development model for the vitality and security of rural populations is questionable (Nash 1994). As households become increasingly dependent on nonfarm income, they may reduce their sensitivity to climatic variability, but they simultaneously increase their exposure to the volatility of international labor markets. As the research in the three communities wound to a close in December of 2000, the U.S. economic recession was already permeating the Mexican economy. Since then, hundreds of maquilas have closed across Mexico, and the productivity in the subsector declined substantially (INEGI 2004). The maquila development model involved no incentives for the foreign-owned factories to invest in regional infrastructure, in the development of domestic input suppliers, or even in the creation of a domestic demand for their products, so as soon as global economic conditions declined, many factories began to close their doors. By mid-2002, the subsector was employing 20 percent fewer employees than it had in 2000 (INEGI 2004), and some editorials in the popular media were calling the maquila model of development a failure (R. G. Amador, *La Jornada*, 24 May 2002; L. Bendesky, *La Jornada*, 27 May 2002).

The relationship of the ejido of Plan de Ayala to the industries of Xicohténcatl I is also complicated by the fact that the industrial city has been gradually expanding onto the ejido's prime cultivated land. Land was taken from the ejido in the first years of its existence to build the two-lane paved road to the industrial complex site. Then, not long after Salinas initiated the reform of article 27 and the ejido's land was officially titled under PROCEDE, the industrial complex purchased part of the ejido's communal lands for the expansion of its operations. Again, in 1995 (or 1997, depending on the source), the factories Kimberly Clark and Dow Chemical, which bordered the ejido to the east, approached three of the ejidatarios to purchase additional land. These households sold off individual parcels of their agricultural property, receiving around 140,000 pesos to 180,000 pesos from these sales.

In the summer of 2000, the community was in the process of debating the sale of an additional 10.25 ha of land by two ejidatarios to

Kimberly-Clark. Contrary to what I expected, almost all the ejidatarios consulted were of the opinion that the sales were not the result of
farmers' discouragement over crop losses or the lack of productivity
of their land, although it is difficult to imagine that such issues did
not play into the decisions. Instead they reported that the farmers
who were selling land were those who were no longer interested in
farming or had succumbed to the "love of money."

Regardless of the motivation for the sale, it is obvious that the
government's land titling program, PROCEDE, and its rural industrialization policy are transforming Plan de Ayala, but perhaps not in
the way that the program was first marketed to farmers. The titling
process is not resulting in private sector–ejido agricultural partner-
ships or in increased access to formal credit, or in the accumulation
of land by more ambitious farmers. Instead, it is resulting in the loss
of relatively productive agricultural land—flat, fertile, and appropriate for mechanization—to a foreign-owned industry.

Some of the ejido's founding members are disturbed by this trend,
feeling that the moral and ideological motivations for the lifestyle
they have chosen are being undermined. Yet many of the youth and
even some of the elders think that the gradual conversion of landscape into industrial zones and satellite settlements is the region's
inevitable future. Some farmers I interviewed predicted almost un-
emotionally that the residential area of the ejido would remain in the
hands of the ejidatarios or their offspring, but that the ejido would
gradually sell itself out of agriculture. As an adaptation to changing
economic opportunities and increasing agricultural uncertainties,
this process seems to be not only inevitable, perhaps, but also desir-
able. Yet, if the success of this development model depends in part
on the continued capacity of the rural population to provide for its
own subsistence, buying farm households out of agriculture without
viable livelihood alternatives to sustain them may only increase economic marginalization, reproducing the chaos of urban poverty that
has characterized Mexico's border cities.

Once again, it is clear that there is no single answer, or one livelihood strategy, that rises above all others as the solution to rural
environmental and economic uncertainties. Instead, programs that
expand the range of livelihood choices available to households appear more promising. Education, for example is a critical asset for a

household to be able to diversify and respond to new opportunities in Mexico's changing economy. Without accessible schools and sufficient cash income to invest in human capital, households will have limited flexibility to cope with change and agricultural uncertainty.

It is also clear that in the immediate future there is a continued role for small-scale agricultural production in the three communities. Just as maize has formed the foundation for agricultural intensification with livestock and has provided an insurance strategy for households entering risky vegetable markets, the benefits of nonfarm activities for the rural households appear to be maximized within (rather than instead of) an agricultural context. Those households that, through a combination of labor, land, livestock, and location, have been able to take advantage of strategies of both agricultural intensification *and* economic diversification are likely to be those that are in the best position to adapt to tomorrow's uncertainties. In the current social and economic context, the alternative scenario, forcing rural households to choose between agriculture and nonfarm wage employment, may simply result in a geographic and sectoral shift of vulnerability that does little to facilitate the adaptive capacity of Mexico's farmers.

10   Flexibility, Stability, and Adaptive Capacity

Agricultural activities, and the individuals and households that depend wholly or partly on agriculture for their survival, are assumed to be vulnerable to climatic variability and change because agricultural production is fundamentally and inextricably linked to the biophysical environment. The sensitivity of crop production to changes in climatic variables has been repeatedly measured and scientifically modeled (IPCC Working Group II 2001). Yet making the leap from the sensitivity of biophysical systems to the vulnerability of farmers and farm systems is not always straightforward, precisely because of the complexity of the organization of farmers' lives, their perceptions and responses to the risks they face, and the values, priorities, beliefs, and ambitions that affect what they do on a daily basis.

From a smallholder's perspective, it is quite difficult to separate climate vulnerability from broader social vulnerability. Farm households are vulnerable to climatic variability and change not only because their crops are dependent on rainfall, soil humidity, and temperature. They are also vulnerable because the range of choice and opportunity they face at any given time is not infinite, and in many cases quite narrow. They are vulnerable because they are simultaneously adjusting to a diversity of uncertainties, shocks, and stresses originating from very dynamic political-economic circumstances as well as from the physical environment. In the current phase of economic globalization, market risks in particular can have unexpected and synergistic implications both for the climate impacts that households experience and for their capacity to cope and, eventually, to adapt.

The economic and institutional context of production is fundamental to understanding vulnerability, and this context is perhaps even more volatile and dynamic than the climatic factors that concern us (Adger 1999: 250). In fact, climatic factors play a relatively minor role in the livelihood strategies of households in the three communities compared with the various other nonclimatic stresses they face daily. Thus it would be erroneous to assume that those households whose crops are most sensitive to climate and most frequently exposed to climate risk are necessarily always the most vulnerable, or that such households can and will have the capability to spontaneously adapt to changes in climate patterns.

In the case of Mexican smallholder agriculture, there are numerous nonclimatic factors that can be considered as structuring vulnerability, ranging from soil erosion and deforestation to the new political plurality in Mexico's government. This book has focused primarily on one nonclimatic dimension of the vulnerability context: neoliberal agricultural reform as a manifestation of the process of economic globalization in Mexico. Proponents of neoliberal economic philosophy argue that with less government intervention, less market regulation, and greater freedom in national and international markets, society should gain. Producers are rewarded for the quality of their products and their comparative market advantages, consumers are assured of the lowest prices, and everyone benefits from more choice, more information, and a higher quality of living.

In theory, the realization of these benefits would appear to reduce vulnerability, at least in an aggregate sense. Undistorted markets may better reflect food demand and improve access to necessary commodities, improving standards of living and overall resilience of poor populations. If free markets are truly more efficient in distributing resources and goods, then overall access to financial and material resources should improve. Handmer, Dovers, and Downing (1999) point out that globalization may increase the strength of international institutions, improve access to insurance, and guarantee human rights—all outcomes that, theoretically, empower populations and increase their capacities to respond positively to change. Yet they and others have also pointed out that the process of globalization is far from uniform, and the benefits are not equally distributed, often with the net effect of *increasing* the marginalization of populations already sensitive to environmental change (Adger 1999; Handmer, Dovers, and Downing 1999; O'Brien and Leichenko 2000).

In Mexico, it is arguable that greater market openness has brought about improved access to some imported commercial goods, and greater general access to information, and it has in part driven a movement toward greater public transparency and political pluralism. As discussed in chapter 9, new incentives for foreign investment have also brought new employment opportunities to some rural areas. Yet so far, at least for the smallholders who were formerly heavily dependent on the public sector for credit, technical assistance, and the marketing of their produce, the benefits of neoliberalism *within the agriculture sector* have not been realized.

There are purportedly new commercial opportunities in niche markets and high-value commodity production, but as the experiences of Nazareno and Plan de Ayala households demonstrated, the quality, volume, and consistency standards for production are high, and access to markets is highly competitive. Basic information about these markets is often lacking for farmers who produce sufficient surplus to commercialize their harvests. For most farmers, production costs have steadily escalated, while the resources to facilitate commercialization and participation in the new agricultural economy have contracted.

Ironically, at the same moment that the agricultural sector was being divided by policy makers into farmers with commercial potential (those who have preferential access to agricultural services) and those without, farmers all over Mexico were also hit with successive droughts, floods, and anomalous frosts that destroyed their harvests and made it even more difficult to meet the requirements of production consistency, volume, and quality necessary for commercial competitiveness. As a result, although a small percentage of farmers have managed to find innovative ways of participating in the new agricultural markets, many, if not the majority, have been excluded, and indeed may now be considered "doubly vulnerable" (O'Brien and Leichenko 2000).

As many others have observed, vulnerability is not an outcome of failed adaptation but rather an ongoing *process*, a condition that is constantly changing and exists whether or not exogenous shocks or stresses bring it into sharp definition (Adger 1999; Kelly and Adger 2000; Ribot 1996). The current moment of rural transformation and political and economic change in Mexico provides an ideal opportunity to explore how farmers are navigating multiple sources of uncertainty and are weighing diverse risks to the basis of their subsistence in their everyday decisions (Nash 1994). Just as it is in moments of social change that vulnerability becomes most obvious, it is also in such moments that the daily livelihood decisions of thousands of farmers take on greater significance and become the bricks and mortar of sector adaptation.

Vulnerability in Central Mexico

Other research on vulnerability has illustrated that economically marginal populations—those with limited access to resources and limited entitlements—are typically also the most vulnerable to climate hazards, and thus often assumed to be the most vulnerable to climatic change (Chen 1994; Downing, Watts, and Bohle 1996; Ribot 1996). The livelihood strategies pursued by the farmers in Plan de Ayala, Torres, and Nazareno do not contest this assumption, but rather highlight the complexity of poverty and vulnerability at the local level in the context of a rapidly changing agricultural sector and national economy. The case studies illustrate that within generally marginalized populations, not all resources and assets are equal; location matters, and the particular ways households relate to the institutions that govern their economic activities make a difference in their vulnerability.

Average income, for example, does not appear to be as important an indicator of adaptive capacities as the flexibility and range of choice provided by particular resources and the overall stability of livelihoods, as reflected in their material wealth and assets. Poor households, such as those of Plan de Ayala that have managed to stabilize their income through a diversity of activities, may be far less vulnerable than households with comparable potential incomes yet whose income is highly variable and whose livelihood strategies are relatively inflexible.

These three concepts—resource access, livelihood flexibility, and stability—are key attributes of adaptive capacity. These three factors are also similar to those that have been recently identified as central to understanding the persistence of rural poverty and the potential for sustainable development, illustrating the strong conceptual links between sustainability, vulnerability, and adaptive capacity (see Bebbington 1999; Ellis 2000; Mortimore and Adams 1999; Scoones 1998; Turner II et al. 2003). Adjustment to dynamic risks is less likely to be successful where choices are limited by lack of available technology, limited land, failures in research, inaccessible credit or insurance, poor transportation, or simply such a high degree of livelihood insecurity that the quickest and most secure route to survival is the only option. A certain degree of livelihood stability, existing without rigidity, offers households the capacity to plan and, with planning, the potential to adjust to future risks or to mobilize to take advantage of new challenges.

In circumstances where there is no assured market for staple crops (although consumer prices have steadily risen), where access to the markets for commercial alternatives is difficult if not impossible, and where the government's rural development policy focuses not on agricultural production but rather "maquilization," being adaptive means having the capacity both to intensify agricultural activities and to diversify economically into activities that are, by definition, less sensitive to the variability and uncertainties of the agricultural sector.

The experience of Plan de Ayala's farmers illustrates that access to nonfarm economic activities is quite important in improving the stability of household economies. Abandoning agriculture, however, is not the solution to rural uncertainty. Although deagrarianization may very well be a long-term solution for many households, in the current environment of high climatic variability and policy uncertainty, a household's diversification into both agricultural *and* nonfarm activities gives it an advantage. This conclusion supports a growing consensus among development practitioners and scholars of rural areas that *diversification matters*, not only for household survival but also for poverty alleviation, rural resilience, and sustainability (Batterbury 2001; Bryceson 2002; Ellis 2000; Francis 2000; Mortimore and Adams 1999).

The cases of Plan de Ayala, Nazareno, and Torres suggest that a certain amount of agricultural flexibility and intensification is necessary in order for households to diversify economically in a pattern that offers them not simply a survival strategy, but a way forward toward increasing stability and security. The challenge for households

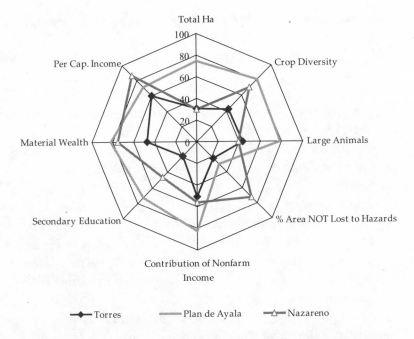

Figure 10.1 Comparison of resources for adaptation. This diagram compares all households in the three communities except the outlier in Nazareno—whose total income distorted the mean of the remaining households—and the outlier household in Los Torres, whose landholding size and income also distorted the mean. The axes represent a uniform scale of 1 to 100 where each point represents the distance of the average value in relation to a maximum value, here defined as the maximum of value of the variable observed in the three communities plus the standard deviation of those three values. *Source*: Household survey data, 2000.

in Mexico's current policy environment is to find the means to pursue such a path.

In the specific context of rural Puebla-Tlaxcala at the turn of the twentieth century, adaptive capacity is associated with a suite of key resources: having sufficient land for one's own subsistence, livestock to provide stability and access to cash, and the education, social connections, and support to take advantage of one's resources and to engage in diversified and occasionally innovative livelihood arrangements. As illustrated in the radar diagram above (fig. 10.1), if the communities are compared in terms of indices of these key resources, it is clear that the majority of households of Torres, with limited landholdings, few animals beyond what is required for production purposes, and limited education, are at a disadvantage.

In the context of Mexico's rapidly transforming economy, access to educational infrastructure is also increasingly critical, perhaps fundamental, to enhancing adaptive capacity to both climatic and economic change. Agronomists and rural development specialists have long known that farmers with higher education are more apt to be receptive to new technologies and adjust more rapidly to change. Educated individuals may also be more likely to be empowered to use institutions and networks to their advantage. In the three case studies, the households with educated adult members are more likely to be those who are complementing their own production with remunerative nonfarm activities, or, in the case of the Fernández family of Torres, for example, are the ones that proactively are addressing both agricultural uncertainties and market opportunities through new entrepreneurial projects.

Households in Nazareno, with the advantage of access to irrigation, are able to reach higher average per capita income levels than their small-scale counterparts in Torres, but their material assets and level of education suggest that the particular demands of vegetable production and the uncertainties in the vegetable markets are at least in part inhibiting them from obtaining the same security of livelihood or undertaking the diversity of activities that are observed in Plan de Ayala.

Although the households in Plan de Ayala have experienced losses similar to those reported by households in Torres, they are more likely to have higher levels of education, larger landholdings, and sufficient animals to complement their income. These resources allow the ejidatarios to make subtle adjustments to their livelihood strategies to cope with climate impacts, such as shifting the emphasis of their income-generating activities from agricultural to nonfarm sources.

None of these resources, either alone or together, represent a recipe for adaptation. As Bebbington argues, assets "are not simply resources . . . they are also the basis of agents' power to act and to reproduce, challenge or change the rules that govern the control, use, and transformation of resources" (Bebbington 1999: 2022). If a household is not able to use its assets to transform its strategies and reinvent its relationship to the institutions that structure its activities, then it is far less likely to be able to negotiate proactively and adapt to environmental and social change. While neither livestock nor education nor having nine hectares instead of four guarantees better livelihood outcomes, these resources do appear to provide households with the opportunity to flexibly negotiate new risks as they arise and evolve.

In a manner similar to the "three-step livelihood diversification" process that Mortimore and Adams (1999) observed in the Sahel, the livelihood strategies of the three communities can also be considered in sequential terms, where landed households slowly accumulate resources (not only material, but also human resources, social connections, financial stocks, etc.) and thus gradually build strategies that are characterized by increasing flexibility and a progressively broader range of choice in the face of any particular crisis (fig. 10.2). The fact that the patterns of subsequent and cumulative adaptive strategies observed in the Puebla-Tlaxcala Valley are relatively similar to what has been observed in the African Sahel (Batterbury and Forsyth 1999; Mortimore and Adams 1999) suggests that such strategies may be broadly characteristic of smallholders farming in marginal environments.

For example, having a minimum of land for subsistence can be considered the foundation of the infrastructure of adaptive capacity for the smallholder farmers in these case studies. Although the technocratic vision of Mexico's rural sector characterizes subsistence production as a sign of poor productivity, nonviability, and inefficiency, its persistence and in many cases intensification may indicate that it should be viewed instead as a core component of the resilience of the rural sector. The capacity to use subsistence production as an asset to access other strategies and resources, however, requires a certain amount of land. Households with minimal landholdings (such as the majority in Torres) or with land of particularly poor quality (such as those who have only rainfed land in Nazareno) lack the basis on which to begin to accumulate wealth and resources to construct a more stable, flexible, and resilient livelihood.

With sufficient land, it may be possible for a household to begin to move beyond a subsistence base and support small numbers of livestock through crop diversification (as in Plan de Ayala), invest-

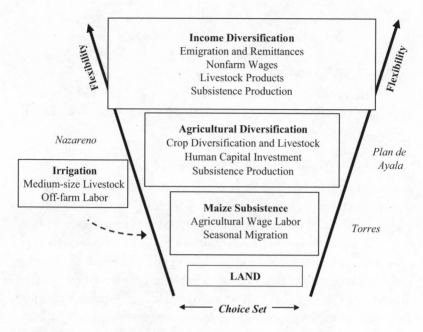

Figure 10.2 Livelihood diversity and flexibility.

ment in commercial crops (as in Nazareno), or in the production of sufficient maize to guarantee more than one season of consumption. These strategies increase the flexibility of households' livelihood strategies and choices and provide more liquidity and security against shocks and hazards as well as capacity to begin investments in such things as secondary school education.

With time, investment in human capital and livestock pays off, allowing diversification into more remunerative nonfarm employment (higher-skilled positions) on a consistent basis. This type of diversification is particularly important because, with nonfarm employment, households enter into a mix of activities that are not necessarily covariate with either climatic risk or agricultural volatility (Adger 1999). Through simultaneous agricultural intensification (crop diversity and livestock) and income diversification, households gain increasing flexibility and, theoretically, adaptive capacity.

Of course it would be simplistic to argue that land, or alternatively greater productivity of land resources (as under irrigation), is the only ingredient necessary to start households on a path toward increasing security and flexibility. As the case of Nazareno illustrates, not all modes of agricultural intensification appear to increase the resilience of rural households. These farmers are inextricably embedded in the free-market and competitive system that has been promoted in Mexico as the solution to the stagnation of the rural economy. Despite their potential for economic gain, the vegetable farmers of Nazareno are perhaps even more vulnerable than their rainfed counterparts. Not only are they still, despite irrigation, sensitive to climatic variability, but this sensitivity is exacerbated by their simultaneous exposure to market risk, both in their use of commercial inputs and in the commercialization of their harvests. Their commitment to irrigation also constrains their ability to diversify into nonfarm activities that might lessen the overall sensitivity of their incomes to the instabilities of irrigated agriculture. For this reason, the irrigation strategies of Nazareno farmers are in constant risk of sudden collapse or retreat into a subsistence strategy that mirrors what is pursued by the more economically marginal households of Torres.

Physical location and the geography of rural development are also instrumental in enhancing the range of choice available to any household, particularly in the current context of rural industrialization, minifundismo, and deagrarianization (Bryceson 1996; de Janvry and Sadoulet 2001). Not only are households in Torres more distant from such essential services as secondary school education, but they also have more difficult access to peri-urban employment opportunities (carpentry, construction, chauffeuring, domestic work) and even to local agricultural markets and services. For these households, the cost of coping with hazards and adjusting to changes in the economic viability of agriculture is exacerbated by the lack of alternative economic opportunities within their community or locality. A nationwide cultural trend toward more urban tastes and preferences has undermined the pulque cottage industry, denying Torres residents their only local source of off-farm income. The combination of this loss and sequential years of poor harvests has forced Torres residents to search out of state for wage income, at considerably greater disruption and cost.

In all three communities it is also clear that the household continues to be particularly valuable as an economically adaptive unit. As Netting illustrated through numerous case studies of smallholder agriculture, the smallholder farm household is "the scene of economic allocation, arranging collectively for the food, clothing, and shelter of its members, and seeking to provide for these needs over the long term with some measure of security against the uncontrollable disruptions of the climate, the market economy, and the state" (Netting 1993: 59). Households that have found a strategy that affords some stability and resilience are also often those that are drawing on the resources of an extended family, all residing within the agriculturally based household. In years of poor harvest, greater emphasis is placed on the contributions of members with nonagricultural wage employment or off-farm (e.g., tractor rental) activities. In years of so-called normal harvests, the household can "get ahead" with investments in equipment, luxury items, or household infrastructure, gradually improving its standard of living. The permanent migration of some household members (as long as some working adults remain) enhances the flexibility of this strategy by providing periodic influxes of remittance income.

This strategy is most widely observed in Plan de Ayala, where the ejido's urban properties and relatively large landholdings, as well as its location on the fringes of a large industrial complex and a commercial town, enable households to expand intergenerationally without undermining their capacity for social reproduction. Although almost every household surveyed in Plan de Ayala reported that some of its members had permanently left to start new households, either within the same ejido or in nearby cities and towns, the households with the highest assets also have relatively large numbers of working adults living in the farm home. Increasingly, researchers of Latin American rural development are emphasizing the adaptive advantage of being able to diversify economically while retaining, and even strengthening, a rural identity and residence (Bebbington 1999). The proximity of Plan de Ayala to urban centers not only decreases the cost of accessing employment opportunities but also allows the ejido to remain relatively intact as an institution. In fact, the benefits of nonfarm employment for the households may depend on the ejido's continued existence.

In contrast, relatively few households in the other two communities appear to be pursuing this type of diversified strategy, largely because of the physical and location constraints in Torres and the intensive labor demands of irrigated agriculture in Nazareno. The drain of adult labor from rural areas through migration not only threatens the viability of labor-intensive production and resource-management practices, but also, because their labor is elsewhere, prevents rural households from directly participating in the regional development of other economic sectors through nonfarm and farm linkages. Even while a substantial flow of remittance income helps such communities enhance consumption, secure inputs, or insure against losses, a lack of viable employment or sources of income within easy access to rural areas may further polarize development paths in Mexico and lead to greater social marginalization of rural communities.

In his study of rural Vietnam, Neil Adger discusses the concept of "collective vulnerability," where inequality between households can either accentuate or mitigate the overall vulnerability of the households within a community (Adger 1999). In the central Mexico case studies, there is some evidence that in communities such as Torres, interhousehold resource inequalities have historically been somewhat beneficial to the community. The two or three wealthy households that were the pulque processors were also those that were able to provide a source of income for the remaining households that collected aguamiel from the maguey plants that bordered their fields. Yet when this market declined, the pulque processors had the social connections, education, and diversified resource base to enter into new activities while the remaining households were left with few options. The rise and fall of pulque processing in Torres illustrates how the collective vulnerability of a community can vary over time as exogenous factors force changes in the internal economic and social relationships within a community.

In Nazareno, inequalities in access to irrigated land and landholding sizes, as well as year-round production, facilitate coping strategies in the community. This inequality ensures that internally the community has an active labor market in which ready cash can be made by vegetable harvesting, weeding, or other agricultural labor. Farmers who face heavy losses can lend out their land to sharecroppers, given the perpetual demand for irrigated land. The volatile fortunes of Nazareno's vegetable farmers also ensure that income levels and livelihoods are relatively fluid: a vegetable farmer today can easily be a day laborer tomorrow, or even a migrant laborer, depending on his or her luck. For this reason, although at any given time particular subsets of the Nazareno community may exhibit high vulnerability and minimal flexibility, collectively the community is probably far better off than a community such as Torres, in the face of the types of socioeconomic changes now occurring in rural Mexico.

It is apparent that the vulnerability and adaptive capacity of the farm households will be a function of their relationship to markets for both inputs and outputs, their sense of security in assuring their basic needs from season to season, the resources and opportunities offered by their location and community, the strength of local institutional networks—be they formal producer associations, the ejido institution, or ethnic organizations—and the degree of diversification of their livelihood systems. While agricultural systems can be considered on a continuum of commercial orientation and scale and in terms of the potential for producing agricultural income, their vulnerability cannot be mapped linearly on the basis of these indicators.

For example, one could consider the vulnerability of some Nazareno households, at some points in time, to be on par with that of the majority of households in Torres, despite, indeed because of, substantial differences in commercial orientation and market involvement. Torres households are classically vulnerable in the sense of being physically, socially, and economically marginal and thus lacking in the necessary resources to mitigate the hazards they face. In contrast, Nazareno households face a different problem: rather than marginalized, they are deeply involved in volatile agricultural markets. They are vulnerable because in these markets they tend to bear the totality of risk. Planting commercial vegetables requires substantial labor and financial commitments and thus gives them little space to adapt to change. Of course the dynamic nature of livelihood outcomes in Nazareno can also be a strength: while some households struggle with losses, others may have "played the lottery" well, providing income-earning options for others.

In order to understand the complexity of the interaction of market risks, political-economic change, and climatic variability, this analysis of vulnerability should be extended to new case studies of still different production systems. Large-scale commercial farmers who produce one or two crops in large volumes are likely to be particularly vulnerable to both market risk (particularly in relation to changes in specific commodity policies) and climatic hazards, but may also have the formal institutional support (e.g., insurance, credit, market contracts, price supports) to mitigate impacts and share risks (Eakin et al. forthcoming). In contrast, small-scale coffee farmers who, under the encouragement of public policy have replaced all subsistence crops with coffee, are inextricably tied to the fluctuations of a particular international commodity market and are less likely to have the same institutional support or livelihood diversity that might help them manage risks (Adger, Eakin, and Winkels forthcoming; Eakin, Tucker, and Castellanos 2005). When these characteristics of scale, institutional context, and market relations are considered together with environmental risks, it is clear that vulnerability is neither static nor linear in nature, and thus assumptions about the uniformity of agricultural risk and the capacity of rural populations to adapt must be made with considerable caution.

Policies for Adaptation or Adaptive Policy?

The broad institutional environment in which farmers make their livelihood decisions determines how they perceive signals of climate change as well as the range of resources they have available to address climatic risk. As adaptation receives more attention in debates over climate change, it will be even more important to understand the dynamics of the institutional environment in creating and reducing vulnerability. Although there is an urgent need for official recognition of climate change and climate risk in national and state policy-making, and specific programs and policies will undoubtedly be required in order to address the problem of climate change in national contexts, it would be unfortunate if "climate policy" were to be created entirely separately from policy to encourage rural economic stability, agricultural sustainability, improved management of natural resources, or greater equity in economic opportunity.

One of the challenges in addressing climatic change and variability through development policy is that the questions "to what are we adapting?" and "who adapts?" remain ambiguous. In the dynamic social and environmental circumstances of Mexico, the answers to these questions are constantly evolving. Smallholder farming is not an activity that is attracting Mexico's youth. Rural landscapes are being transformed through remittances, necessity, new opportunity, and the information age. Any climate scenario projecting increased climatic variability would imply that Mexico's populations will need to adapt to a variety of climate outcomes simultaneously. With such uncertain scenarios for the future, perhaps the best hope is to pursue development policies that encourage a diversity of alternative paths toward growth and stability, based on what is already working well for vulnerable populations.

Instead of searching for the ideal or optimal agricultural adaptation to projected change—be it oats instead of maize, earlier planting, or more efficient irrigation—perhaps the goal should be to create adaptive policies, policies that evolve over time with the changing goals and vulnerability of populations, while maintaining the overall objective of improving the range of choices available and the long-term sustainability of rural livelihoods. In other words, although it may be difficult, even unwise, to propose specific adaptations to climate and socioeconomic circumstances not yet known or experienced, it may be possible to use analyses of climate trends and simulations of climate change to avoid making decisions that will result in a narrower range of choices for the future.

Ironically, although the aims of neoliberalism are to *increase* choice and opportunity by removing obstacles to the efficient functioning of markets, in practice the types of policies implemented in Mexico under the broad framework of neoliberalism may be having the opposite effect for smallholders. The persistence of the belief that one model of production—capital intensive, large scale, and run as part of the global food industry—is the future of agriculture leads naturally to policies that ease the functioning of such agribusinesses, although it may do so at the expense of rural economic security for the farmers who are following more traditional agricultural models.

It is important to recognize that the policy decision to orient public support for production only toward farmers who fall within a narrow definition of *commercially viable* has significant welfare and economic consequences for those who are by definition excluded. If smallholder agriculture has truly been written off, then the opportunities to develop viable alternative (rural) livelihood strategies must be supported. If, however, the evidence from the central Mexico case studies described in this study holds true more generally, then in the near future small-scale agriculture still has a role to play, perhaps not as an economic force in its own right, but as a potential springboard into other activities for the younger generations in rural areas. Facilitating processes of economic diversification that do not undermine the fundamental viability of family-farm production not only helps households deal with the environmental uncertainties that have persistently faced agriculture, but also conversely provides rural households with the subsistence security (maize, beans, and livestock) to mediate survival in the evolving economy.

In order to facilitate adaptive responses of households to the environmental changes that they experience—in other words, to expand their coping range over time—it is thus critical to recognize the importance of nonagricultural and local off-farm activities in the livelihoods of rural households and the contribution of these activities to the viability of their agricultural security (Bebbington 1999; de Janvry and Sadoulet 2001). Rural education, such as is being promoted in Mexico through the PROGRESA/Oportunidades program, may eventually make a substantial contribution to the capacity of households to broaden the range of choices available to them and thus their capacity to address stresses and shocks.

Yet trends such as the conversion of agricultural land—land that is actually fertile and amenable to mechanized agriculture as in Plan de Ayala—to factory construction and industrial use are perplexing. The land-titling program, PROCEDE, is facilitating this land conversion, propelled by the neoliberal idea that the market can decide the most efficient use of the rural landscape. Yet if the story of Plan de Ayala reflects other development patterns in the region, the "efficiency" of this policy implicitly depends on the availability of local subsistence food production and the ejido landholdings to subsidize industrial wages and livelihoods. In this sense, the institution of the ejido is not necessarily slowing down the process of rural development (as the reform of article 27 might have us believe), but in some cases may be one source of rural resilience.

It is important to separate agricultural outcomes and trends from those of rural areas and livelihoods. In fact, Bebbington goes so far as to argue that livelihood patterns that allow households to maintain their rural residencies permit the continued reproduction of cultural practices associated with specific places, and that this "cultural capital" can alone play a significant role in providing meaning and a source of empowerment to rural households, regardless of agricultural efficiency or productivity (Bebbington 1999: 2034). Thus the gradual expansion of rural industry onto agricultural lands at the expense of local production may prove counterproductive by undermining the types of rural livelihood strategies that appear to be most constructive for managing risk and adapting to change.

Given that the era of agrarian reform has been given its postmortem in Mexico (DeWalt, Rees, and Murphy 1994), and that the promotion of economically competitive land use appears to be central to current development policy, expanding the size of agricultural landholdings to permit the type of diversification and flexibility that was observed in Plan de Ayala is unlikely and unfeasible. There are, however, other ways in which the current development programs might be managed so that rural adaptive capacity is not undermined but rather enhanced, while economic objectives are maintained. A few case studies have shown that when rural populations have been empowered to participate in the changing economy on their own terms and at their own pace, they have been able to do so in ways that may even have increased their sense of local identity and reinforced their traditional practices (Bebbington 1993, 1996; Nigh 1997; Wilkinson 1997). Yet such participation and empowerment will be difficult if large segments of the rural population are dismissed as having "no commercial potential" and thus no rural future.

If rural industrial growth is going to be a future focus of Mexico's economic policy, then such policies need to provide better support for the flexibility and adaptive capacity of the rural populations that will supply the industries with cheap labor. Mutually beneficial relationships between farmers and industry might allow farmers to take advantage of recycled water for irrigation, for example. If industries could be encouraged to invest in local education, agricultural extension, or roads and market infrastructure, their actions would facilitate the development of a diversified rural economy, particularly one that includes subsistence and regional commercial agriculture; such involvement might also improve industries' production processes and lower their transaction costs. For such far-sighted investment to occur, industries would have to be interested in more than taking advantage of cheap labor, and regional and national governments would need to value the rural sector as a source of human capital, environmental services, and even agricultural innovation.

In terms of specific agricultural adaptations—more climatically appropriate crops, flexibility in the timing of planting, diversification into livestock activities, better management of land and water resources, and perhaps the use of climate information for agricultural planning—it is clear that the production practices currently pursued by farmers should not be considered part of the problem but rather a source of solutions. The farmers of the three communities are pursuing the strategies that make the most sense according to their subsistence and livelihood priorities and their resources and opportunities. To enhance the capacity of these households to respond to climate variability and change, it would be more constructive to work within the structure of these strategies, rather than seek to change them entirely.

In this perspective, useful and practical investments to promote adaptive capacity in agriculture might entail, for example, research into rapid-maturing maize varieties that tend to resist frost impacts and irregular rainfall, are preferred food crops, and also have commercial value. Colored maize already has a niche market in Mexico City and perhaps even abroad, should farmers be able to gain access to the market and produce the quality of harvest necessary. While there was little attention to climatic sensitivity in the initial maize breeding programs of the Green Revolution, in recent years "drought resistance" has once again surfaced on the agenda of Mexican academic institutions such as the University of Chapingo, international organizations such as the Center for Research on Improved Maize and Wheat (CIMMYT), as well as local nongovernmental organizations. Far more could be done if federal and state governments more actively supported such initiatives. It is less likely that these projects will flourish on a broader scale if such support is left to private sector agribusiness.

Efforts to help commercialize locally produced milk and cheese might also provide households with diversification opportunities while not threatening their subsistence base. In its policy documents, Tlaxcala's agriculture ministry recognizes the importance of livestock as a "complement" to rural livelihoods and incomes, and promotes improved livestock management, breeding, and marketing through the Alianza program. Yet access to this support is not easy, and the current paucity of technical assistance and poor market infrastructure inhibits investment by depressing the prices farmers receive for the animal, meat, or milk sales.

The current emphasis of the Fox administration on agro-enterprise and commodity-chain development could conceivably be supportive of such initiatives, if, and only if, the smallholders who might benefit from such programs are not dismissed from the start as lacking in productive potential. Support for local markets is critical: the future of Mexico's farmers cannot depend on opportunities with multinational agribusinesses or international markets alone. A further obstacle is the reluctance of farmers to make the transition from being smallholder producers of raw agricultural produce to small-scale business owners of agricultural products. This transition not only requires some training to meet product standards and access specialized markets, but it also requires farmers to establish themselves as taxable businesses under Mexico's fiscal authorities (Secretaría de Hacienda). While this change may seem a formidable task, the success of PROCEDE, the land-titling program, suggests that when public resources are dedicated to informing rural households of their options, and when support is provided for technical assistance, households are not entirely resistant to change.

For those households that are already trying to survive in Mexico's increasingly competitive markets, policies that help such farmers reduce their cost of production and improve their access to the information they need for making their decisions not only enhance their contribution to the local economy but give them the extra margin of flexibility to better manage both climatic and economic risks. The pursuit of economic comparative advantage and a competitive edge need not be at the expense of rural security. As the story of Don José illustrates, smallholder farmers such as those of Nazareno are in good position to apply labor-intensive production techniques such as organic agriculture (and thus diminish their risk of debt and economic crisis after crop losses), but their livelihoods would be that much stronger if they also had access to preferential prices, niche markets, credit, insurance, and agricultural extension to enhance and reward their efforts. And without a broader vision of seasonal price variations, market demand, or climate variability, the most considered decisions of the vegetable farmers are often undermined. Without access to such information, planning, whether for the next month, the next year, or the next five years, is nearly impossible.

"Es Otra Libertad"

Despite significant advances in modeling climate processes and the physics of climate change, anticipating the direction and pace of social change remains in the realm of science fiction. Yet rather than ignore the dynamic social context of our decision making, or simplify it to a narrow suite of indicators of economic growth and population, we must directly confront and attempt to map its complexity. There are many ways to go about such research, and the debate continues over what combination of methods, whether statistical and physical models, historical analogues, detailed ethnographies, or some other approach, is most appropriate for understanding our collective vulnerability and possible futures. All these methods and approaches add some new knowledge and provoke discussion. There is a need, however, to remember that ultimately the future is constructed by the daily decisions of a multitude of actors, ranging from subsistence farmers to world leaders, and we cannot begin to grasp the meaning of our future vulnerability if we do not understand the decision-making processes.

I have found that one of the best ways to appreciate farmers' decisions and strategies is by working directly with them. This means sitting at their tables to share tortillas and black beans, discussing school fees, production costs, and family illnesses; hiking to their fields to see frost-damaged maize or a new crop of peaches; washing, picking, and packing zucchini for market and then experiencing the disappointment of receiving "no price"; attending school graduations and weddings; and lots of mutual patience and listening. I now feel I have begun to understand the daily lives, dreams, and frustrations of a very small number of households in central Mexico. When we are faced with large uncertainties about the future, coupled with the urgency to act now, the knowledge and experience of these and other farmers like them can provide the basic elements from which we can begin to construct a realistic understanding of the meaning of change and adaptation, and an idea of what might be required to mitigate vulnerability over the longer term.

Rural livelihoods are the obvious place to start building grounded theories of the critical elements of adaptive capacity and vulnerability. Although segments of urban populations can be highly sensitive to heat waves, floods, and storms, for many urban residents climate impacts are experienced indirectly. More important than the obvious biophysical sensitivity of rural livelihoods to climate events is the perhaps unexpected fact that rural areas around the world are the locus of rapid change. In many developing countries, rural areas are not the sleepy backwaters they are often purported to be. In rapidly industrializing countries such as Mexico, rural populations are increasingly mobilized. As agricultural supports have been withdrawn, rural-urban migration has increased and new areas of unrest and protest have erupted. Urban development projects—airports, highways, and industrial zones—while bringing new opportunities, can also threaten the integrity of rural communities and cultures, and there is a risk that some populations may become increasingly alienated and marginalized.

The challenge is to seize the opportunity provided by the direct experience of this process of change, and to learn from it about our own decision-making processes, our own tolerances of uncertainty, and our struggles to meet present goals and future ambitions. I have always had a huge respect for those whose food comes directly from their own toil and labor and, as an (ironic) consequence, are perhaps less in command of their sustenance than those of us, like myself, whose dinner is relatively easily purchased. Rather than dismissing rural livelihoods as "backward," "inefficient," and thus a threat to social progress, we may actually have much to learn from rural households about survival, adaptation, and resilience. There is a meaning to these livelihoods that escapes quantification and simulation. This is perhaps no better expressed than by the words of Don Carlos, who, after recounting the ejido of Plan de Ayala's struggle for land, its success in obtaining it, and the various hardships brought on by political unfairness and climatic events, shrugged and said that he still preferred his work to anything else: "Ni por todo el mundo de dinero que llegue—prefiero tener terreno que trabajar para alguien más. . . . Aquí no hay quien que me reine. No es lo mismo comprar todo. . . . Es otra libertad." (Not for all the money in the world—I prefer to have land than to work for somebody else. . . . Here no one rules me. It is not the same buying everything. . . . It's a different kind of freedom.)

Appendix A / Glossary

a medias A form of sharecropping in which the landowner typically supplies the land and water for production and the tenant supplies the labor and inputs. The harvest is split between the two parties.

Alianza para el Campo The suite of government agricultural programs designed to encourage commercialization and modernization of peasant agriculture.

campesino A widely used term in Mexico, roughly translated as "peasant farmer." A campesino can be an ejidatario or farmer with individual titled land.

canícula The period of the rainy season (typically from mid-July to the end of August) in which there is a decrease in rainfall.

ejido An agrarian community organized as part of the land reforms after the 1910 revolution. Community members (*ejidatarios*) have usufruct rights to cultivation, typically on individual plots. The communities often include an urban area as well as collectively managed pasture or forested land. The communities are administered by the *comisariado ejidal*.

milpa The land used to produced maize, or maize and beans, typically for domestic consumption.

minifundio A landholding (or owner of such land) that has been repeatedly subdivided so that individual plots are quite small (e.g., <2 ha)

municipio An administrative jurisdiction in Mexico, roughly equivalent to a U.S. county.

pequeña propiedad Privately owned landholdings

pulque The local alcoholic beverage made from the sap (*aguamiel*) of the *maguey* plant in Tlaxcala.

rastrojo The dry maize stalks and maize plant residue left after harvesting the grain, used as animal feed.

temporal Land used for rainfed crop production. Also the term for the rain of the rainy season (the *temporada*).

yunta The general term for draft animal power, often signifying one or two mules or horses and a plow.

Appendix B / Methodological Notes

The material presented in this book was compiled over the course of eighteen months of fieldwork, beginning in January 2000. Over this period I interviewed dozens of farmers, their families, agricultural merchants, extension staff in public and private agencies, academics, and other specialists; implemented a household survey in a subset of households in each community; organized participatory exercises and structured discussions with groups of farmers; and spent hours collecting data in the archives and offices of local newspapers, libraries, and public institutions. Yet some of my greatest insights into the livelihoods of farmers in the Puebla-Tlaxcala Valley came from simply being there: helping with the harvest, chatting with mothers outside the primary school, attending a wedding celebration or school graduation. Alone, none of these methods and data sources would have been sufficient to understand the full complexity of the farmers' vulnerability.

The year 2000 was a presidential election year, and, given that it was Mexico's first attempt at democratic elections, it was a tense and expectant year as well. Any outsider's presence and persistent questions could be perceived as suspicious. In fact, in one of the communities a rumor started that linked me to former president Salinas de Gotari, who apparently had also begun his career with an academic thesis on Tlaxcaltecan agriculture. I made every effort convince the farmers and their families that my ambitions were purely academic and that I had no political ambitions or connections. I also said I would do what I could to communicate their stories and opinions (anonymously) to a wider audience. This promise is in part what motivated their open and considered responses to my many questions, and what has motivated me to publish this book.

Aside from the names of the states and communities in which the research was conducted, I have used pseudonyms to protect the identities of all the people I interviewed for this project, except in one case where my informant requested that his name be used. The fragments of interviews that I present occasionally in the text are taken from my field notes, in those cases where I had successfully captured the actual language and sentence construction used by the interviewee. I used a tape recorder for documentation only in group interviews. I take full responsibility for any errors in my reporting of the interviews.

To implement the survey in Torres and Nazareno, I used sketch maps provided to me by INEGI (the National Institute of Statistics, Geography, and Information) and divided each community into quadrants. I developed a sampling plan based on an estimation of the density of housing in each quadrant. The households were selected for the survey at regular intervals. In Plan de Ayala, my intention was to survey all ejidatarios in the community. In the end, I surveyed all who were willing to be surveyed, and, with the exception of one household, for those who did not wish to participate, I requested (and was granted) qualitative interviews.

While undertaking the surveys in Nazareno, I was often accompanied by the two daughters of a farmer to whom I am particularly indebted, Don Manuel Santos. In Plan de Ayala I worked alone, and in Torres I was fortunate to have the help of José Jimenez López, a graduate student in agrobiology from the Autonomous University of Tlaxcala. The household survey consisted of eleven sections, entailing demographic characteristics, crop production and land use, agricultural investment, commercialization, farm decision-making, livestock activities, credit, participation in public sector programs, farm organization, risk perception, and use of climate information. In the course of the survey, the respondent also drew a map of his or her fields, indicating the fields' location, soil type, relative sensitivity to climate hazards, and the characteristics of the harvests associated with each field for the previous two years.

There are many ways to define and describe livelihoods. In some cases measures of household income have been used as proxies for measuring the livelihood strategy outcomes (Ellis 2000). In these cases income is disaggregated into its various sources in order to determine the composition of a household's strategy. Households can then be classified on the basis of their income class, on the basis of the composition of their income sources, or on the basis of some combination of source and total income.

Measures of monetary income, however, fall short of describing the complexity of household sensitivity to climate impacts and their adaptive capacity. In interviews it was clear that farmers' vulnerability was not a simple function of income but rather a product of a complex combination of household resources, their production practices, their expectations and priorities, as well as the physical exposure of their incomes and crops to risk. After some time in the communities I felt I had a good idea of the resources available to households and the range of economic activities they engaged in. What I needed was a heuristic tool that would enable me to capture this complexity while also allowing me to classify households in livelihood groups to facilitate my analysis.

After experimenting with a variety of options, I settled on a two-stage classification procedure. I first selected a series of variables in the survey that described different household characteristics, production, and resources (e.g., age of household head, land per household member, total land area owned, number of livestock, household dependency ratio, percent of land planted in maize, etc.). I used the normalized values of these variables in a principal components analysis, in order to identify those variables that were most associated with the interhousehold variance within each community (table B.1). These were the variables that loaded highly on the first components that together explained just over 50 percent of the total variance in each community's sample. For example, components 1, 2, and 3 accounted for 61.8 percent and 55 percent of the variance in Plan de Ayala and Torres, respectively, and components 1, 2, 3, and 4 accounted for 55.4 percent of the variance in Nazareno.

The highly loaded variables for each community were then used to classify the households in each community through a k-means cluster analysis. The variables associated with the greatest amount of interhousehold difference in Plan de Ayala were not necessarily the same for Torres or Nazareno and vice versa (e.g., landholding size was relatively uniform in Plan de Ayala while varying considerably in Nazareno and Torres). K-means cluster analysis requires that the researcher define the number of clusters or classes desired. Some experimentation was required to identify an appropriate number of household classes within each community. I first explored how the normalized data clustered in both dendrograms and icicle graphs, in order to identify a number of household classes that appeared to make sense according to the natural grouping of the data without creating an unmanageable or unreasonable number of household classes (particularly given the small samples of each community).

Once the clusters were established, average values for all the original variables (including those not used in the cluster analysis) were analyzed in order to characterize the households in each group. Having spoken at length to all the households surveyed, I also had personal insight into the appropriateness of the classifications that resulted from this analysis.

Most of the variables used in the classification were self-explanatory (e.g., number of hectares planted in 1999, number of different crops planted, number of the households with secondary education, etc.). The income variables were more complex. The survey respondents were asked to pro-

Table B.1 Survey Variables Used to Classify Households

	Torres	Plan de Ayala	Nazareno
Explained variance by first three components (%)	55.0	61.8	55.4
Total income	C1: 0.949*	C1: 0.922	
% Crop sales	C1: 0.930		C1: 0.887*
% Nonfarm		C1: 0.801	C1: -0.444*
% Government transfer		C1: -0.885	
% Off-farm		C2: 0.695	C3: -0.856
% Animal sales	C1: 0.718		
Per capita income	C1: 0.979*		C2: 0.822*
Total ha	C1: 0.930*		C1: 0.832*
% ha in maize	C3: 0.799	C3: 0.718	C1: -0.843*
% ha affected 1999	C3: 0.662	C2: -0.911*	C4: -0.454
% ha irrigated			C1: 0.710
Total irrigated ha			C1: 0.883*
Material goods index	C2: 0.729*	C1: 0.701	C1: 0.470
Land per capita	C1: 0.955*		C2: 0.850*
Members of household with secondary school education	C2: 0.918*	C3: -0.713*	C4: 0.836
Number of return migrants in household		C2: -0.595	C4: 0.766
Large animals	C3: -0.789	C2: 0.894*	
Medium animals	C2: 0.917*		
Dependency ratio		C3: 0.832	
# of crops planted	C3:-0.647	C3: -0.613	C1: 0.853*
# persons sending remittances		C3: 0.586	

Notes: The values in each cell are the factor loadings from the principal component analysis for each variable and the component (e.g., C1 or C2) on which the variable loaded highly. The variables with relatively high factor loadings for each community were used to classify the households in a cluster analysis.

The factor loadings marked with * are those for which the F ratio was relatively large (>10). The F ratio is the ratio of the variance within each cluster to the variance not explained by each cluster (error variance). The larger this ratio, the greater the role played by the variable in separating the clusters.

vide an estimate of any wage income earned by themselves or household members in all economic activities they engaged in. I later classified these data into nonagricultural activities (nonfarm wage or self-employment), the gross income they received from crop sales, income received from animal sales (also gross income), and income received in off-farm activities. The respondents were also asked to estimate any income (either cash or as food rations) received via government transfers through programs such as PROCAMPO, PROGRESA, or emergency employment. Finally, an attempt was made to estimate income coming into the household from relatives and offspring living outside the household. This latter income source proved to be very problematic—either the respondents were reluctant to reveal this information, or they had difficulty estimating it because the influx of cash and goods from this source was highly variable. As a result, I used a measure of the number of people sending support to each household as a rough indicator of the participation of remittances in household income.

There were undoubtedly sources of income entering the household that I failed to record (or were not revealed to me), and as with any research of this nature, it is difficult to be fully confident that the respondent's own estimates were accurate. For example, I feel that there was a general underreporting of income from seasonal work as day laborers, particularly in Nazareno and Torres (Plan de Ayala households did not generally work as day laborers). Many households worked only occasionally as day laborers, and were unsure of the frequency of this work, or did not separate this work from their work on their own farms and thus failed to report the income. The income reported from animal sales may also distort the estimation of total income of each household. Households with an apparently high income from animal sales in 1999 may actually be materially poor: they sold their livestock in 1999 to cover debts or recuperate crop losses, resulting in an income peak that would not be reflected in the income of previous or subsequent years.

Despite these caveats, all the surveys were conducted inside or in the immediate vicinity of the respondents' homes, and the income data are compatible with my own observations of the relative poverty of each household (building construction, utilities, furniture, and equipment). The average incomes calculated for each community are also within the range of incomes calculated in the region in other studies (Aquirre Alvarez et al. 1999). To strengthen my estimation of relative wealth, I also included an index of material wealth in the survey with the idea that, as a measure of accumulation, this index would more accurately reflect wealth over time.

References

Acuna-Soto, R., D. W. Stahle, M. D. Therrell, S. Gomez Chavez, and M. K. Cleaveland. 2005. Drought, epidemic disease, and the fall of classic period cultures in Mesoamerica (AD 750–950). Hemorrhagic fevers as a cause of massive population loss. *Medical Hypotheses* 65 (2):405–9.

Adger, N. W. 1999. Social vulnerability to climate change and extremes in coastal Vietnam. *World Development* 27:249–69.

Adger, N. W., N. Brooks, G. Bentham, M. Agnew, and S. Eriksen. 2004. *New indicators of vulnerability and adaptive capacity: Final project report.* Norwich, UK: Tyndall Centre for Climate Change Research.

Adger, N. W., H. Eakin, and A. Winkels. Forthcoming. Nested and networked vulnerability in South East Asia. In *Global environmental change and the South-East Asian region: An assessment of the state of science,* ed. L. Lebel. Washington, DC: Island Press.

Aguirre Alvarez, L., B. A. Salcido Ramos, M. E. Meneses Álvarez, and F. Álvarez Gaxiola. 1999. *Planificación de actividades de desarrollo para productores de hortalizas en el Centro Este del Estado de Puebla.* Puebla: SAGAR/Colegio Postgraduados/ICRA/RIMISP.

Alland, A. 1975. Adaptation. *Annual Review of Anthropology* 4:59–73.

Altieri, M., and J. Trujillo. 1987. The agroecology of corn production in Tlaxcala, Mexico. *Human Organization* 15:189–220.

Antle, J., S. M. Capalbo, E. T. Elliot, and K. H. Paustian. 2004. Adaptation, spatial heterogeneity, and the vulnerability of agricultural systems to climate change and CO_2 fertilization: An integrated assessment approach. *Climatic Change* 64:289–315.

Appendini, K. 1992/2001. *De la milpa a los tortibonos: La reestructuración de la política alimentaría en México.* México, DF: El Colegio de México, Centro de Estudios Económicos: Instituto de Investigaciones de las Naciones Unidas para el Desarrollo Social.

———. 1994. Transforming food policy over a decade: The balance for Mexican corn farmers in 1993. In *Economic restructuring and rural subsistence in Mexico: Corn and the crisis of the 1980s,* ed. C. Hewitt de Alcántara, 145–60. [San Diego]: Ejido Reform Research Project, Center for U.S.–Mexican Studies, University of California, San Diego; Geneva: United Nations Research Institute for Social Development; [Mexico, DF]: Centro Tepoztlán.

———. 1998. Changing agrarian institutions: Interpreting the contradictions. In *The transformation of rural Mexico: Reforming the ejido sector*, ed. W. Cornelius and D. Myhre, 25–38. La Jolla: Center for U.S.–Mexican Studies, University of California, San Diego.

Austin, J. E., and G. Esteva, eds. 1987. *Food policy in Mexico: The search for self-sufficiency*. Ithaca, NY: Cornell University Press.

Barkin, D. 1990. *Distorted development*. Boulder, CO: Westview Press.

Barlett, P. F. 1980. Adaptive strategies in peasant agricultural production. *Annual Review of Anthropology* 9:545–73.

Bassett, T. J., and K. S. Zimmerer. 2003. *Political ecology: An integrative approach to geography and environment-development studies*. New York: Guilford Press.

Batterbury, S. 2001. Landscapes of diversity: A local political ecology of livelihood diversification in South-western Niger. *Ecumene* 8:437–64.

Batterbury, S., and T. Forsyth. 1999. Fighting back: Human adaptations in marginal environments. *Environment* 41:7–30.

Batterbury, S., T. Forsyth, and K. Thomson. 1997. Environmental transformations in developing countries: Hybrid research and democratic policy. *Geographical Journal* 163:126–32.

Bebbington, A. 1990. Farmer knowledge, institutional resources, and sustainable agricultural strategies: A case study from the eastern slopes of the Peruvian Andes. *Bulletin of Latin American Research* 9:203–28.

———. 1993. Modernization from below: An alternative indigenous development? *Economic Geography* 69: 274–92.

———. 1996. Movements, modernization, and markets: Indigenous organizations and agrarian strategies in Ecuador. In *Liberation ecologies*, ed. R. Peet and M. Watts, 86–109. New York: Routledge.

———. 1999. Capitals and capabilities: A framework for analyzing peasant viability, rural livelihoods, and poverty. *World Development* 27:2021–44.

———. 2000. Re-encountering development: Livelihood transitions and place transformations in the Andes. *Annals of the Association of American Geographers* 90:495–520.

Bebbington, A., and S. Batterbury. 2001. Transnational livelihoods and landscapes: Political ecologies of globalization. *Ecumene* 8:369–80.

Bellon, M. R. 1991. The ethnoecology of maize variety management: A case study from Mexico. *Human Ecology* 19:389–418.

Bennett, J. W. 1976. *The ecological transition*. Oxford: Pergamon Press.

Berdegué, J., T. Reardon, and G. Escobar. 2001. Rural non-farm employment and incomes in Chile. *World Development* 29:411–25.

Blaikie, P. 1999. A review of political ecology. *Zeitschrift für Wirtschaftsgeografphie* 43:131–47.

Blaikie, P., T. Cannon, I. Davis, and B. Wisner. 1994. *At risk: Natural hazards, people's vulnerability, and disasters*. London: Routledge.

Brklachich, M., D. McNabb, C. Bryant, and J. Dumanski. 1997. Adaptability of agriculture systems to global climate change: A Renfrew County, Ontario, Canada pilot study. In *Agricultural restructuring and sustainability: A geographical perspective*, ed. B. Ilbery, Q. Chiotti, and T. Rickard, 185–200. Oxon: CAB International.

Brush, S. 1977. *Mountain, field, and family: The economy and human ecology of an Andean valley.* [Philadelphia]: University of Pennsylvania Press.

Brush, S., M. Bellon Corrales, and E. Schmidt. 1988. Agricultural development and maize diversity in Mexico. *Human Ecology* 16:307–28.

Bryant, R. 1998. Power, knowledge, and political ecology in the third world: A review. *Progress in Physical Geography* 22:79–94.

Bryant, C. R., B. Smit, M. Braklachich, T. R. Johnston, J. Smithers, Q. Chiotti, and B. Singh. 2000. Adaptation in Canadian agriculture to climate variability and change. *Climatic Change* 45:181–201.

Bryceson, D. F. 1996. Deagrarianization and rural employment in sub-Saharan Africa: A sectoral perspective. *World Development* 24:97–111.

———. 2002. The scramble in Africa: Reorienting rural livelihoods. *World Development* 30:725–39.

Burton, I. 1997. Vulnerability and adaptive response in the context of climate and climate change. *Climatic Change* 36:185–96.

Burton, I., S. Huq, B. Lim, O. Pilifosova, and E. L. Schipper. 2002. From impact assessment to adaptation priorities: The shaping of adaptation policy. *Climate Policy* 2:145–59.

Burton, I., G. White, and R. Kates. 1978. *Environment as hazard.* New York: Oxford University Press.

Buttel, F. H. 1997. Some observations on agro-food change and the future of agricultural sustainability movements. In *Globalising food*, ed. D. Goodman and M. Watts, 344–65. New York: Routledge.

Calva, J. L. 1994. La reforma neoliberal del régimen agrario mexicano. In *Estado y agricultura en México: Antecedentes y implicaciones de las reformas Salinistas*, ed. E. Ochoa and D. E. Lorey, 143–66. Azcapotzalco, México, DF: Universidad Autonoma Metropolitana, Unidad Azcapoltzalco.

Cancian, R. 1980. Risk and uncertainty in agricultural decision making. *Agricultural decision making: Anthropological contributions to rural development*, ed. P. Barlett, 161–76. San Diego: Academic Press.

Carswell, G. 2000. *Livelihood diversification in southern Ethiopia.* IDS Working Paper 117. Brighton, UK: Institute of Development Studies at the University of Sussex.

Carter, T. R., M. L. Parry, H. Harasawa, and S. Nishioka. 1994. *IPCC technical guidelines for assessing climate change impacts and adaptations with a summary for policy makers and a technical summary.* London: University College London and National Institute for Environmental Studies, Japan.

Castro Morales, E. 1972. Comentarios. In *Los recursos naturales del Estado de Puebla y su aprovechamiento: El hombre y su medio ambiente: Aspectos antrop-*

ológicos e históricos. Décima Sexta Serie de Mesas Redondas. Ciudad de Puebla: Instituto Mexicano de Recursos Naturales Renovables.

Cebreros, A. 1990. La reorganización productiva del campo mexicano: El caso del minifundio. *Comercio Exterior* 40:849–52.

Centro Estatal de Desarrollo Municipal. 1987. *Enciclopedia de los municipios de Puebla.* Puebla: Gobierno del Estado de Puebla.

Chen, R. 1994. The human dimension of vulnerability. In *Industrial ecology and global change,* ed. R. Socolow, C. Andrews, F. Berkhout, and U. Thomas, 85–105. Cambridge: Cambridge University Press.

Chen, R., and R. Katz. 1994. Climate change and world food security. *Global Environmental Change* 4:3–6.

Chiotti, Q., T. Johnston, B. Smit, and B. Ebel. 1997. Agricultural response to climate change: A preliminary investigation of farm-level adaptation in southern Alberta. In *Agricultural restructuring and sustainability: A geographical perspective,* ed. B. Ilbery, Q. Chiotti, and T. Rickard, 201–18. Oxon: CAB International.

Comisión Económica para América Latina y el Caribe (CEPAL). 2000. *Panorama social de América Latina.* Santiago de Chile: Naciones Unidas.

Comisión Nacional del Agua. 2002. *Determinación de la disponabilidad de agua en el acuífero valle de Tecamachalco, Estado de Pueblo.* México, DF: Comisión Nacional del Agua, Gerencia de Aguas Superficiales.

Conde, C., and H. Eakin. 2003. Adaptation to climatic variability and change in Tlaxcala, Mexico. In *Climate change, adaptive capacity, and development,* ed. S. Huq, 241–59. Potsdam: Potsdam Institute for Climate Impact Research.

Conde, C., R. M. Ferrer, and C. Gay. 1998. Variabilidad climática y agricultura. *GeoUNAM* 5 (1):26–32.

Conde, C., R. M. Ferrer, and D. Liverman. 2000. Estudio de la vulnerabilidad de la agricultura de maíz de temporal mediante el modelo CERES-Maize. In *México: Una visión hacia el siglo XXI: El cambio climático en México,* ed. C. Gay Garcia, 119–41. México, DF: Universidad Nacional Autónoma de México.

Consejo Nacional de Población (CONAPO). 1998. *Índice de marginación, 1995.* México, DF: Secretaria de Gobernación.

Copans, J. 1983. The Sahelian drought: Social sciences and the political economy of underdevelopment. In *Interpretations of calamity,* ed. K. Hewitt, 83–97. Boston: Allen & Unwin.

Corbett, J. 1988. Famine and household coping strategies. *World Development* 16:1099–1112.

Cornelius, W., and D. Myhre, eds. 1998. *The transformation of rural Mexico: Reforming the ejido sector.* La Jolla: Center for U.S.–Mexican Studies, University of California, San Diego.

Corral, L., and T. Reardon. 2001. Rural nonfarm incomes in Nicaragua. *World Development* 29:427–42.

Cotter, J. 1994. Salinas de Gotari's agricultural policy and scientific exchange: Some lessons from before and during the green revolution. In *Estado y agricultura en México: Antecedentes e implicaciones de las reformas Salinistas,* ed.

E. C. Ochoa and D. E. Lorey, 39–55. Azcapotzalco, México, DF: Universidad Autónoma Metropolitana, Unidad Azcapoltzalco.

Crosson, P. 1993. Impacts of climate change on the agriculture and economy of the Missouri, Iowa, Nebraska, and Kansas (MINK) region. In *Agricultural dimensions of global climate change*, ed. H. M. Kaiser and T. E. Drennen, 117–35. Delray Beach, FL: St. Lucie Press.

Dahlin, B. H. 1983. Climate and prehistory on the Yucatan Peninsula. *Climatic Change* 5:245–63.

Davies, S. 1996. *Adaptable livelihoods: Coping with food insecurity in the Malian Sahel*. London: Macmillan Press.

De Grammont, H. C., M. A. Gómez Cruz, H. González, and R. Schwentesius Rindermamm, eds. 1999. *Agricultura de exportación en tiempos de globalización*. Chapingo, Mexico: Centro de Investigaciones Económicas, Sociales y Tecnológicas de la Agroindustria y la Agricultura Mundial; México, DF: Instituto de Investigaciones Sociales: Centro de Investigaciones y Estudios Superiores en Antropología Social: Juan Pablos Editor.

De Janvry, A., M. Chiriboga, H. Colmenares, A. Hintermeister, G. Howe, R. Irigoyen, A. Monares, F. Rello, E. Sadoulet, J. Secco, T. van der Pluijm, and S. Varese. 1995. *Reformas del sector agrícola y el campesinado en México*. San José, Costa Rica: Fondo Internacional de Desarollo Agrícola y Instituto Interamericano de Cooperación para la Agricultura.

De Janvry, A., G. Gordillo, and E. Sadoulet. 1997. *Mexico's second agrarian reform: Household and community responses*. La Jolla: Center for U.S.–Mexican Studies, University of California, San Diego.

De Janvry, A., and E. Sadoulet. 2001. Income strategies among rural households in Mexico: The role of off-farm activities. *World Development* 29:467–80.

De Janvry, A., E. Sadoulet, and G. Gordillo de Anda. 1995. NAFTA and Mexico's maize producers. *World Development* 23:1349–62.

Delgadillo Macías, J., T. Aguilar Ortega, and D. Rodríguez Velázquez. 1999. Los aspectos económicos y sociales de El Niño. In *Los impactos de El Niño en México*, ed. V. Magaña Rueda, 189–210. México, DF: Secretaria de Educación Pública-Consejo Nacional de Ciencia y Tecnología (SEP-CONOCYT).

Denevan, W. M. 1980. Latin America. *World systems of traditional resource management*, ed. G. A. Klee, 217–56. New York: Halsted Press.

DeWalt, B., M. W. Rees, and A. D. Murphy. 1994. *The end of the agrarian reform in Mexico*. [La Jolla]: Center for U.S.–Mexican Studies, University of California, San Diego.

Díaz-Cisneros, H. 1994. The impact of support prices for corn on small farmers in the Puebla Valley. In *Economic restructuring and rural subsistence in Mexico: Corn and the crisis of the 1980s*, ed. C. Hewitt de Alcántara, 37–54. [La Jolla]: Ejido Reform Research Project, Center for U.S.–Mexican Studies, UCSD; Geneva: United Nations Research Institute for Social Development (UNRISD); [Mexico, DF]: Centro Tepoztlán.

Dilley, M. 1997. Climatic factors affecting annual maize yields in the valley of Oaxaca, Mexico. *International Journal of Climatology* 17:1549–57.

Doolittle, W. 1989. Arroyos and the development of agriculture in northern Mexico. In *Fragile lands in Latin America: Strategies for sustainable development*, ed. J. O. Browder, 251–61. Boulder, CO: Westview Press.

———. 2000. *Cultivated landscapes of native North America*. Oxford: Oxford University Press.

Dow, K. 1992. Exploring differences in Our Common Future(s): The meaning of vulnerability to global environmental change. *Geoforum* 23:417–36.

Downing, T. E., M. J. Gawith, A. A. Olsthoorn, R.S.J. Tol, and V. Pier. 1999. Introduction to *Climate, change, and risk*, ed. T. E. Downing, A. A. Olsthoorn, and R. S. J. Tol, 1–18. London: Routledge.

Downing, T. E., M. J. Watts, and H. G. Bohle. 1996. Climate change and food insecurity: Towards a sociology and geography of vulnerability. *Climate change and world food security*, ed. T. E. Downing, 185–206. Berlin: Springer-Verlag.

Dussel Peters, E. 2000. *El Tratado de Libre Comercio de Norteamérica y el desempeño de la economía en México*. Report LC/MEX/L.431. México, DF: United Nations, Comisión Económica para América Latina y el Caribe, Sede Subregional en México.

Dyer-Leal, G., and A. Yúnez-Naude. 2003. NAFTA and conservation of maize diversity in Mexico. Paper presented at the Segundo Simposio de América del Norte sobre Evaluación de los Eflectos Ambientales del Comercio, of the Commission on Environmental Cooperation for North America, 23 March 2003. Mexico City. Accessible at www.cec.org/files/pdf/ECONOMY/Dyer-Yunez_ExSum_fr.pdf.

Eakin, H. 1998. Adapting to climate variability in Tlaxcala, Mexico: Constraints and opportunities for small-scale maize producers. Master's thesis, University of Arizona, Tucson.

———. 2000. Smallholder maize production and climatic risk: A case study from Mexico. *Climatic Change* 45:19–36.

———. 2002. Rural households' vulnerability and adaptation to climatic variability and institutional change. PhD diss., University of Arizona, Tucson.

———. 2003. The social vulnerability of irrigated vegetable farming households in Central Puebla. *Journal of Environment and Development* 12:414–29.

Eakin, H., C. Tucker, and E. Castellanos. 2005. Market shocks and climatic variability: The coffee crisis in Mexico, Guatemala, and Honduras. *Mountain Research and Development* 25:304–9.

Eakin, H., M. Wehbe, C. Ávila, G. Sanchez Torres, and L. Bojórquez-Tapia. Forthcoming. Social vulnerability and key resources for adaptation: Agriculture producers in Mexico and Argentina. AIACC Working Papers. http://www.aiaccproject.org.

Easterling, W. 1996. Adapting North American agriculture to climate change in review. *Agricultural and Forest Meteorology* 80:1–53.

Ellis, F. 2000. *Rural livelihoods and diversity in developing countries*. Oxford: Oxford University Press.

Escalante, R., and T. Redón. 1987. Neoliberalismo a la Mexicana: Su impacto sobre el sector agropecuario. *Problemas del Desarollo* 75:115–51.

Escobar Ohmstede, A. 1997. Las "sequías" y sus impactos en la sociedad en México decimonónico, 1856–1900. In *Historia y desastres en América Latina*, Vol. 2, ed. V. García Acosta, 219–57. Lima, Peru: La RED/CIESAS, ITDG.

Felstehausen, H., and H. Díaz-Cisneros. 1985. The strategy of rural development: The Puebla initiative. *Human Organization* 44:285–92.

Famine Early Warning System (FEWS). 1999. *FEWS current vulnerability assessment guidance manual*. Washington, DC: U.S. Agency for International Development/Famine Early Warning System.

Florescano, E. 1980. Una historia olvidada: La sequía en Mexico. *Nexos* 32:9–18.

Flynn, M. 2001. Fox strives to spread maquiladoras south. *Borderlines UPDATER* 7 August. http://www.usmex.org/borderlines/updater/2001/aug7ppp.html.

Foley, M. 1995. Privatizing the countryside: The Mexican peasant movement and neoliberal reform. *Latin American Research Review* 22:59–76.

Fox, J. 1995. Governance and rural development in Mexico: State intervention and public accountability. *Journal of Development Studies* 32:1–30.

Fox Quesada, V. 2003. *Tercera informe del gobierno*. México, DF: Presidencia de la Republica.

———. 2004. *Cuarto informe del gobierno*. México, DF: Presidencia de la Republica.

Francis, E. 2000. *Making a living: Changing livelihoods in rural Africa*. London: Routledge.

Friedmann, H. 1994. Distance and durability: Shaky foundations of the world food economy. In *The global restructuring of agro-food systems*, ed. P. McMichael, 258–76. Ithaca, NY: Cornell University Press.

Fritscher Mundt, M. 1999. El maíz en México: Auge y crisis en los noventa. *Cuadernos Agrarios* 8–9:142–63.

García Güemez, A. 1998. Puebla en el contexto nacional, una visión general. In *Puebla, un modelo para armar*, ed. G. Sánchez Daza and J. Ornelas Delgado, 13–26. Puebla: Benemérita Universidad Autónoma de Puebla.

García Zamora, R. 1994. Crisis agrícola y nuevos subsidios al campo. In *Estado y agricultura en México: Antecedentes e implicaciones de las reformas Salinistas*, ed. E. Ochoa and D. E. Lorey, 73–100. Azcapotzalco, México, DF: Universidad Autónoma Metropolitana, Unidad Azcapoltzalco.

Gates, M. 1989. Codifying marginality: The evolution of Mexican agricultural policy and its impact on the peasantry. *Journal of Latin American Studies* 20:277–311.

Gerber, J., and W. A. Kerr. 1995. Trade as an agency of social policy: NAFTA's schizophrenic role in agriculture. In *NAFTA in transition*, ed. S. J. Randall and H. W. Konrad, 93–111. Calgary: University of Calgary Press.

Gifford, R. M., B. D. Campbell, and S. M. Howden. 1996. Options for adapting agriculture to climate change: Australian and New Zealand examples. *Greenhouse: Coping with climate change*, ed. W. J. Bouma, G. I. Pearman, and M. R. Manning, 399–416. Collingwood, VIC, Australia: CSIRO.

Gledhill, J. 1995. *Neoliberalism, transnationalization, and rural poverty*. Boulder, CO: Westview Press.

Gobierno del Estado de Puebla. 1999. *Alianza para el Campo: Puebla Apoyos 1999*. Puebla: Gobierno del Estado de Puebla.

Gobierno de Tlaxcala. 2000. *Alianza para el Campo 2000, presupuesto convenido*. Tlaxcala: Secretartía de Fomento Agropecuaria.

———. 1998. Altzayanca. In *Los municipios de Tlaxclala: Monografías*. CD-ROM. Tlaxcala: COPLADET.

———. 1998. Huamantla. In *Los municipios de Tlaxclala: Monografías*. CD-ROM. Tlaxcala: COPLADET.

Gómez Cruz, M. A., R. Schwentesius Rinderman, M. Muñoz Rogríguez, V. H. Santajo Cortés, and C. Flores Valdez. 1993. *¿Procampo o anticampo?* Texcoco: CIESTAAM, Universidad Autónoma Chapingo.

González López, G. 1990. Lecciones del Plan Puebla para el cambio tecnológico en el campo mexicano. *Comercio Exterior* 40:962–67.

Goodman, D., and M. Watts, eds. 1997. *Globalising food: Agrarian questions and global restructuring*. London: Routledge.

Greenburg, J., and T. Park. 1994. Political ecology. *Journal of Political Ecology* 1:1–13.

Hammer, G. L., J. W. Hansen, J. G. Phillips, H. Hill, A. Love, and A. Pogieter. 2001. Advances in application of climate prediction in agriculture. *Agricultural Systems* 70:515–53.

Handmer, J. W., S. Dovers, and T. E. Downing. 1999. Societal vulnerability to climate change and variability. *Mitigation and Adaptation Strategies for Global Change* 4:267–81.

Hanemann, W. M. 2000. Adaptation and its measurements. *Climatic Change* 45:571–81.

Heath, J. R. 1992. Evaluating the impact of Mexico's land reform on agricultural productivity. *World Development* 20:695–711.

Helms, S., R. Mendelsohn, and J. Neumann. 1996. The impact of climate change on agriculture. *Climatic Change* 33:1–6.

Hernández Cerda, M. E., L. A. Torres Tapia, and G. Valdez Madero. 2000. Sequía meteorológica. In *México: Una visión hacia el siglo XXI: El cambio climático en México*, ed. C. Gay García, 25–39. México, DF: Instituto Nacional de Ecología.

Hewitson, B., and R. Crane. 1992. Large-scale atmospheric controls on local precipitation in tropical Mexico. *Geophysical Research Letters* 19:1835–38.

Hewitt de Alcántara, C. 1994. Introduction to *Economic restructuring and rural subsistence in Mexico: Corn and the crisis of the 1980s*, ed. C. Hewitt de Alcántara, 1–24. [La Jolla]: Ejido Reform Research Project, Center for

U.S.–Mexican Studies, UCSD; Geneva: United Nations Research Institute for Social Development (UNRISD); [Mexico, DF]: Centro Tepoztlán.

Hewitt, K. 1983. *The idea of calamity in a technocratic age. Interpretations of calamity*, ed. K. Hewitt, 3–32. Winchester: Allen & Unwin.

Hodell, D., J. Curtis, and M. Brenner. 1995. Possible role of climate in the collapse of Classic Maya civilization. *Nature* 375:391–94.

Hussein, K., and J. Nelson. 1998. *Sustainable livelihoods and livelihood diversification*. IDS Working Paper 69. Brighton, Eng.: Institute of Development Studies, University of Sussex.

Industrial Development Ministry. 2000. *Tlaxcala Mexico profile*. CD-ROM. Tlaxcala: Government of the State of Tlaxcala.

Instituto Nacional de Estadística, Geografía e Informática (INEGI). 1992a. *Puebla: Perfil sociodemográfico: XI censo general de poplacion vivienda 1990*. México, DF: INEGI.

———. 1992b. *Tlaxcala: Perfil sociodemográfico: XI censo general de poplacion vivienda 1990*. México, DF: INEGI.

———. 1999a. *Perspectiva estadística Puebla*. Aguascalientes: INEGI.

———. 1999b. *Censos económicos 1999: Enumeración integral: Parques, ciudades y corredores industriales de México: Resultados oportunos*. Aguascalientes: INEGI.

———. 2000a. *Anuario estadístico Puebla: Edición 2001*. Aguascalientes: INEGI.

———. 2000b. *Anuario estadístico Tlaxcala: Edición 2000*. Aguascalientes: INEGI.

———. 2001a. *Estados Unidos Mexicanos: Tabulados básicos: XII Censo General de Población y Vivienda 2000*. Aguascalientes: INEGI.

———. 2001b. *Estadística de la industria maquiladora de exportación 1995–2000*. Aguascalientes: INEGI.

———. 2004. *Estadística de la industria maquiladora de exportación. Banco de información económica*. [Online database] INEGI. http://dgcnesyp.inegi.gob.mx/bdiesi/bdie.html.

Instituto Nacional de Investigaciones Forestales, Agrícolas y Pecuarias (INIFAP). 1998. *Conversión productiva en temporal para el estado de Tlaxcala*. Tlaxcala: INIFAP-Tlaxcala.

Intergovernmental Panel on Climate Change (IPCC) Working Group I, ed. 2001. *The scientific basis*. Geneva: IPCC.

Intergovernmental Panel on Climate Change (IPCC) Working Group II, ed. 2001. *Climate change 2001: Impacts, adaptation, and vulnerability*. Geneva: IPCC.

Jennings, B. H. 1988. *Foundations of international agricultural research: Science and politics in Mexican agriculture*. Boulder, CO: Westview Press.

Jones, J. W., J. W. Hansen, F. S. Royce, and C. D. Messina. 2000. Potential benefits of climate forecasting to agriculture. *Agriculture, Ecosystems, and Environment* 82:169–84.

Kaiser, H. M., S. J. Riha, D. S. Wilks, and R. Sampath. 1993. Adaptation to global climate change at the farm level. In *Agricultural dimensions of global climate change*, ed. H. M. Kaiser and T. E. Drennen, 136–52. Delray Beach, FL: St. Lucie Press.

Kandlikar, M., and J. Risbey. 2000. Agricultural impacts of climate change: If adaptation is the answer, what is the question? *Climatic Change* 45:529–39.

Katz, F. 1988. Rural rebellions after 1810. In *Riot, rebellion, and revolution: Rural social conflict in Mexico*, ed. F. Katz, 521–60. Princeton, NJ: Princeton University Press.

Kelly, P. M., and W. N. Adger 2000. Theory and practice in assessing vulnerability to climate change and facilitating adaptation. *Climatic Change* 47:325–52.

Kelly, T. 2001. Neoliberal reforms and rural poverty. *Latin American Perspectives* 28:84–103.

Krippner, G. 1997. The politics of privatization in rural Mexico. *Politics and Society* 25:4–34.

Leff, E. 1995. *Green production: Toward an environmental rationality*. New York: Guilford Press.

Licate, J. A. 1981. *Creation of a Mexican landscape: Territorial organization and settlement in the eastern Puebla basin, 1520–1605*. Department of Geography Research Paper #201. Chicago: University of Chicago, Department of Geography.

Liverman, D. 1991. Global change and Mexico. *Earth and Mineral Sciences* 60:71–76.

Liverman, D., M. Dilley, K. O'Brien, and L. Menchaca. 1992. *The impacts of global warming on Mexican maize yields: Report for the U.S. Country Studies Program*. Washington, DC: Environmental Protection Agency.

Liverman, D., and K. O'Brien. 1991. Global warming and climate change in Mexico. *Global Environmental Change* December: 351–64.

Loker, W. M. 1996. "Campesinos" and the crisis of modernization in Latin America. *Journal of Political Ecology* 3:69–88.

Magaña, V. O., ed. 1999. *Los impactos de El Niño en México*. México, DF: SEP-CONACYT.

Magaña, V. O., J. Amador, and S. Medina. 1999. The midsummer drought over Mexico and Central America. *Journal of Climate* 12:1577–88.

Magaña, V. O., C. Conde, O. Sánchez, and G. Carlos. 1997. Assessment of current and future regional climate scenarios for Mexico. *Climate Research* 9:107–14.

Magaña, V. O., and Quintanar, A. 1997. On the use of a general circulation model to study regional climate. In *Numerical simulations in the environmental and earth sciences*, ed. F. García García, G. Cisneros, A. Fernández-Equiarte, and R. Álvarez. Cambridge: Cambridge University Press.

Marsden, T. 1997. Creating space for food: The distinctiveness of recent agrarian development. In *Globalizing food: Agrarian questions and global restructuring*, ed. D. Goodman and M. Watts, 169–91. London: Routledge.

Marsh, R., and D. Runsten. 1998. Smallholder fruit and vegetable production in Mexico: Barriers and opportunities. In *The transformation of rural Mexico: Reforming the ejido sector*, ed. W. Cornelius and D. Myhre, 277–306. La Jolla: Center for U.S.–Mexican Studies, University of California, San Diego.

Martínez Saldaña, T. 1997. *La diáspora Tlaxcalteca*. Tlaxcala: Gobierno del estado de Tlaxcala.

Masera, O., and S. López-Ridaura, eds. 2000. *Sustentabilidad y sistemas campesinos: Cinco experiencias de evaluación en el México rural*. México, DF: PUMA, Mundi-Prensa México and Universidad Nacional Autónoma de México.

McCabe, J. T. 1990. Success and failure: The breakdown of traditional drought coping institutions among the pastoral Turkana of Kenya. *Journal of Asian and African Studies* 25:146–60.

McMichael, P. 1994. Introduction to *The global restructuring of agro-food systems*, ed. P. McMichael, 1–17. Ithaca, NY: Cornell University Press.

Mendoza, B., E. Jáuregui, R. Diaz-Sandoval, V. García-Acosta, V. Velasco, and G. Cordero. 2005. Historical droughts in Central Mexico and their relation with El Niño. *Journal of Applied Meteorology* 44 (May):709–16.

Mjelde, J. W., S.J.H. Harvey, and J. Griffith. 1998. A review of current evidence on climate forecasts and their economic effects in agriculture. *American Journal of Agricultural Economics* 80:1089–95.

Morales Flores, M. 2000. *Informe del Gobierno 1999*. Puebla: Gobierno del Estado de Puebla.

Morales, T., and V. Magaña. 1999. Unexpected frosts in central Mexico during the summer. *Proceedings of the Tenth Symposium on Global Change Studies*, 262–63. Boston: American Meteorological Society.

Mortimore, M. 1989. *Adapting to drought: Farmers, famines, and desertification in West Africa*. Cambridge: Cambridge University Press.

Mortimore, M., and W. M. Adams. 1999. *Working the Sahel: Environment and society in northern Nigeria*. London: Routledge.

Mosiño Aleman, P., and E. García. 1974. The climate of Mexico. In *Climates of North America*. Vol. 11 of *World survey of climatology*, ed. R. A. Bryson and F. K. Hare, 345–404. Amsterdam: Elsevier.

Moss, R. H., A. L. Brenkert, and E. L. Malone. 2001. *Vulnerability to climate change: A quantitative approach*. Report prepared for the U.S. Department of Energy, PNNL-SA-33642. Oak Ridge, TN: Battelle and U.S. Department of Energy.

Murphy, S. J., R. Washington, T. E. Downing, R. V. Martin, G. Ziervogel, A. Preston, M. Todd, R. Butterfield, and J. Briden. 2001. Seasonal forecasting for climate hazards: Prospects and responses. *Natural Hazards* 23:171–96.

Myhre, D. 1994. The politics of globalization in rural Mexico: Campesino initiative to restructure the agricultural credit system. In *The global restructuring of agro-food systems*, ed. P. McMichael, 145–69. Ithaca, NY: Cornell University Press.

———. 1998. The Achilles' heel of the reforms: The rural finance system. In *The transformation of rural Mexico: Reforming the ejido sector*, ed. W. Cornelius and D. Myhre, 39–68. La Jolla: Center for U.S.–Mexican Studies, University of California, San Diego.

Nadal, A. 1999. *Maize in Mexico: Some environmental implications of the North American Free Trade Agreement (NAFTA)*. Environment and Trade Series #6

Issue Study 1. Commission on Environmental Cooperation. http://www.ced.org/pubs_docs/documents/index.cfm?varlan=english&ED=1398.

Nash, J. 1994. Global integration and subsistence insecurity. *American Anthropologist* 96:7–30.

Netting, R. 1993. *Smallholders, householders: Farm families and the ecology of intensive, sustainable agriculture.* Stanford, CA: Stanford University Press.

Nigh, R. 1997. Organic agriculture and globalization: A Maya associative corporation in Chiapas, Mexico. *Human Organization* 56:427–36.

Nolasco, M., and G. Bonfil Batalla. 1972. Comentarios. In *Los recursos naturales del Estado de Puebla y su aprovechamiento: El hombre y su medio ambiente: Aspectos antropológicos e históricos.* Décima Sexta Serie de Mesas Redondas. Ciudad de Puebla: Instituto Mexicano de Recursos Naturales Renovables.

O'Brien, K. L., and R. M. Leichenko. 2000. Double exposure: Assessing the impacts of climate change within the context of economic globalization. *Global Environmental Change* 10:221–32.

———. 2003. Winners and losers in the context of global change. *Annals of the Association of American Geographers* 93:89–103.

Ochoa, E. C. 1994. The urban roots of Mexican food policy: The state and basic grains since 1934. In *Estado y agricultura en México: Antecedentes e implicaciones de las reformas Salinistas,* ed. E. C. Ochoa and D. F. Lorey, 17–38. Azcapotzalco, México, DF: Universidad Autónoma Metropolitana, Unidad Azcapoltzalco.

Organization for Economic Co-operation and Development (OECD). 1997. *Globalization and environment: Preliminary perspectives.* OECD Proceedings. Paris: OECD.

———. 1997. *Review of agricultural polices in Mexico.* Paris: OECD.

Ornelas Delgado, J. 1994. Tlaxcala y sus retos. In *Estudios regionales: Ensayos sobre cinco estados de la república,* ed. J. M. Flores Osorio, M. A. López Hernández, G. Luo Vera, J. Ornelas Delgado, and A. Yamasaky, 81–115. Tlaxcala: Universidad Autónoma de Tlaxcala.

Parry, M. 1990. *Climate change and world agriculture.* London: Earthscan.

Parry, M., and T. Carter. 1998. *Climate impact and adaptation assessment.* London: Earthscan.

Perales R. H., S. B. Brush, and C. O. Qualset. 2003. Landraces of maize in central Mexico: An altitudinal transect. *Economic Botany* 57:7–20.

Pessah, R. 1987. Channeling credit to the countryside. In *Food policy in Mexico: The search for self-sufficiency,* ed. J. E. Austin and G. Esteva, 92–110. Ithaca, NY: Cornell University Press.

Polsky, C. 2004. Putting space and time in Ricardian climate change impact studies: Agricultura in the U.S. Great Plains. *Annals of the Association of American Geographers* 94:549–64.

Ramírez Juárez, J. 1999. Ajuste estructural y estrategias campesinas de reproducción en el Valle de Puebla, Mexico. PhD diss., Enseñanza e Investigación en Ciencias Agrícolas, Colegio de Postgraduados, Puebla.

Ramirez Rancaño, M. 1990. *El sistema de haciendas en Tlaxcala*. [Mexico]: Consejo Nacional para la Cultura y las Artes, Dirección General de Publicaciones.

Reardon, T., J. Berdegué, and G. Escobar. 2001. Rural nonfarm employment and incomes in Latin America: Overview and policy implications. *World Development* 29:395–409.

Redclift, M. 1983. Production programs for small farmers: Plan Puebla as myth and reality. *Economic Development and Cultural Change* 31:551–70.

Reilly, J. M. 1999. Climate change and agriculture: The state of the scientific knowledge. *Climatic Change* 43:645–50.

Reilly, J. M., and D. Schimmelpfenning. 1999. Agricultural impact assessment, vulnerability, and the scope for adaptation. *Climatic Change* 43:745–88.

———. 2000. Irreversibility, uncertainty, and learning: Portraits of adaptation to long-term climate change. *Climatic Change* 45:253–78.

Reyes Castañeda, P. 1981. *Historia de la agricultura: Información y síntesis*. México, DF: AGT Editorial.

Ribot, J. C. 1996. Introduction to *Climate variability, climate change, and social vulnerability in the semi-arid tropics*, ed. J. C. Ribot, A. R. Magalhaes, and S. S. Panagides, 1–10. Cambridge: Cambridge University Press.

Richards, P. 1985. *Indigenous agricultural revolution*. London: Hutchinson & Co.

Risbey, J., M. Kandlikar, and H. Dowlatabadi. 1999. Scale, context, and decision making in agricultural adaptation to climate variability and change. *Mitigation and Adaptation Strategies for Global Change* 4:137–65.

Robbins, P. 2004. *Political ecology*. Malden, MA: Blackwell.

Rojas, T. 1991. La agricultura en la época prehispánica. In *La agricultura en tierras mexicanas desde sus orígenes hasta nuestros días*, ed. T. Rojas, 15–118. México, DF: Grijalbo.

Romero, M. 1991. La agricultura en la época colonial. In *La agricultura en tierras Mexicanas desde sus orígenes hasta nuestros días*, ed. T. Rojas, 139–216. México, DF: Grijalbo.

Roncoli, C., K. Ingram, and P. Kirshen. 2001. The costs and risks of coping with drought: Livelihood impacts and farmers' responses in Burkina Faso. *Climate Research* 19:119–32.

Rosenzweig, C. 1990. Crop response to climate change in the southern Great Plains: A simulation study. *Professional Geographer* 42:20–37.

Rosenzweig, C., and M. Parry. 1993. Potential impacts of climate change on world food supply: A summary of a recent international study. In *Agricultural dimensions of global climate change*, ed. H. Kaiser and T. E. Drennen, 87–116. Delray Beach, FL: St. Lucie Press.

Sánchez Daza, G. 1998. Características de la industria manufacturera en Puebla. In *Puebla, un modelo para armar*, ed. G. Sánchez Daza and J. Ornelas Delgado, 121–42. Puebla: Benemérita Universidad Autónoma de Puebla.

Scoones, I. 1996. *Hazards and opportunities: Farming livelihoods in dryland Africa: Lessons from Zimbabwe*. London: Zed Books.

———. 1998. *Sustainable rural livelihoods: A framework for analysis*. IDS Working Paper No. 72. [Brighton, Eng.]: Institute of Development Studies.

Secretaría de Fomento Agropecuaria (SEFOA). 2000. Internal document (Overview of Agricultural Sector and State Policy), photocopy. Version February 2000.

Secretaría de Medio Ambiente y Recursos Naturales (SEMARNAT). 2002. *Compendio de estadísticas ambientales 2002*. México, DF: SEMARNAT.

Secretaría de Programación y Presupuesto (SPP). 1981. *Síntesis geográfica de Tlaxcala*. México, DF: Secretaría de Programación y Presupuesto.

Sen, A. 1981. Ingredients of famine analysis: Availability and entitlements. *Quarterly Journal of Economics* 96:433–63.

———. 1990. Food, economics, and entitlements. In *The political economy of hunger*, ed. J. Dreze and A. Sen, 50–67. Oxford: Clarendon Press.

Sistema Integral de Información Agroalimentaria y Pesquera (SIAP). 2003. Sistema de Información Agrícola de Consulta (SIACON). México, DF: Secretaría de Agricultura, Ganadería, Desarrollo Rural y Alimentación (SAGARPA).

Smit, B., D. McNabb, and J. Smithers. 1996. Agricultural adaptation to climatic variation. *Climatic Change* 33:7–29.

Smithers, J., and B. Smit. 1997. Human adaptation to climatic variability and change. *Global Environmental Change* 7:129–46.

Snyder, R., ed. 1999. *Institutional adaptation and innovation in rural Mexico*. La Jolla: Center for U.S.–Mexican Studies, University of California, San Diego.

Trenberth, K. E., and T. J. Hoar. 1996. The 1990–1995 El Niño–Southern Oscillation event: Longest on record. *Geophysical Research Letters* 23 (1):57–60.

———. 1997. El Niño and climate change. *Geophysical Research Letters* 24:3057–60.

Trujillo, J. A. 1990. Adaptación de sistemas tradicionales de producción de maíz a las condiciones 'siniestrantes' de Tlaxcala. In *Historia y Sociedad en Tlaxcala: Memorias del 1º Simposio Internacional de Investigaciones Socio-Históricas sobre Tlaxcala*, 67–70. 14–16 October 1988. México, DF: Universidad Iberoamericana, Gobierno del Estado de Tlaxcala and Universidad Autónoma de Tlaxcala.

Tsonis, A. A., A. G. Hunt, and J.B. Elsner. 2002. On the relation between ENSO and global climate change. *Meteorology and Atmospheric Physics* 84:229–42.

Tuirán, R. 2002. Migración, remesas y desarrollo. In *La situación demográfica en México, 2002*, 77–87. México, DF: Consejo Nacional de Población.

Turner, B. L., and S. B. Brush. 1987. *Comparative farming systems*. New York: Guilford Press.

Turner II, B. L., R. E. Kasperson, P. A. Matson, J. J. McCarthy, R. W. Corell, L. Christensen, N. Eckley, J. X. Kasperson, A. Luers, M. L. Martello, C. Polsky, A. Pulsipher, and A. Schiller. 2003. A framework for vulnerability analysis in sustainability science. *PNAS* 100:8074–79.

Von Wobeser, G. 1991. La agricultura en el Porfirato. In *La agricultura en tierras mexicanas desde sus orígenes hasta nuestros días*, ed. T. Rojas, 255–300. México, DF: Grijalbo.

Watts, M. 1983. Hazards and crises: A political economy of drought and famine in northern Nigeria. *Antipode* 15:24–34.

Watts, M., and H. G. Bohle. 1993. The space of vulnerability: The causal structure of hunger and famine. *Progress in Human Geography* 17:43–67.

Weber, E. U. 1997. Perception and expectation of climate change: Precondition for economic and technological adaptation. *Psychological perspectives to environmental and ethical issues in management*, ed. M. Bazerman, D. Messick, A. Tenbrusel, and K. Wade-Benzoni, 314–41. San Francisco: Jossey-Bass.

Wheaton, E. E., and D. C. Maciver. 1999. A framework and key questions for adapting to climate variability and change. *Mitigation and Adaptation Strategies for Global Change* 4:215–25.

White, G. 1973. Natural hazards research. In *Directions in geography*, ed. R. J. Chorley, 193–216. London: Methuen.

Whitmore, T. M., and B. L. Turner II. 1992. Landscapes of cultivation in Mesoamerica on the eve of the conquest. *Annals of the Association of American Geographers* 82:402–25.

Wilken, G. 1987. *Good farmers: Traditional agricultural resource management in Mexico and Central America*. Berkeley and Los Angeles: University of California Press.

Wilkinson, J. 1997. Regional integration and the family farm in the Mercosul countries. In *Globalising food*, ed. D. Goodman and M. Watts, 35–55. London: Routledge.

Wilson, E. O. 1992. *The diversity of life*. New York: W. W. Norton.

Yapa, L. 1996. Improved seeds and constructed scarcity. *Liberation Ecologies*, ed. R. Peets and M. Watts, 69–85. New York: Routledge.

Yates, P. L. 1981. *Mexico's agricultural dilemma*. Tucson: University of Arizona Press.

Yúnez-Naude, A., and E. J. Taylor. 2001. The determinants of nonfarm activities and incomes of rural households in Mexico, with emphasis on education. *World Development* 29:561–72.

Zimmerer, K. 1991. Wetland production and smallholder persistence: Agricultural change in a highland Peruvian region. *Annals of the American Association of Geographers* 81:443–63.

Index

About the Author

Hallie Eakin is an assistant professor in the Department of Geography at the University of California, Santa Barbara. Eakin's research focuses on economic globalization, agricultural change, and adaptation and vulnerability to climate risk in Latin America and specifically in Mexico, where she has collaborated with the Center for Atmospheric Sciences of the National Autonomous University of Mexico since 1997. Eakin has also worked as a consultant to international and bilateral development agencies on projects related to agricultural development, the use of seasonal forecasting in drought risk mitigation, and adaptation to climate change.